The
Real Estate
Agent's
Field Guide

The
Real Estate Agent's Field Guide

Essential Insider Advice for Surviving in a Competitive Market

BRIDGET MCCREA

AMACOM

American Management Association

New York • Atlanta • Brussels • Chicago • Mexico City • San Francisco
Shanghai • Tokyo • Toronto • Washington, D.C.

Special discounts on bulk quantities of AMACOM books are available to corporations, professional associations, and other organizations. For details, contact Special Sales Department, AMACOM, a division of American Management Association, 1601 Broadway, New York, NY 10019.
Tel.: 212-903-8316. Fax: 212-903-8083
Web site: www.amacombooks.org

This publication is designed to provide accurate and authoritative information in regard to the subject matter covered. It is sold with the understanding that the publisher is not engaged in rendering legal, accounting, or other professional service. If legal advice or other expert assistance is required, the services of a competent professional person should be sought.

REALTOR® is a registered collective membership mark that identifies a real estate professional who is a member of the NATIONAL ASSOCIATION of REALTORS® and subscribes to its strict code of ethics.

Library of Congress Cataloging-in-Publication Data

McCrea, Bridget.
    Real estate agent's field guide : essential insider advice for surviving in a competitive market / Bridget McCrea.
        p. cm.
    Includes index.
    ISBN-10: 0-8144-0809-5
    ISBN-13: 978-0-8144-0809-4
    1. Real estate business—Vocational guidance.   I. Title.

HD1382.M365 2004
333.33—dc22
                                                        2004000116

Printing number

10 9 8 7 6 5 4 3 2

Contents

Part 4: Bracing for Success   **243**

Foreword

By John Foltz, President,
Realty Executives Phoenix

Look around you. The real estate industry as you know it is undergoing substantial changes that are affecting everyone from the large franchise conglomerate to the independent broker to the individual real estate agents who are out working in the field. No longer the keepers of information that they once were, those agents are among the most affected by these changes, yet they appear to be the least aware of them.

Over the years, I've watched the real estate industry evolve into a powerful force, where entrepreneurial types tend to excel. I myself began selling real estate in college as a way to circumvent the "nine-to-five, hourly wage" treadmill that many of my colleagues were stuck on. In 1966, at the age of eighteen, I held a real estate apprentice license. I graduated with a master's degree in finance from the University of Wisconsin and went into the securities business for six years.

In 1978, the lure of the real estate industry was too much to resist, so I went back into commercial and residential real estate sales for eleven years for Realty Executives, an affiliation that's lasted twenty-six years and counting. I was a top-producing agent for several years, then I moved up into a supervisory position. In total, I've reviewed over 300,000 transactions for Realty Executives Phoenix, of which I'm currently president.

All along, my love of real estate went far beyond just making money. It was about selling homes and making people's personal dreams come true, something that few professionals these days can boast. But after thirty-seven years of working in and around the business, I now know that at least one constant has remained: that real estate is all about relationships. Real estate is truly a people business, and one that requires personal contact, relationships, and communication to be done correctly.

What has changed dramatically is the speed at which that communication takes place. When I started in the business, it was a "door knocking" business. You would go into a neighborhood that you wanted to specialize in and knock on doors to develop your business base. Car phones were still a long way from being developed, e-mail wasn't even a legitimate word, and laptops hadn't yet been invented.

Today, the process has been streamlined by the Internet, which has created dramatic change both in the communications and in the transaction time itself. Everything is expedited, which means that agents must also "expedite" in order to keep up with and attempt to stay ahead of consumers, other business service providers, and, of course, their competitors.

Through it all, however, the basic way in which a real estate transaction is handled hasn't changed much at all. You still have to fill out a contract, put the funds through escrow or an attorney (depending on what state you're doing business in), and go to the closing table to seal the deal. The transaction really isn't that complex, nor has it been simplified much over the last two decades, but the amount of information that consumers have at their fingertips has virtually exploded during that time.

It's a far cry from the 1960s real estate landscape, when multiple listing services (MLS) were not that popular. Most companies at that time had their own listings and just kind of kept them to themselves. Slowly, they began to realize the value of sharing listings and using co-brokerage techniques to provide a broader market for selling properties. MLSs began to dot the landscape, and soon every agent in town had access to the property listings.

Fast-forward to the 2000s, and the rules have changed drastically.

Now, every person in town—real estate agent or not—has access to that kind of information via desktop computers and an Internet connection. Systems like Internet Data Exchange (IDX), broker reciprocity, and virtual office web sites (VOWs) have become the starting point of choice for buyers looking for homes, and the advertising vehicle of choice for sellers trying to unload their dwellings.

As a result, total transaction time has become compressed, particularly because a buyer no longer has to wait for an agent to sift through the MLS for good candidates, then drive around on a Sunday afternoon touring homes. Instead, a consumer can access homes via the Web, view virtual tours of these homes online, and eliminate undesirable properties with the click of a few keystrokes. What's left are the homes they'd like to see in person and possibly bid on, with the help of a real estate professional.

In theory, it really sounds like the industry has come of age and learned how to operate in a technologically advanced environment, right? Maybe, but along with these fundamental changes came a slew of concerns that all agents should be thinking about right now. Because they're no longer the keepers of secret information, agents have had to position themselves as valued counselors and negotiators, then convey that position to a public that once viewed them as, well, keepers of secret information.

At the same time, agents are watching their piece of the real estate pie being picked away at by a number of forces. While median home sales prices have risen significantly over the last forty years, so too have the number of outside forces that are ready to grab a piece of the real estate commission. They range from discount and flat fee brokers to the new crop of referral companies that demand a flat fee or percentage of the sales price in exchange for leads. So even though home prices are on the rise, the net fee that an agent takes home is actually smaller today than it was ten years ago.

Part of that comes from the new breed of real estate brokerages that has hit the scene with the help of the Internet. Take unbundled or "menu" services, for example. These agents typically lack the skills and courage that it takes to become a trusted adviser, so they basically compete with one another based on pricing and discounts. What they don't realize is that pricing and discounts are an issue only in the absence of the client's perceiving value. Those agents who do well over the years do not talk about commission rates, but they do consistently offer value as trusted advisers to their clients.

Most agents these days become top producers because they combine that trusted adviser role with determination, experience, and expertise that sets them ahead of the pack. The problem is, I've found that most agents believe that a full day of work begins at 9:30 a.m., with a break at 11 a.m. for lunch with friends and a golf game later that afternoon. In today's economy, it just doesn't work that way. There are literally thousands of agents out there who are willing to work with your customer—and who will gladly take your customer's call for you while you're out on the fairway at 3 p.m. on a Monday afternoon.

For that reason, most agents—no matter how ambitious their aspirations might be—are destined to be average or worse. It's true. Most will be not more than mediocre. Because there are very few barriers to entry in this industry, and because the real education of a real estate licensee doesn't start until he or she hits the ground running, looking for prospects, calling FSBO signs, and handing out business cards at local networking meetings, most don't realize the harsh realities of the business until they've already invested the time and money in it.

Where real estate agents are also facing challenges these days is in the legalities of doing business. There are regulatory challenges, licensing laws, codes of ethics, and liability risks that all agents should be thinking about as they go about their business. The "blame someone else" culture is growing like a virus, and the agent's role as a guardian and trustee has put somewhat of a target on the agent's back. Salespeople tend to be unrealistically optimistic, thinking that they'll never be sued for anything because they're well-intentioned people who are out there doing the right thing. What they don't realize is that about 90 percent of the lawsuits are frivolous, and that they happen randomly.

Of course, there is still a great joy that comes from helping a family purchase its first home, unload an existing dwelling to move up to larger digs, or sell a large home in an attempt to simplify and downscale their lives. As trusted advisers who for decades have been helping people do that and more, real estate agents play a critical role in a very important process that most individuals undertake only a few times. Unfortunately, most agents believe that the key to success in this industry is to simply learn how to do a transaction and adopt appropriate sales tactics. While these abilities are certainly important, agents must also act ethically and responsibly, stay on top of the key trends in their industry, and be ready to adapt when the time comes.

PART 1

DRIVING
FORCES

CHAPTER 1

Facing the Forces of Change

TURBULENT WATER AHEAD

Fifteen years ago, a freshly minted residential real estate license hung on the right broker's wall virtually ensured success in a field known for its low barriers to entry and high financial rewards. With the closely guarded multiple listing service (MLS) books—delivered weekly only to members of the Realtors' association—tucked under their arms, agents held the keys to the entire home-selling industry. They were the keepers of information, and pretty much everyone knew it.

With the advent of the Internet came a dramatic shift. Quite literally overnight, a new breed of brokers came on the scene. They tapped the Internet as both a marketing tool and a vehicle for gaining access to those guarded MLS books, which quickly went the way of the eight-track. A more knowledgeable and tech-savvy set of consumers quickly followed, bringing with them a determination to challenge every traditional agent's way of doing business.

But the Internet isn't the only driving force behind the monumental changes in the residential real estate industry. Demanding consumers, commission compression, the rise of alternative brokerage methods, industry consolidation, and increased legal risks are all causing agents to rethink the way they do business. Combined, these forces of change are altering the real estate landscape as we know it and forcing agents and their brokers to operate in a Wild-Wild-West-like environment.

TWO DECADES AND COUNTING

Since the 1980s, the residential real estate industry has demanded higher commission rates, which in turn meant higher agent incomes. Driving those increases were agent-only access to the MLS, which contained valuable data about every home that had been listed with an agent in a particular region or city. Commissions stayed steady, since agents held all the cards, so to speak, and top producers were fairly easy to come by.

In the late 1990s the MLS information that agents had been holding close to the vest slowly became available to a much wider audience via the Internet. MLS systems began showing their listings to home buyers, who at the time were just beginning to turn to their computers for home data. As it turned out, those consumers enjoyed the access and demanded more. Most recently, the National Association of Realtors® (NAR) approved rules that make listings even more accessible to consumers, who now come to agents more informed. (See Chapter 3.)

Throughout the 1990s, MLS data were online, but in a format that still was accessible only to real estate agents. Agents would boot up their computers every morning, log into a password-protected system, and get an eyeful of the most updated listing information. That went on for several years until the late 1990s, when the rest of the world caught its first glimpse of the highly coveted information that agents and brokers had been hiding for so many years.

In June 2003 NAR announced that by the following year, buyers would be able to access as much information online as local agents *allow* (a word that shows just how protective agents still are of the information). To access the information, consumers must register for a password and relinquish some personal tidbits, essentially making that consumer a customer, with whom an agent would probably share that information anyway.

So what does this mean for the real estate agent who's trying to make a good buck by helping buyers into homes and sellers out of them? Well, it's a double-edged sword. Being able to collect consumer data before the buyers even tap into the MLS means that agents will be well positioned to help these consumers once they get to the hard part of the transaction: home showings, negotiations, mortgages, and property disclosures.

Since 80 percent of home buyers use real estate agents, and because agents use the MLS to search for homes, it only makes sense to close the loop and give consumers access to the MLS directly. On the other hand, it's also another chink in the armor of traditional real estate agents, who—in much the way that auto dealers were once the only keepers of the Kelly Blue Book (which is now online for anyone to access)—have had to reposition themselves to operate in a marketplace where the value they bring to the table goes far beyond showing homes.

"They really let the cat out of the bag on this one," one long-time agent wrote on a RealTalk chat board in 2002, apparently wistful for the days when only MLS members could access MLS data. Too late. Technological innovation has increased the availability of information in nearly all industries, and real estate is no exception.

Gone too, or soon to be, are the days when you loaded a family into your Mercedes Benz for a Sunday afternoon of driving around looking at a list of homes. Today, a consumer can access basic listing information on a local MLS through processes known as broker reciprocity, IDX, and virtual office Web sites (VOWS) (we'll get into what these are later); view an entire home online via a virtual tour; and check out the selling price, neighborhood, schools, and other pertinent information—all before they ever set foot in a real estate office.

This is a fundamental, but again not insurmountable, change that some feel has actually strengthened the position of the agent in the marketplace. After all, someone has to help home buyers and sellers decipher all of the new laws and regulations that surround the purchase of a home, and someone has to help them wade through the paperwork, figure out what the market will really pay for their homes, and prepare their homes for sale.

LOW BARRIERS TO ENTRY

Real estate is a pretty easy business to get into, but a pretty difficult one to survive in. Newly licensed agents quickly find themselves operating in an industry where titles like "million-dollar producer" are thrown around on Web sites and in newspaper ads, yet are rarely applicable to the average agent, who earns about $41,000 a year, according to the National Association of Realtors' latest statistics. The Bureau of Labor Statistics (BLS) pegs the number even lower, stating that the median annual earnings of the real estate agent was $27,640 in 2000, the latest year for which statistics are available (see Figure 1-1).

According to the BLS, the middle 50 percent of real estate agents earn between $19,530 and $45,740 a year. Assuming that $1 million in sales nets about $15,000 in commissions, that means that agents would have to sell about seven median-priced homes at $135,000 each to become million-dollar producers (assuming that an agent earns the typical 3 percent commission for her or his side of the transaction, then splits it with

Figure 1-1.

HOW THE MONEY BREAKS DOWN

According to the Bureau of Labor Statistics, the median annual earnings of salaried real estate agents, including commission, were $27,640 in 2000. The middle 50 percent earned between $19,530 and $45,740 a year, while the lowest 10 percent earned less than $14,460 and the highest 10 percent earned more than $78,540. Median annual earnings in the industries employing the largest number of salaried real estate agents in 2000 were as follows:

Residential building construction	$44,940
Subdividers and developers	32,030
Real estate agents and managers	27,770
Real estate operators and lessors	20,770

Source: Bureau of Labor Statistics

the broker) and make that $15,000 in gross commissions. That means that in order to survive and thrive, agents need to either do volume or find a broker who doesn't take such a big cut of the commissions.

Daryl Jesperson, CEO of RE/MAX International, Inc., advises agents to look beyond the numbers to find their true earning potential. The average salesperson at RE/MAX, for example, makes $121,000 a year but pays for personal expenses and a share of office overhead. Also factor in that those averages are less likely to include most of the industry's heavy hitters than they are those who are barely scraping by, and it's clear why Jesperson warns agents to take such surveys with a grain of salt.

"The groups will send out tens of thousands of these and get a small number of them back," he says. "The people who answer them, however, are the ones who are managing offices or that have time on their hands. The agents earning the most money along with designations and other credentials most likely can't afford the time to answer them."

Still, one can't ignore the facts. The BLS says that the business of real estate sales has a significant turnover rate, and it describes the industry as a highly competitive field in which "many beginners become discouraged by their inability to get listings and to close a sufficient number of sales." The common assumption is that only two out of every five agents will make it—a dismal ratio for the new agent, but comparatively good news for the existing agent who would rather not see the industry fill up with more top producers.

BOOM TIMES

Regardless of earnings potential—or lack thereof—people are flocking to the real estate industry like never before. Those low barriers to entry are certainly one good reason, but another driver is the economic downturn that started in 2000 and that hadn't let up as of early 2004. Pushed out of cushy executive jobs in industries like high-tech, many experienced sales-people and executives, as well as new college graduates, have turned to real estate as their first or second career (see Figure 1-2).

Figure 1-2.

GETTING STARTED AIN'T CHEAP

The barriers to entry for someone who is looking to become a sales agent may be minimal, but most new agents will feel a pinch on their wallets until they get their first transaction closed. A bare-bones estimate for getting started is about $1,500, according to Sherry Weston, a Fort Worth, Texas–based real estate instructor who teaches at Tarrant County College and Leonard-Hawes Real Estate School. Weston breaks down the costs for a new agent in the state of Texas as follows (check with your local or state board of Realtors for more specific information for your own state):

❑ $500: For four real estate classes, including books. (Weston says the cost of education may be higher if the student does not already have some college credit. Texas, for example, requires a total of 120 classroom hours of core real estate courses, plus another 60 hours of "acceptable" other courses.)

❑ $77.50: Application fee for state license

❑ $20: Transcript fee

❑ $20: To process required broker sponsorship

❑ $60: For real estate exam (taking into account the fact that many applicants fail the first time, and many students also take an exam prep course at a cost of about $100).

❑ $300: Annual dues to the local board of Realtors (includes membership in the Texas Association of REALTORS® and NAR)

❑ $100: Board of REALTORS® member application fee

❑ $125: Per quarter for multiple listing service

❑ $75: For a key card to show houses (an electronic "lockbox" system used profusely in some states/regions, and not at all in others)

❑ $125: Annual fee for keycard maintenance

❑ $75: For a key box to list houses (price is per key box, and agents need one for each listing)

❑ $36 to $50: For each sign (some brokers provide signs).

In addition, Weston says some offices charge "office fees" and that amounts vary between brokers and range from zero to $2,500 per month. The biggest expenses most agents incur relate to marketing, and other such fees include advertising (some brokers do institutional advertising), computer equipment for the home and/or car, telephone lines, and cell phones.

Why the influx? Simple. Real estate is a booming market in an era when almost every other industry is down in the dumps, or struggling to emerge from them. Real estate has been one of the primary drivers of the U.S. economy through the most recent downturn. People see properties continuing to change hands, they see that the barriers to entry for agents are fairly low, and they want in. Sniffing out opportunity, they decide to enroll in a course and sit for the real estate exam.

And it's no wonder, really. In 2002, more than 5.57 million existing homes and 974,000 new homes were sold in the United States, up from 5.3 million existing homes and 908,000 new homes in 2001. Low mortgage rates were undoubtedly the key drivers nationwide, with rates dropping below 5 percent as of June 2003. Also fueling the boom are the myriad immigrants and multicultural buyers who have discovered the value of American homeownership, and the fact that owning a home became less expensive than renting.

According to NAR, more than 5.76 million existing homes and 1.03 million new homes will exchange hands in 2003, making it the best year since 1968, when NAR began tracking housing data. The housing sector set another record in 2003, according to NAR, based on stronger-than-expected homes sale through midyear and a continued drop in mortgage interest rates. In fact, David Lereah, NAR's chief economist, said the forecast was steadily upgraded all year.

"The performance of the current housing market is nothing short of astounding," says Lereah. "Record low mortgage interest rates, a growing number of households, rising consumer confidence, and an improving economy mean we probably will set a third consecutive record for both existing- and new-home sales this year."

If the volume of homes sold is high, so too are the prices that such properties are fetching, thus creating another draw for folks seeking a career in real estate. Higher home prices mean fatter commission checks, more room to negotiate commission rates without cutting one's own throat, and extra cash to dole out to the new breed of "referral" companies that have their hands out at the closing table (read more about these forces of change in Chapter 4). The national median existing-home price was projected to rise 6.6 percent in 2003 (over 2002) to $168,600, according to NAR, while the median new-home price was to grow by 3.0 percent in 2003 to $193,200. "Although existing-home price gains this year will be less than the 7.0 percent overall rise in 2002," says Lereah, "they'll still rise above historic norms."

HIGHER DEMANDS

If the opportunities for new agents are great, so too are the outside forces that can quickly force them to retreat back to the corporate world. First and foremost, there's the consumer, who no longer has to sit and wait for the phone to ring with property information from the real estate agent. A quick flip of a computer switch and the right keywords can put an area's entire MLS (multiple listing service) in front of the consumer within a few seconds. The trend is positive in that it alleviates much of the early research (i.e., driving around on weekends looking at homes) that agents had to do, yet it is challenging in that agents are forced to deal with a more demanding, knowledgeable consumer.

Perhaps that's why the old axiom that "20 percent of the agents do 80 percent of the business" isn't valid anymore. RE/MAX cofounder Dave Liniger remembers a time thirty years ago when a top-performing agent really stood out from the rest of the industry. Back then, he says quality agents snagged the majority of the business—or, as the axiom goes, a full 80 percent of it—simply because they looked better and their competition was lacking in quality and customer service.

"Today the competitive influences that have come about have made everybody be much better or they can't compete at all," says Liniger.

Today, the scales have tipped, and he estimates that the top 50 percent of agents are now doing 80 percent of the business. So while opportunities to succeed have increased, so has the amount of competition that even the best agents have to deal with.

And those top producers are pulling in more transactions than ever, according to Liniger, who started RE/MAX in 1973 after realizing that really good agents didn't want to split their commissions 50/50 with their brokers. His idea: Pay them 100 percent of their commissions, then have them pay their own overhead, from telephone service to desk space to paperclips.

The idea worked, and it spawned a change in the industry. Traditional brokers now offer commission splits that are fairer to agents, like 80/20 or 60/40. When RE/MAX got going, Liniger says his agents averaged ten transaction sides (either the listing or the selling side of the deal) apiece each year, while the industry average was five. Today, RE/MAX agents complete twenty-four sides a year on average in an industry that averages seven a year—including RE/MAX production.

STILL, THEY FLOCK

Despite the kind of challenges that are never mentioned in the typical real estate license educational course, new agents are flocking to the real estate industry in droves. In doing so, they're creating competition within their respective geographies that is all the more fierce, although most established agents would dismiss that notion. Still, the fact that new agents are swarming into the business makes one wonder if they're really doing their homework on their new career, particularly on the income side.

Evidently they're either ignoring it or hoping it isn't accurate, since membership in the National Association of Realtors rose 10 percent during the first quarter of 2003—twice the rate of the same period in the previous year. Nationally, NAR reports that 78,000 new members were added to real estate agents' ranks between 2001 and 2003, representing a significant increase to 948,000 members. Individual states are experiencing their own boom in people interested in real estate careers. In Texas, for example, nearly 5,000 new members had joined the state's roster of 118,859 licensed agents as of January 2003, up from 113,942 in January 2002, a 4 percent jump.

Most agree that the low barriers to entry combined with thoughts of pocketing 6 percent of a home's sales price make the field particularly attractive. Add in the fact that many other job sectors have suffered since the nation's economic malaise took hold in 2000 and it's not hard to see why real estate is so alluring.

While many professions require years of graduate school, becoming a real-estate agent is fairly simple in most states, requiring as few as twenty hours of classes and a one-day exam. States like South Dakota have tightened the reins a bit in recent years, adding forty hours of classroom instruction and phasing out the entry-level salesperson's test in favor of a broker's test, but in states like Utah licensees don't even need high school diplomas. In Maine and Vermont, new licensees can simply take the test and pass with a 75 or higher—without taking any specific coursework.

New agents typically face their first challenges out in the field, where thousands of competitors are vying for the same pool of home buyers and sellers. With the number of new agents swelling in most states—in 2003, California saw a 105 percent hike in the number of people taking the real estate license exam for the first time, according to the California Department of Real Estate—that competition is only getting fiercer. Other states that reported increases in 2003 were Arizona, Florida, New Jersey, New York, North Carolina, Ohio, Tennessee, Texas, West Virginia, and Washington, D.C., according to the Association of Real Estate License Law Officials (ARELLO).

In North Carolina, the Carolina Multiple Listing Service and the Charlotte Regional Realtor Association (CRRA) have posted membership gains over the last five years, both nearly doubling their ranks during that time. The CRRA has approximately 5,000 members, and the MLS has about 6,100. Five years ago, membership in both groups was about half of what it is now, according to Anne Marie Howard, executive director for CRRA, who attributes much of the growth to cutbacks in the manufacturing sector and mergers in the banking industry.

ADAPTATION EQUALS SUCCESS

What the influx of new real estate agents probably doesn't realize is that they're coming into an industry where even the most experienced agents are trying to figure out how to deal with issues like evolving consumer preferences, technology, commission compression, industry consolidation, discount brokerages and brokerages offering menu-based services, risk management, increased regulations, and a slew of outside forces ranging from financing to taxes. Digging down deeper, issues like skyrocketing homeowner's insurance rates, tax increases, toxic mold cases, BRRETA, RESPA (see Chapter 8), and other issues are all affecting the way agents do business.

Most of these issues start and end with consumers, who ultimately determine the way in which real estate is bought and sold. Their tech-savvy ways have forced agents to use technology, their complaints force regulators to make new rules, and their demands for more service for less money have spawned a plethora of new brokerage models. Steve Murray, editor at residential real estate news, research, and information service REAL Trends in Littleton, Colorado, says that today's consumer is looking beyond the service package historically supplied by the real estate professional. Studies from Harris Interactive, NAR, and the California Association of Realtors all found that consumers want more assistance in the sale and purchase of homes.

"While they want more service, they also want more involvement in the process, they also want to understand what is going on," says Murray. "They also want 'one-stop shopping.'" Murray is quick to point out that consumers don't want limits on their choices of settlement services— meaning that they don't want to limit themselves to only those providers of ancillary services that an agent suggests—but they do want a simple process that's facilitated by the agent.

"Once they pick a real estate agent and brokerage, the consumer expects them to manage and handle the process through to closing," says Murray. "In all of these studies, it came through loud and clear that consumers prefer the full-service, full-price brokerage offer."

That should be music to the ears of any agent working in a company like Coldwell Banker, RE/MAX, or Century 21, right? Wrong, says Murray, because even these age-old brokerages can't always produce what consumers are demanding. "It's equally clear that what we offer today is not what consumers consider to be full service," says Murray.

As a result, consumers are taking a "we'll pay for what we get" attitude toward real estate professionals, and are hitting agents in their wallets to make up for the services that they don't feel they're getting. "They're pushing for lower commissions and lower cost because they are not getting what they consider to be full service," Murray says.

The numbers prove it. "The average commission rate that consumers are paying for services to sell their homes has dropped for 11 years in a row, with the single biggest year of decline in that 11-year period taking place in 2002," says Murray, who points to the robust real estate market as an influencer of the commission compression, but says the "decline cannot be laid solely there." In other words, discount brokerages, hard-negotiating consumers, and competition among brokers for listings have all taken their toll on the commission rate.

At the root of the problem is the fact that for the last twenty years, agents have been trained to prospect, farm, and market and to ensure that a growing pile of disclosure statements and contracts get filled out properly. What they haven't been trained on—like many professionals, including dentists, doctors, and lawyers—is how to present their "value proposition" to the customer. While some companies and professionals excel at positioning themselves in a place of value, agents tend to take for granted the fact that people are somehow going to figure out on their own just why they need agent representation in the first place

To improve their image in the customers' eyes and ensure that everyone knows just how much value they're providing, Murray advises agents to start working more closely with their brokers to help customers manage their way efficiently through the process of buying a home. "Brokers and agents could work together to actually disclose to a buyer or seller all the things they are prepared to do to help that person buy or sell a home," says Murray, "in a step-by-step transparent process. That would be a good start."

Russell Capper, who heads up Houston-based eRealty, Inc., says that real estate agents who lack proper access to the advanced technology tools they need in order to operate in a changing environment are the ultimate losers. "If I were a traditional, full-service agent right now I'd be screaming holy terror that someone should be implementing a technology process that brings me up to speed with everyone else," says Capper. "Nearly every other industry and sector in today's economy is rapidly developing and employing new market exchanges. Real estate is the only one that seems to be wanting to destroy and make less effective their market exchange because of Internet technology."

Of course, that's coming from a man who is sitting on the leading edge of technology in an industry that still seems to long for the days when paper-based MLS books were the industry's sacred bibles. Capper himself has had many debates with old-school brokerages over the years—some of them even culminating in lawsuits—but has consistently come out on top. Read more about him in Chapters 4 and 5, where we delve into the pressures that discount and Internet brokerages are putting on traditional agents.

CHANGING APPROACH

It's already been proven that the Internet cannot—and will not—replace the qualified agent at any level. According to the National Association of Realtors' 2003 Profile of Home Buyers and Sellers, nearly 86 percent of sellers use a real estate agent to assist in the process, regardless of the vast array of marketing choices available to them. Nearly four out of five home buyers used an agent as an important information source and to assist in the transaction, NAR reports, even though 42 percent of them also used the Internet as an information source.

Liniger sees the trend for consumers to use the Internet first—before calling an agent—as a positive. He says every industry study shows that even the most tech- and Internet-savvy buyers prefer to use agents, despite the fact that they're doing their initial home searches on the Web and winnowing down their choices before picking up the phone to make that initial call to the agent.

Liniger says this is good for agents, because they no longer have to show a hundred properties in person in order to find the right one. "Internet-savvy buyers look at about half as many listings with the agent," he says, "and are basically more confident because they can look at a hundred properties online in a few hours and narrow it down themselves."

According to NAR's 2003 Profile of Homebuyers and Sellers, 2003 marks a milestone in the technological evolution of the real estate industry. For the first time, more buyers used the Internet as an information source than used newspaper advertisements. In 2003, 65 percent of all home buyers used the Internet, while 49 percent searched newspaper advertisements—what used to be thought of as a mainstay in the real estate business (it was a weekly ritual at most offices in the early 1990s, for example, to pull out the photos and type up ads for the newspapers' advertising departments to pick up).

Use of the Internet among home buyers has increased consistently over the last eight years. In 1995 only 2 percent of home buyers used the Internet in their home search. Other popular sources of information included yard signs (69 percent), open houses (48 percent), builders (37 percent), and home books or magazines (35 percent).

VIRTUAL, PLEASE

The good news, according to NAR, is that those home buyers who searched the Internet were actually *more* likely to use a real estate agent to complete the home search and close the transaction. NAR expects the numbers to rise, with more potential buyers expecting to see homes on the Internet, often with a virtual home tour, before they spend time driving around town.

So that means that even though consumers have what seems like the world at their fingertips thanks to the Internet, they're not sure how to manipulate the information to either buy or sell a home on their own—

despite early beliefs about disintermediation, or elimination of the middleman—the agent, in this case.

On the negative side for agents, NAR acknowledges that the captive "car time"—which was often used to bond with customers, prequalify them, and get a true feel for their hot buttons—has been greatly reduced, making the agent's job much different from what it was just ten years ago. In Chapter 3 we'll take a more in-depth look at how the Internet and technology—both the consumer-facing tools and those used internally at real estate offices—are altering the business landscape.

For now, it's important to know that industry experts agree that the Internet has inflicted major changes on the real estate industry. The trend has been particularly pertinent for older agents who are used to handling everything manually, and who are having circles run around them by younger, tech-savvy agents who are quick to load up their briefcases with digital cameras, personal digital assistants, and electronic lockboxes.

But while the industry has changed and technology has expedited many of its processes, there are still only twenty-four hours in a day. "The agents who are focused on getting listings and making sales are often blissfully unaware of many of the distractions," says Jesperson. "If you look at the most successful real estate agents, they're the ones who spend the vast majority of their time face-to-face with buyers or sellers—that's how they make money. The diversions of the Internet and everything else are just that—a new diversion for the same people who had to find things to keep themselves busy ten years ago."

Liniger says that the most valuable weapon in any successful agent's arsenal right now is simply the knowledge that real estate is a person-to-person business. Unlike airline tickets, books, or even automobiles, houses simply cannot be bought and sold without some sort of personal interaction. "The real estate industry is in a league of its own, and it's very complex," says Liniger, who for nearly thirty years has watched the industry evolve and morph, but who still knows deep down that it's the same people business it was when he founded RE/MAX in 1973.

TAKE A STAB

Combine low interest rates with climbing home prices and the unlikelihood of a real estate bubble (a comparison is often made to the "tech bubble," because of real estate's growing returns through the early 2000s) anytime soon and it's not hard to see why real estate is such an attractive career choice. After all, how hard could it be to list a few homes, walk a few buyers through them, and show up at the closing table for your commission check?

Unfortunately, it's not that easy. Roles have shifted, and an increasing number of outside forces have erected stumbling blocks for the agent. Still, people are flocking to the profession in droves, and it's no wonder, really, when real estate schools like one in Orlando, Florida, have telephone hold messages that claim that "Once licensed, a real estate agent's earning potential is virtually limitless." Not so fast, Mr. Educator. Remember that the average real estate agent has to hustle to make $41,000 a year. And while it's only fair for them to present the salary on a "gross" basis—as any other professional would—this deserves a closer look, particularly if you're an agent who is trying to survive in a changing industry. So take out the taxes (estimate 30 percent) and overhead, such as travel expenses and other out-of-pocket costs (10 to 20 percent), and the net income for the average agent is $20,500, or about $10 an hour based on a 2000-hour work year (unlikely, as most agents are regularly called out to show homes and do makeup work on nights and weekends).

Does this mean that the average agent is destined to wallow in mediocrity for an entire career? Not at all. It does, however, mean that all agents have to pay attention to more than just listing, sales, and negotiation techniques. Most important, it means staying on top of the fact that strong forces of change are reshaping the real estate industry as we know it.

Take the commission-only structure, arguably one of real estate's most difficult obstacles. A double-edged sword, the process can make big winners out of those who sell a lot, and losers out of those who do not. Put simply, success is hard to come by and highly coveted, particularly by new and hungry agents. Still, salaried agents haven't caught on yet, and probably won't anytime soon, because of the independent nature of the real estate business and that "unlimited earning potential" that everyone talks about.

"If you're unemployed, having just come from a salaried job, you can be broke by the time you pick a real estate school and take your licensing exam," says Jesperson. "Anyone working in real estate knows today's business is more competitive than it has ever been, and that the knowledge factor has to be so much greater."

By knowledge factor, Jesperson is referring to the lengthy laundry list of things an agent must know about each and every transaction that she helps close. These things range from financing to legalities, risk management to disclosures, and everything in between.

"Twenty years ago there was a VA loan, an FHA loan, and a conventional loan, and that was it," says Jesperson. "Today there are probably twenty different FHA-type loans, not to mention the disclosures of everything from radon to toxic mold. All of these factors have made the process much more complex."

THE FUTURE, AND BEYOND

NAR knows that its 948,000 members nationwide are heading into an uncertain future marked by industry consolidation, technology, changes in the broker-agent relationship, and regulatory impacts. To help agents break down the changes that they need to be worried about most, the group released "The Future of Real Estate Brokerage" in 2003, which highlights challenges and opportunities for Realtors®.

"Even in the face of change, agents and brokerage firms are tied to the demands of consumers, and successful real estate professionals work continuously to serve their clients," NAR reports. "The successful business model is the one that provides a service for which consumers are willing to compensate."

Calling agents "irreplaceable" in the marketplace, NAR points to documented consumer loyalty as proof: In 2001, 67 percent of sellers surveyed said that they would use the same real estate agent again. Sounds simple enough, right? Think again. Though many full-service brokerages (those offering the full menu of services for a fee that ranges from 5 to 7 percent of the home's sales price) refuse to admit it, they are losing business to a new breed of real estate firms that cater to customer demands for more service for less money. Their strategies range from 3.5 percent commission to flat fees of $399 for simply listing a home on the MLS to fees for each "unbundled" service ($200 to hold an open house, $500 to do the paperwork for the transaction, and so on).

Most of these companies have also discovered the Internet as a vehicle for change in real estate, and have taken full advantage of its low overhead to go up against the likes of traditional brokerage offices like those of RE/MAX or Coldwell Banker. They've also tapped a market that some agents never get to see: the FSBO, or "for sale by owner" set.

When you start with technology, add in a dash of low-end competition, toss in a few new regulatory hurdles, and top it all off with a more demanding customer base, it's easy to see why agents need help navigating the changing waters of the industry (see Figure 1-3). To survive and thrive in the marketplace, agents must address these key issues right now. They must also understand and adapt to the changes in the marketplace. This book will help you do just that.

ADAPTING TO CHANGE

J. Lennox Scott, chairman and CEO at John L. Scott Real Estate in Seattle, is another long-time real estate veteran who sees technology as the ultimate facilitator for agents. His company, which today has 120 offices and 3,300 agents, was founded by his grandfather in 1931, then headed up by his father from 1967 to 1980, when Scott took over as president.

The company is well known for its progressive thinking when it comes to technology, and it sits in an area of the country that was the first to adopt broker reciprocity (see Chapter 3 for more information on this "sharing of listing" data between competitive brokers). According to

Figure 1-3.

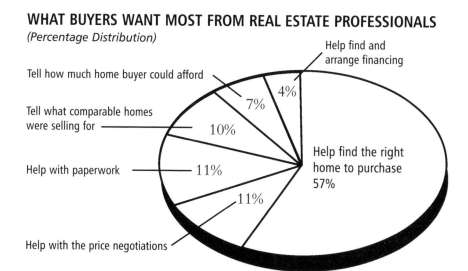

WHAT BUYERS WANT MOST FROM REAL ESTATE PROFESSIONALS
(Percentage Distribution)

Help find and arrange financing

Tell how much home buyer could afford

Tell what comparable homes were selling for — 10%

7%

4%

Help find the right home to purchase 57%

Help with paperwork — 11%

11%

Help with the price negotiations

Source: *The 2003 National Association of REALTORS Profile of Home Buyers and Sellers. Used with permission.*

Scott, technology not only has helped agents be more productive, but has also helped them lead more balanced lives.

"Years ago, being a highly productive agent meant working sixteen-hour days, six or seven days a week," Scott recalls. "Now, thanks to the efficiencies they've gained through technology and the Internet, they can live life with 'purpose and passion' with a balanced spiritual, personal, family, work, and community life."

Scott, who knows full well that his own agents are grappling with challenging issues in the marketplace these days, says that that seemingly simple achievement goes a long way toward creating a successful agent who is successful not only in his job, but also in his life. Such achievements shine through to consumers looking for capable, knowledgeable agents to help them with one of the biggest financial decisions they'll ever make in their lives.

"From their real estate agents, people are looking for communication, delivery of the services, and the experience level of the individual agent," says Scott. "By finding a broker who supports you in terms of branding, coaching, mentoring, marketing, and technology, then combining those tools with your own goals and focused approach to the market, you'll not only succeed, you'll be giving consumers exactly what they want."

SIX THINGS TO REMEMBER FROM CHAPTER 1

- ❑ The real estate industry has been in a state of flux for at least twenty years, and counting.
- ❑ The average real estate agent—though promised "unlimited income potential" by educators and mentors—nets $21,500 a year, or roughly $10 an hour for a full workweek.
- ❑ A large influx of agents became licensed in the 2002–2003 time frame, but many of them will fail because of low barriers to entry, high expectations, and the assumption that the industry yields big profits for everyone involved.
- ❑ Technology and the Internet have pushed customers to find alternative research avenues when buying or selling, but 80 percent of them continue to use real estate agents to seal the deal.
- ❑ Resourceful agents have found ways to harness technology and make it work for them, without having it cut into their profits.
- ❑ To survive and thrive in the future, real estate agents will have to deal with some or all of the following forces of change: changing customer preferences, technology, commission compression, discount and menu brokers, risk management, and outside forces such as industry consolidation and licensing issues.

CHAPTER 2

Changing Consumer Demands

THE BALANCING ACT

Ask Carole Caborn what customers want from her these days and she blurts out her answer pretty quickly. "Blood," she says, acknowledging that while some customers are still "nice to work with," a good portion of them are out to pay as little as possible and eke the most production possible out of her as a real estate agent.

Take Caborn's repeat customer, who asked if this Realtor® associate with Coldwell Banker Residential Real Estate in Longwood, Florida, would give his newly licensed son 25 percent of her commission when his home sold. To make matters worse, he also wanted to list the property at a lower commission percentage (a rate she'd previously extended to him, with her broker's permission, on her first-ever listing as a real estate agent). While it looks like "just a percentage point" to an outsider, a lower commission brings with it the stigma of "undercutting" the 6 or 7 percent that the majority of full-service agents have become accustomed to receiving over the last few decades. (Agents and brokers are not allowed to discuss or "set" commission rates—by law—but it's common knowledge that the going rate in most areas ranges between 6 and 7 percent.)

For a home priced at $150,000, the sale would have netted an agent a whopping $937.50, assuming the broker's cut is 50 percent. Her broker's answer: "No way."

"I told them that I could take it at the going rate and give his son 30 percent of my cut," says Caborn. "He had a fit and said no, it won't work that way. It's either the percent commission he wanted and 25 percent for his son, or nothing." After more negotiations, Caborn and the homeowner agreed to do the deal at the lower rate, but with no cut for the son.

"He then went on to tell me how upset his son was going to be about that, so I called his son and he told me that he wasn't upset at all," Caborn says. "I suspect that will be the last business deal I do with that customer, who obviously wanted me to work for nothing. That really goes against my principles as a real estate agent. Plus, none of us enjoy working for nothing."

Armed with a background in consumer retailing, Caborn has a thick skin when it comes to negotiations and selling. In the business for three years, she closed $2.5 million worth of business in 2002. She says that over just the last three years she's seen consumer tastes change and transform, but she sticks to her guns in saying that the majority of them are still enjoyable to work with, despite their increasingly demanding ways—particularly when it comes to asking for lower rates in exchange for more work.

FICKLE CUSTOMERS

Real estate is a relationship-based business, so it's only natural that an agent's customers would be first on the list of outside pressures affecting an agent's success right now. When it comes to product marketing, it's the product, stupid. But if there's one key, driving force behind the changes in a service-based industry like real estate, it's the customer, stupid.

Changing consumer preferences and the vast amounts of information that are now available at everyone's fingertips via the Internet have been the driving forces behind most of the recent changes in the market. Those changes include technological innovations, increased competition among brokers, commission compression, the increase in online and discount brokers, and even industry consolidation.

All companies know that their customers want everything yesterday, but home sellers and buyers, it seems, also want it for free, or at least for less than the typical 6 to 7 percent commission that real estate agents are accustomed to. Again, agents and brokers are not allowed to set any kind of commission, but it's common knowledge that in some markets the going rate is 5.5 percent, and in others the going rate is 7 percent. Unlike lawyers, real estate agents are not accustomed to doing pro bono work, thus causing something of a conflict between agents' desire to satisfy their clients' needs and the requirement that they also make a living.

The simple fact is that economic conditions, the Internet, and higher levels of consumer confidence do not make the task of buying or selling a home any easier. Commonly known as one of the biggest decisions that any consumer will make in a lifetime, buying a house is daunting—from selecting a neighborhood and a specific house, to figuring out how much one can afford, to sitting down at the closing table to sign a mile-high stack of contracts and documents.

The challenges that go along with selling a home range from pricing the home competitively (but not out of the market) and selling it within a reasonable time frame to figuring out the best way to market it (is it through newspaper ads, open houses, the Internet, or a combination of all three?). Put simply, consumers may be more educated and knowledgeable about the behind-the-scenes aspect of the real estate industry, but they're still as confused as ever.

According to a 2003 survey conducted by LandAmerica Financial Group, Inc., of Richmond, Virginia, consumers are perplexed by the mountain of forms, processes, and legal jargon that come along with the home purchase process. LandAmerica reports that 86 percent of home buyers report difficulty and confusion in the process and more than one-third of them experienced delays in closing on their house purchase.

"Clearly, though they are buying homes in record numbers, home buyers are in need of education and guidance from their real estate advisers," says Janet Alpert, president of LandAmerica. "The onus then falls on those real estate professionals to answer questions and provide clarity to make the home-buying process go as smoothly as possible."

The survey found that consumers think that the hardest part of buying a home is managing the sheer number of separate steps or processes necessary to close the purchase without a delay. LandAmerica found that respondents voiced most concern over the process of establishing an escrow account (49 percent), followed by negotiating a contract (46 percent), ensuring that appraisals are conducted properly (42 percent), and buying title insurance (42 percent).

The level of confusion that exists as a result of a lack of understanding of the home-buying process differed little on the basis of age, income, or home-buying experience, the survey found. In fact, nearly eight of ten previous home buyers (those who had been through the process at least once before) found the experience confusing despite their experience, but first-time home buyers were most likely to experience difficulty or confusion.

The percentage that found managing the processes difficult remained high across all age groups. The survey found that 95 percent of 18- to 29-year-olds found it difficult, compared with 84 percent of 30- to 49-year-olds and 79 percent of those aged 50 and older. A full 43 percent of respondents look to their real estate agent to ensure a smooth home-buying experience, and another 42 percent rely on the advice of lenders and attorneys.

Perhaps that's why nearly four out of five home buyers in 2001 used a real estate agent as an important information source and to assist in the transaction, according to NAR, and only 13 percent of all homes sold were sold by the owner directly (also known as an FSBO, or for sale by owner).

YOU'RE NOT ALONE

The fact that home buyers and sellers need all the help they can get with the real estate transaction hasn't stopped them from "asking for blood," as

Caborn put it. And if you thought you were the only agent with more demanding customers landing on your doorstep, think again.

According to the Council of Residential Specialists, a Chicago-based not-for-profit affiliate of NAR with about 40,000 members worldwide, a 2002 online, random-sample survey of its members showed that virtually all have experienced rising customer demands over the past five years, for reasons that include easy Internet access to real estate information and expectations of "24/7" service as a result of technological advances.

About 60 percent of survey respondents said that customer demands have "increased greatly" since 1997, whereas 40 percent say that they have "grown somewhat." Major factors stimulating rising demands are "access to market data on the Internet," cited by 87 percent of respondents; "technological advances causing the public to expect service and availability '24/7,'" cited by 84 percent; and "increasing familiarity with the sales process," cited by 58 percent.

Lesser factors include a "growing number of inexperienced first-time buyers," cited by 22 percent; "increasing exposure to other customer-centered service industries (e.g., hotels, fine restaurants)," cited by 17 percent; the "increased age of customers," cited by 12 percent; and the "decreased age of customers," cited by 10 percent.

Above all, the single most important factor fueling intensifying customer demands was "Technological advances causing expectations of service and availability '24/7,'" chosen by 50 percent of respondents, with "access to market data on the Internet" taking 37 percent of the vote.

The CRS survey revealed that in order to cope, participants are dealing with more demanding customers in several ways, most notably by working longer hours (67 percent). And while 25 percent of those surveyed say they are operating with existing employees, 31 percent are hiring additional assistants, 32 percent are making referrals to outside vendors, and 31 percent are forging formal alliances with outside service providers.

Agents are also racking up more designations, credentials, and education in an effort to better prepare themselves to operate in the industry. For thirteen years, Jesse Acevedo was content with the Realtor designation after his name. But in 2001, Acevedo found himself competing in a tougher market and working with a broader range of home buyers with different needs. To deal with the changing tides, this Realtor and office manager with ERA Ace Realty and Investments Inc. in Plantation, Florida, set out to add some new credentials after his name by investing time and money in continuing education.

For Acevedo, it started in September 2001 when he spent two weeks and about $1,400 to obtain his broker's license. He says that the course provided valuable information on legal matters, escrows to deposits, and contract writing. A trainer for ERA on a national basis, in September 2002 Acevedo took the company's thirty-five-hour Train the Trainer course, which teaches new ERA agents what it takes to sell residential real estate. Five months later he obtained his SRES (Senior Residential Specialist) designation, which he says "helps him better serve the senior community" in Florida. Acevedo also has his eBuyer designation, is a WebEx trainer and an ABR (Accredited Buyer Representative), and was recently selected as an elite member of ERA's National Training Advisory Council.

Acevedo says that his significant investment in education over the last two years has resulted in a 20 percent increase in business. "It has made me more knowledgeable about the entire industry," says Acevedo. "Customers these days want to deal with professionals who have titles, so this gives me a definite edge in the marketplace" (see Figure 2-1).

TECHNOLOGY-DRIVEN?

Consumers today know that they can sell their homes on their own, should they wish to. They can turn to a $299 flat-fee broker to at least get their property in the MLS; or they can hire an agent who sells her services on a piecemeal or "menu" basis. Put these possibilities together and the traditional, full-service real estate agents find themselves in a precarious position, struggling to stay one step ahead in a consumer-centric industry, and earning less in commissions that they're accustomed to making. Most top-producing agents (I've interviewed many of them on this very topic over the

Figure 2-1.

RISING OUT OF THE SLUSH PILE

Real estate agents who are interested in gaining an edge through education, credentials, and designations should investigate the following options:

☐ *CRS (Certified Residential Specialist).* To accommodate the residential needs of home buyers and sellers, the Residential Sales Council of the National Association of Realtors instituted a class of expert real estate professional known as the CRS. Every CRS has undergone a rigorous, specialized course of detailed training aimed at making residential transactions as smooth and worry-free as possible (www.crs.com).

☐ *GRI (Graduate Realtors Institute).* Conferred by NAR, the GRI is presented to Realtors who have completed a comprehensive education program in residential real estate. The program's focus is on practical real estate training (www.realtor.org).

☐ *e-PRO.* Agents who have successfully completed the e-PRO training program for real estate professionals are considered to have above-average knowledge in the area of online real estate. Endorsed by NAR, the e-PRO course teaches professionals the nuts and bolts of working with real estate online, including Web sites, e-mail, online tools, and consumer preferences (www.realtor.org).

☐ *CRB (Certified Real Estate Broker Manager).* This designation is the highest designation a broker manager, owner, or qualifying broker can earn. It takes years of practical experience and hours of formal classroom instruction and training to earn this designation, which allows for more skillful management of an office or business (www.crb.com).

☐ *ABR (Accredited Buyer Representative).* This designation is the benchmark of excellence in buyer representation and is awarded by the Real Estate Buyers Agent Council (REBAC) of NAR to agents who meet the specified educational and practical experience criteria (www.rebac.net).

☐ *CRPP (Certified Relocation Professional Program).* Established in 1990, the Employee Relocation Council's (ERC) Certified Relocation Professional Program formally recognizes those who have mastered extensive knowledge on the principles and practices of relocation (www.erc.org).

last seven years) will scoff at the idea that they're somehow being disinter-mediated by a mix of technology and smarter consumers, but any middle-of-the-road or low-producing agent will spill his guts on how tough the business has become over the last five years.

INFORMATION OVERLOAD

Call it information overload if you will, but today's consumer is pretty savvy when it comes to the house hunt. Should they be so inclined, buyers can pull up a local MLS, search for homes by criteria, figure out the addresses, look at the homes, and even line up services like financing and appraisals on their own, online. Ambitious sellers are setting up Web sites, uploading virtual tours of their homes to the Net, managing their own open houses, and using a title company and/or an attorney (depending on state laws) to close their homes.

It's enough to make a real estate agent gasp.

According to J. Lennox Scott, chairman and CEO at John L. Scott Real Estate in Seattle, in the age of the Internet the public wants a quick response, which can be difficult for some agents.

"Customers want instant information and communication through the Internet, by phone, and in person," says Scott. "Our industry took a bad rap for years about agents not returning e-mail, but that's because most agents are out in the field—not sitting behind the desk all day."

Scott points to wireless devices, such as the Treo, through which agents can send and receive e-mail while on the road, as a true savior for the real estate professional who has only a small window of time in which to respond to customer inquiries. Also helpful are e-mail notification pro-grams, such as John L. Scott's Home Delivery system, which notifies a consumer immediately via e-mail when homes come onto the market that fit the consumer's search parameters.

Not all agents are intimidated by their knowledgeable, tech-savvy cus-tomers. One successful agent in Sacramento, California, calls the Internet an "incredible thing" for the industry, noting that a full 85 percent of all buyers are currently using the Internet to educate themselves. "Buyers are coming to us so much better prepared," he says. "In a way, it's kept our cost of doing business in check."

The fact that consumers can find their own information without an agent has put the real estate professional in much more of an educational role. Take the time a home buyer kept bringing Toni K. Napolitano long lists of property information printed out from the Internet. A Realtor associate with The Keyes Co./Realtors in Fort Lauderdale, Napolitano knew that her challenge was to help that buyer focus, or risk spending months scouring the entire county for the right home.

"Home buyers, and particularly the younger ones, are so computer literate that they're doing searches long before they even come to me," says Napolitano. Getting those buyers focused takes guidance and education. "It was a matter of helping this customer realize what lifestyle she really wanted, then determining what area would best fit that lifestyle," says Napolitano. "The key in working with any young buyer is helping them pinpoint exactly what they want to accomplish through homeownership, then fitting a particular property to their desired lifestyle."

What Napolitano also knows is that despite the growing presence of the Internet, agents like herself continue to be the key information source that home buyers turn to for help, and that sellers rely on to market their homes to the masses. To sift through the chaos of newspaper ads, yard signs, and real estate magazines, the vast majority of consumers still prefer working with an agent. NAR's 2003 profile of home buyers and sellers proved the point: Nearly 90 percent of consumers who visit the Internet for home information end up working with an agent anyway.

NAR also found that nearly three out of four home buyers now use the Internet as a tool when searching for a home, and that those who use the Internet are more likely to use real estate professionals. The survey showed that 71 percent of home buyers used the Internet in their search for a home during the first quarter of 2003, up from 41 percent during 2001. In total, three out of four buyers purchased a home through a real estate agent or broker, up from 69 percent in 2001; 14 percent bought from a builder, and 9 percent bought directly from an owner. Of buyers who used an agent, 63 percent chose a buyer representative. Satisfaction with the agent was high for both buyers and sellers.

The findings are particularly encouraging to the over 432,000 (BLS, 2000) working real estate agents in the United States who once viewed the Internet as a threat to their livelihood, like Caborn, who says the more computer-savvy a customer is, the harder she has to work to close the deal. These days, when such customers outline their criteria for neighborhood, home price, and home size, they also hand Caborn a stack of potential properties that they've already found on the Web.

"When working with a buyer, along with all of the listings that I pull up, they come up with their own. Most of the latter are not based on the criteria that they've given me," says Caborn. "As an agent I can't really refuse to show them those properties, which means double work for me during the process."

Take the customer who tells Caborn that he wants a concrete-block home, then pulls up a frame house online because the virtual tour was attractive and the size was right. "I have no problem with them changing the criteria," she says, "but it does become difficult to sort of convince them that maybe they don't want to see those listings because that's not what they've told me that they want. It's really kind of a fine line, to some degree. Overall, however, real estate is a very enjoyable and fulfilling profession."

PLAYING THE ROLE

Ten years into her role as a Realtor associate with RE/MAX Suburban in Chicago, Mary Zentz has seen a major shift in customer preferences, demands, and likes and dislikes. In the past, a "nice client" would almost always refer another "nice client" to her, thus keeping the chain of business tightly linked together with little or no advertising and marketing fees. The result was that a full 90 percent of her business came from referrals.

In the last two years, Zentz says, the landscape has changed as the economy has put a damper on the number of executives who are buying homes and/or moving up into larger ones. Zentz sold $15 million worth of property in 2002, most of it still through referrals, but her primary market, which consists of buyers of $400,000 to $500,000 homes, has been affected by the nation's economic uncertainty, and these people aren't talking with one another about the house-hunting process as much. "It's decreasing referrals in this price range," says Zentz, whose business has doubled as a result of the productivity of her Web site and prospect incubation systems. "Since these are not referrals, my overall referral percentage is down."

"A lot of books these days tell consumers how they can save money on anything they do in their entire lives, and buying a house is one of them," says Zentz, who in 2003 worked with a client who phoned her no less than three to four times a day in the preliminary stages of the home search—long before the client had even picked a home and started the actual process.

"When you're in the actual buying process, it's normal to talk to someone several times a day," Zentz says. "But when someone is just in the looking stage, I don't expect to talk to them three or four times a day because I don't have anything to tell them." To maximize her productivity, Zentz relies on automated systems like Fusion MLS (available through many local MLS systems) to spit out new listing data to customers via e-mail, based on their house-hunting criteria, every twenty-four hours.

But once a day isn't good enough for most customers anymore, according to Zentz, who winds up telling her consistent callers that she just doesn't have any more information to share. Some would argue that Zentz risks having that client call another agent who will somehow pull the information out of his hat, although most agents put trust in the fact that once they've agreed to work with a client, that client will stick with them. (To prevent losing clients, she says, most agents use buyers agency contracts.)

When a client is in "buying mode," you can find Zentz checking the MLS four to five times a day for that client and personally delivering him or her the most updated market information available. "This is where it's really important to have an assistant attached to a real-time MLS data-base," says Zentz, who recently sold a property within an hour and a half of its becoming available on the MLS. "It became a dual offer, and if my assistant and I had been fielding unproductive calls we would not have had the opportunity to secure this property for our buyer," says Zentz.

To make sure she takes care of her top clients, Zentz keeps a list of "top ten buyers" (those who are ready to buy and totally motivated), for whom she and her office manager conduct several daily searches—on top of the Fusion MLS system search—through the system to see what's come up for sale that meets their criteria. If there's a match, she contacts the client immediately to get a head start on the automated system, which doesn't send out notifications until 4 a.m. each morning.

Zentz says she's pleased with the stronghold she's carved out in her market. As a RE/MAX agent, she takes home 100 percent of the commissions she earns, and she says that she understands her clients' anxiousness about possibly missing out on a great buying opportunity in the hot Chicago marketplace. The combination of Fusion and her top ten list prevent that from happening. "I go to great lengths to secure my buyers their dream homes," says Zentz, who like all business owners must earn a certain income level to support her activities. Her typical day comprises ten to twelve hours of work, and she considers herself lucky to have one day off out of ten workdays.

SURPRISE, SURPRISE

Sometimes a customer can surprise you, even in these changing times. Caborn says she recently sold a home to a twenty-nine-year-old man who called on her when the listing agent for a certain property was otherwise occupied and unable to show it to him. It turned out that the property wasn't what he was looking for, so Caborn accessed the local MLS system and pulled up a variety of other properties for sale in his price range and desired neighborhood.

"He found one that he absolutely loved, and I acted as the selling agent on the sale," says Caborn, who sees her role as being an educator and support system for such clients, who have a broad idea of what they want but who truly don't know how to go about closing one of the most important deals they'll ever make in their lifetime. "After the closing, he told me that he could have never found that on his own, and thanked me for my services," says Caborn.

Not all clients offer such gratitude, says Caborn, who works with a wide range of buyers and sellers and prefers not to focus on any particular niche (something many real estate experts advise, as evidenced in the next section). She says that trial and error has led her to be choosier about the customers she works with. Take the homeowner who called her out to a home in Orlando for a listing appointment. Caborn drove over to see that house and wound up speaking to the person who was renting it, only to find out that the homeowner was interviewing several agents and expected to pit them against one another to get the lowest commission percentage.

"I knew right off the bat that I wouldn't get that listing because I don't take listings for less than the going rate (typically 6 to 7 percent in most areas of the nation, though most state laws dictate that all commission rates are negotiable)," says Caborn. "We work very hard as agents, and my philosophy is that if you don't make a living at it, then there's really no reason to be doing it."

But just because you're a full-service real estate agent doesn't mean that you have to wait until the closing to get compensated. Just ask Ann Leviton, broker/owner at Mavrik Realty in Minneapolis/St. Paul, Minnesota, who collects a $250 retainer fee up front from home buyers when they decide to work with her and sign a contract for exclusive buyer representation.

Roughly 70 percent of Leviton's business comes from working with buyers, of which 70 percent are first-time home buyers. In the real estate business since 1994, she completed thirty-seven transaction sides in 2002 for a total of $6.5 million on an average home price of $176,000. She says the knowledge she's gained from working with such buyers has positioned her as an expert in that niche, thus paving the way for the nominal retainer fee.

"I'm very knowledgeable on both the housing and the financing side, and I'm especially good at helping first-time buyers—who are often short on cash—find special financing to maximize their purchasing power," Leviton explains. "I also work hard to make the often-stressful home-buying process fun by exposing my playful side to prospects and clients alike, most notably through my personal promotion and marketing, which jokes about it and sometimes pokes fun at it." (Her newspaper ads, for example, often include headlines like "Happy Hour Is a Smooth Closing," "Plays Well with Others" and "Had It with Renting? Dump the Landlord."

In exchange, Leviton says she gets a loyal, appreciative client referral base that's always willing to refer new business her way—one of the key business channels that all agents strive for. She doesn't let the $250 retainer fee—which she refunds at the closing table if she receives her full commission from the seller—stand in the way of doing business. She does, however, strive to professionalize the agent-client relationship by collecting the retainer fee and to make her buyers realize that she's work-ing for them and their best interests at all times and that she too is devot-ing considerable time and energy to their home hunt from start to finish. (She notes that in Minnesota, buyer representation agreements may be cancelled at any time, so full compensation for services rendered is never a sure thing; should an agreement be cancelled, at least she gets to keep the retainer fee.)

"Every once in a while someone might be cash poor, and be getting most of their down payment and closing costs covered by the lender, a grant, or gift funds, so I let the retainer fee slide until the closing," Leviton says. "But I've had clients so happy with the job I've done find-ing them the right home that in the end they plead with me at the clos-ing table to take the money."

HOW ABOUT A NICHE?

Caborn may be steaming along without a niche, servicing a wide variety of home buyers and sellers, but many other agents prefer to pick a niche and stick with it. It can be a geographic niche, a job-related niche (an ex-teacher, for example, would do well by working with educators), a certain ethnic group, a neighborhood, or some other specialty area. The value? A niche allows an agent to become a true expert in that specialty area and helps deflect those learning curves thrown at them by demanding consumers.

For David Mohabir, there's nothing quite like sitting across the closing table from a pair of young home buyers who have just had the keys to their new abode handed to them. "To see that sense of accomplishment—that happiness on their faces—is always a thrill," says Mohabir, a Realtor with ERA All Action, Inc., in Sunrise, Florida.

For Mohabir, that thrill comes several times a month. In 2002, roughly 70 percent of his $8 million in sales was generated by deals involving home buyers in their twenties and thirties. A Realtor for four years, Mohabir intentionally courts younger buyers by specializing in condominiums, townhouses, and starter single-family homes ranging in price from $80,000 to $200,000.

Thanks to the low-interest-rate environment of the early 2000s, Mohabir's niche was a good one. He says he's seen a marked increase in the pool of young buyers. Those who would typically be renters, for example, are taking advantage of low mortgage interest rates and flexible lending programs and becoming homeowners at a younger age than in the past. When they jump into the home-buying process feet first, Mohabir is there to brace their fall.

"Younger people realize the affordability of owning a home versus renting," says Mohabir, who has even placed young buyers into town-houses or condos at about the same monthly cost as renting. "When they stop paying someone else's mortgage, they end up with tax advantages and equity buildup—all at just about the same price as they would pay while renting."

Other agents may pick geographic niches, such as a certain neighborhood or region, where they can really concentrate their farming and marketing efforts and establish themselves as "the person to go to" when you want to buy or sell a home in these areas. A highly successful agent in

Boca Raton, Florida, for example, does 80 percent of her thirty-three transactions a year in a pair of twenty-three-story towers with 378 units situated right on the beach.

Over the last sixteen years, this agent has become the "best in the marketplace" and has made her name synonymous with real estate at that condominium. She lives on site and considers that choice yet another edge when it comes to meeting and mingling with potential customers. She says other agents had the edge in the condo when she moved in, so penetrating that business took time, patience, and a plan for success.

"During the early years, I learned the skills of successful condo farming by starting with simple steps like mailing out flyers to residents, then slowly progressed to learning the nuances of the building and units," she says. "From there, I built valuable, long-term relationships with clients, met their individual needs, and followed up on every business detail."

The agent warns that success doesn't come easy or quickly for agents breaking into a new niche. "Be willing to spend both money and time on the farming process, and don't expect to get deluged by phone calls after handing out a stack of flyers and business cards once or twice," she warns. She adds that the trick is to keep your name and reputation out there and in front of the customer at all times. Depending on the time of year, for example, she distributes calendars, thank-you notes, and sometimes even music CDs during the holidays. She also factors fifteen extra minutes into her schedule in the morning because she frequently gets waylaid in the parking garage, talking to potential and existing customers.

Greg Herder, CEO at Hobbs/Herder Training, says that finding a target market is one of the first steps any agent should take, even though some may balk at having to exclude certain markets or specialty areas in favor of their niche. Herder, whose Newport Beach, California, advertising agency specializes in marketing materials for residential real estate agents, dismisses their objections as hogwash. That's because it's much easier to be a big fish in a small pond, rather than the other way around.

"You can't go for the whole world," says Herder. "Yet most agents have the mentality that says, 'If I limit myself, I'm going to miss out.' Unfortunately, the exact opposite happens." Herder points to one of the nation's top real estate agents, Allan Domb of Philadelphia, who calls himself "the Condo King" and works with buyers and sellers in a handful of condominium complexes. Today, he's the city's largest luxury condo real estate agent.

"You have to pick a niche—be it geographic, lifestyle, or professional. Just pick something that's a natural part of your personality or past job background and exploit it," says Herder, adding that those agents who do focus on a particular group can then provide services and products that are of real value to that group. Web sites that reach out to a general audience are a dime a dozen, for example, but one that caters specifically to Hispanic home buyers will certainly get attention if it is positioned correctly.

"Agents who limit themselves tend to do extraordinarily well," says Herder. "When they can put together a message that's targeted and appropriate for that group, that has a specific appeal that really will make them stand out so much more effectively than just being another real estate agent." And remember, Herder says, that a title like "service specialist" is not a niche. "I've never actually seen a campaign that says, 'I'm a liar and a cheat,' have you?" (See Figure 2-2.)

THE MULTICULTURAL NICHE

There are hundreds of different niches for agents to explore, but we'll look here at one that is both growing and ripe for the picking: the multicultural home buyer market. Ten years ago, Don Ware was a new real estate agent in need of a niche. Being situated near the Saddleback Valley area of Mission Viejo, California, he picked up on a trend that would take more established agents a couple more years to notice: that California's Hispanic, Asian American, African American, and other multicultural markets were growing both in size and buying power.

Two years into his real estate career, that early revelation led Ware to the business niche he was looking for. "I started working with the multicultural market by default," says Ware, a Realtor with RE/MAX in Mission Viejo. "They were just out there, looking for properties to buy."

Figure 2-2.

JUST THE FACTS, MA'AM

NAR's 2003 "Profile of Home Buyers and Sellers" found that:

❑ The typical buyer walked through ten homes and searched for eight weeks before finding the home that was ultimately purchased.

❑ Eighty-six percent of buyers used a real estate agent during their search.

❑ Three-quarters of buyers bought their home with the assistance of an agent.

❑ Forty-one percent of home buyers first found out about the home they purchased through an agent.

❑ Forty-two percent of buyers used the Internet frequently as part of their home search.

❑ Buyers typically searched for homes on their own for two weeks before contacting an agent.

❑ Forty-four percent of buyers found their real estate agent through a referral from a friend, neighbor, or relative.

❑ Eighty-nine percent of home buyers who used a real estate professional would definitely use, or consider using, that agent again.

❑ Eighty-three percent of sellers sold their homes with the assistance of an agent.

❑ Sixty-nine percent of sellers contacted only one agent before listing their home.

❑ Forty percent first found their listing agent through a referral from a friend or family member.

❑ When choosing an agent, 62 percent of sellers thought that the agent's reputation was the most important factor.

❑ Seventy percent of home sellers reported that they would definitely use the same agent in their next sale or recommend the agent to a friend.

❑ Nearly one-third of "for-sale-by-owner" (FSBO) sellers thought that understanding and completing the necessary paperwork was the most difficult task in selling a home themselves.

Today, 95 percent of Ware's sales, which totaled $5.5 million in 2002, came from working with multicultural buyers and sellers. His typical client is a multicultural family looking for a single-family home. Most become long-term clients, referring both family and friends to Ware, who speaks both Vietnamese and Spanish fluently.

Ware credits his ability to be culturally sensitive and the way he's gone the extra mile to learn the ins and outs of the multicultural market with helping him find this lucrative niche. "I have clients who have been with me for ten years," says Ware, "and I handle their entire family's real estate transactions."

Ware is one of a growing number of real estate agents who have come to realize the ethnic melting pot in which they're operating in the United States. They know that it takes more than just a surface knowledge of these customers' wants, needs, and buying habits to effectively reach out to them and retain them as lifelong clients. It's become a niche in itself, mainly because these customers are both plentiful and in need of help during the home-buying and home-selling process.

In July 2003, the U.S. Census Bureau reported that the nation's Hispanic population had grown much faster than the population as a whole, increasing from 35.3 million on April 1, 2000, to 38.8 million on July 1, 2002. Among the race groups, Asians had the highest rate of growth, at 9.0 percent. The Census Bureau estimates that the nation's foreign-born population in 2002 numbered 32.5 million, accounting for 11.5 percent of the total U.S. population. Among the foreign-born population, 52 percent were born in Latin America, 26 percent in Asia, 14 percent in Europe, and the remaining 8 percent in other regions of the world, such as Africa and Oceania.

That spells opportunity for agents who take the time and care to learn how to work with those buyers, says Michael Lee, a Castro Valley, California–based diversity consultant and author of *Opening Doors: Selling to Multicultural Real Estate Clients*. In fact, Lee says, agents who ignore the nation's increasingly diverse population risk missing opportunities. NAR, for example, estimates that between now and 2010, 60 percent of all home buyers will be minorities. The problem is, agents tend to lean toward treating everyone the same way, even if this means handing a list of potential properties to someone accompanied by a seeing-eye dog, according to Lee. "What agents really need to do is customize their services to meet the unique needs of each client," says Lee, who has been a licensed real estate broker since 1976.

For one Coldwell Banker broker, catering to the Hispanic market means taking Spanish lessons three times a week to reach her goal of being fluent in the language by the end of the year. She says that knowing the language will give her the communication tools she needs in order to truly understand her area's growing multicultural market. "It's a challenge, but I have a real passion about it and want to be able to understand the people that I'm working with," says the broker, whose firm has 850 agents and 25 offices. "I feel I can do that best by understanding their language and being able to communicate with them."

Lee warns agents to brace themselves for a very different experience from what they're used to. Most multicultural buyers, for example, make large purchases not on emotional instincts, but for investment purposes. "Caucasians tend to get emotionally involved and fall in love with their homes, while buyers from diverse cultures look at them more as an investment in America," Lee says. "They're more analytical about the purchase, and if one property doesn't satisfy them, they know another will come along."

In other words, telling Asian American clients that they'll "just love this home" probably isn't a good sales pitch, says Lee, who advises agents to both understand and accept the differences, then learn to distinguish each individual culture's "buying signs" or "hot buttons."

Ware says that multicultural buyers are also sensitive about the geographic locations of their investments. Most of them want a certain neighborhood, school district, and location, for example, while some have special requirements about the direction in which their house faces, based on beliefs like feng shui.

Such challenges aside, the rewards of working with the multicultural market include a steady stream of referrals and possibly a lifetime of working with an entire family of potential home buyers and sellers. "The biggest reward comes when the multicultural clients are grateful enough to refer their friends and family members to you," says one real estate agent. "That's truly when I know I've done a good job."

For agents interested in learning more about how to work with the multicultural market, NAR's "At Home with Diversity: One America" certification was created by NAR and approved by the U.S. Department of Housing and Urban Development (HUD). It's a diversity certification course for real estate professionals that gives participants insight into the thought patterns and behavior of a diverse client base. Learn more online at www.realtor.org/divweb.nsf. NAR also recommends the book *Kiss, Bow, or Shake Hands: How to Do Business in Sixty Countries* by Terri Morrison, Wayne A. Conaway, and George A. Borden (Adams Media Corporation, 1995), which offers advice on business etiquette in dozens of countries.

BUILDING A CUSTOMER BASE

So, you know that your customers' preferences are changing and that you must cater to them as specifically as possible, while always walking a fine line between your own needs and their wants and demands. You also know that finding one or more niches to go after is probably a better approach than shooting darts at one big dartboard, and that working with a customer base that you have some sort of connection with is a good idea. The good news is that you don't have to compromise yourself or your ethics to meet those demands and still turn a profit as an agent, but you do have to know how to play the game right.

One of the cornerstones is a good referral pipeline, says David Jenks, vice president of research and development for the sixth largest real estate company in North America, Austin, Texas–based Keller Williams Realty International. In other words, you need a well-populated list of customers that you've done business with and the friends and family they've shared your business cards or Web site with. Your goal is to get those referrals to think of you when it comes to time to buy or sell a home.

"What differentiates the agents who are doing sixty, a hundred, or more transactions a year from those who are doing one a month (the industry norm) is referrals," says Jenks. "The key to staying in the top 20 percent of agents is to sustain a good flow of business that's driven by word-of-mouth referrals from a client base that you stay in touch with in a targeted way that consistently markets your services."

That's a mouthful, but what Jenks is saying is this: Pick a good crowd of close business contacts that you can reach out to on a consistent basis (via an e-mail newsletter, postcards, flower seeds, and so on) with something that is of value to them. The idea is to build up business with customers who will think of you when it comes time to buy or sell—or when someone asks them for the name of a good real estate agent—thus significantly reducing your need to haggle with demanding, cutthroat customers with whom you have no established relationship.

The practice is working in the field. Several years ago, ERA American Realty of Northwestern Florida in Fort Walton Beach, Florida, launched a client follow-up program that its seventy agents can sign up for and never have to think about again. For $20, agents submit clients for one of the three categories in the Sold Program (past clients, current clients, and potential clients), which begins with a simple "How did we do?" survey sent out after the transaction is completed. For the next five years, clients receive six mailings a year, including postcards, magnetic memo boards, a four-year subscription to *Today's Living* magazine, a yearly anniversary card, and customized return address labels—all sent in the name of the original agent.

In 2001, ERA American Realty extended the program to eight years and added cross-sales buyers to its database. "We found that a lot of customers were still in their homes five years later, so we extended it," says Gloria Frazier, president and broker. "The 'cross-sales' buyer category allows agents to stay in touch with buyers whose properties we listed but didn't sell." Managed on an ACT! database by one part-time employee, the Sold Program has paid off for the company, which has watched its repeat referral business grow from 40 percent of its business to 58 percent since 1995.

Here's another good example of how a targeted approach to customer farming can work in your favor as an agent. The Family Team at Keller Williams Realty in Palm Harbor, Florida, had never tracked its sources of business until 2002, when a thorough review revealed that a whopping 87 percent of the team's business came from referrals. Eager to capitalize on that already-high number, the Family Team assembled in January 2002 to figure out a way to "touch" those valuable customers on a more regular basis. It created an aggressive program that reaches out and touches all one thousand of its past and present clients thirty-three times a year.

"In order to really make someone remember you, you have to hit them every twenty-one days," says SuzAnne Mabus, Realtor. "That's where the thirty-three-touch program comes in." The "touching" includes sending out calendars, football schedules, daylight saving time cards, and twelve newsletters annually. The Family Team also delivers bags of candy on holidays like Easter and creates and mails out music CDs (holiday music for Christmas, love songs on Valentine's Day) four times a year. At the bottom of every item is this note: "If you know of anyone who wants to buy or sell real estate, would you please let The Family Team know?"

Mabus says the team spends 13 percent of its income on advertising, and "if it costs more than 50 or 75 cents, we won't do it." To make the yearlong process easier, the group plans out its entire year every October. The payoff has been significant: Sales have grown from $3 million in 2001 to $7 million in 2002 to an expected $10 million in 2003. "And we're not working as hard to constantly generate new business," Mabus says, "because our referrals are calling us."

REMEMBER: YOU'RE THE PRO HERE

The Internet is a great place to preview homes, watch virtual home tours, and get the lowdown on every property within a certain MLS's jurisdiction, but how does a potential buyer know that that home isn't located in a sinkhole area? And how does a single home seller know that it's safe to let someone in to look at her home at 9 p.m. at night? That's where you, the agent, come in. So no matter how many reams of paper a customer comes at you with, or how tough the customer is at negotiating, you're the one who took the time to get educated, apply your knowledge from your past life and work experience, bone up on technology, and learn your geographical region inside and out. You did all this to make the customer's home buying or selling process that much easier, and you'll need to both show and tell your customers that during the course of business.

Real estate agents are hardly alone in their plight of wrangling with increasingly demanding customers. Frugal, discerning consumers are everywhere—at flea markets, in the aisles of the Best Buy store, and dealing one-on-one with the independent carpet cleaners of the world. They're everywhere, and no business can afford to avoid them, so businesses are all learning to work with them and meet their demands without losing their shirts. Just think, by the year 2014 it will probably be possible to purchase and finance a home online, conduct an "electronic closing," and sign all documents via a video screen, so the best is yet to come.

Through it all, it's those agents who nurture relationships with their consumers and communities who will prevail, despite the challenges that new technology, consumer demands, and changing business environments throw at them. "The top-producing agents are still going to be the ones who can fulfill the role of lifelong, trusted adviser," says John Foltz, president of Realty Executives in Phoenix. He himself has worked with the same family seven times over the last eleven years, and he says, "They would go nowhere else, not because of our friendship, but because they saw me as a trusted adviser."

Dave Liniger, RE/MAX International cofounder and chairman of the board, advises agents to remember that while consumers' expectations have gone up, so has the individual agent's ability to serve as that adviser. "Most fascinating is the speed at which you can deal with consumers now, thanks to e-mail, faxes, overnight mail, and other technological advances," says Liniger, who has been in the business nearly forty years. "So customers' expectations may have gone up, but the agent's ability to fulfill those expectations is much greater today than ever before."

Six Things to Remember from Chapter 2

- ❑ Customer preferences are constantly changing and are driven primarily by access to technology, information, and more choices during the process of buying or selling a home.

- ❑ Just because customers are knowledgeable doesn't mean that the real estate transaction is any easier for them, as evidenced by the fact that four out of five consumers use agents to assist them with the process.

- ❑ Agents who feel that they're working with increasingly demanding customers are not alone. Sources ranging from international real estate groups to individual agents concur that the average home buyer or seller is becoming more difficult to do business with.

- ❑ In order to provide valuable information and services to their clients, many real estate agents prefer to drill down on a specific customer niche, be it geographic, demographic, or some other strategy. Others fare just as well by working with a broader, more general market.

- ❑ The real estate industry offers a wide range of professional designations that have been created to help agents stand out in the marketplace and display their expertise in areas like relocation and technology.

- ❑ As consumers have become more demanding, real estate agents have become more able to meet their needs by using tools like voice mail, e-mail, and fax transmissions to communicate and share information quickly with one another and with their clients.

CHAPTER 3

Jumping on the Technology Train

GET ON BOARD

Edward Krigsman rode the technology wave right into the real estate industry. He caught the wave in 1997, which means that acronyms like VOW (virtual office web site) and IDX (Internet data exchange) are second nature for him, as are technology gadgets like wireless personal digital assistants, electronic MLS systems, and electronic lockboxes.

As associate broker with John L. Scott Real Estate in Seattle, Krigsman heads up a four-person team that ranked tenth out of 3,000 company agents in 2002 by netting sales of about $27 million. Krigsman counts his personal Web site, local online MLS service, Compaq laptop computer (which he regularly boots up and connects to the Internet at the local Starbucks coffee shop during the day), an IPAQ PDA, and Microsoft Office suite with MS Outlook among his most valuable tech tools.

"Technology basically overlays my entire marketing plan—which is to work with the mid- to high-end urban properties in the city," says Krigsman. "Because I myself am tech-savvy, I tend to attract the types of clients who are also familiar with technology, more efficient, and more appreciative of the technology and how it facilitates the real estate transaction."

Technology also helps agents like Krigsman connect with buyers and sellers before he even meets them. When they visit his Web site they can view not only his firm's listings, but also those in the entire Seattle area through a concept known as *broker reciprocity*, in which competitive firms agree to have a portion of their listing information accessible through a search function on each other's Web sites. (Note: The Pacific Northwest happens to be one of the more progressive areas when it comes to technology adoption and broker reciprocity in that much of the region introduced, accepted, and used the system years before the rest of the country caught on to its value.)

Unlike some real estate agents, who immediately saw such technological innovations as a threat to their very existence, Krigsman says that he knows no other way. "I'm always seeking out new efficiencies, new ways to sell more houses and make more money using technology," he says. "I've never really thought of it in any other way."

TECH TRANSITIONS

For every Krigsman there is an agent who really likes the "old way" of doing things and therefore has yet to fully embrace the power of technology. Human nature comes into play here, and since many of us are afraid of the unknown, those agents who are behind the technology curve view the concept as a threat to the industry and its function. Throw in the fact that most people over the age of 35 were never introduced to computers in school (I was among the first wave of college students to get my hands on an Apple IIE for word processing in college back in 1987), and it's easy to see why technology is throwing a learning curve at some agents.

While younger agents tend to jump right into technology without looking back, older agents—which make up the bulk of the profession—are fearful of it, viewing it not as a business tool but as a force for change in a profession that they dominated pretty well into the early 1990s. With the average agent getting older (from 42 in 1978 to 51 in 2003, according to NAR), the resistance is bound to grow, although agents overall seem to be catching on to the fact that tech can be more friend than foe.

Bryan Foreman, president of Vienna, Virginia–based MLS systems and real estate software provider Interealty Corp., talks to real estate agents and brokers on a daily basis and says there's a clear split between the tech-savvy and the tech-averse in the industry. He sees age and number of years in the industry as the dividing factors, and he says that younger agents are usually more than willing to integrate technology into their operations. "The older agents go into it kicking and screaming, and they don't necessarily see the value of it," says Foreman. "But there is definitely a new crop of agents out there who are much more open and are starting to use technology to their advantage."

But working against the older agent who doesn't use technology is the fact that the age of the first-time home buyer has dropped to 31, which creates an even wider technology divide. Many first-time home buyers are in need of professional expertise during the house hunt and subsequent transaction, and first-time buyers made up 40 percent of all home buyers nationwide, according to NAR (see Figure 3-1).

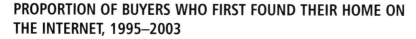

Figure 3-1.

PROPORTION OF BUYERS WHO FIRST FOUND THEIR HOME ON THE INTERNET, 1995–2003

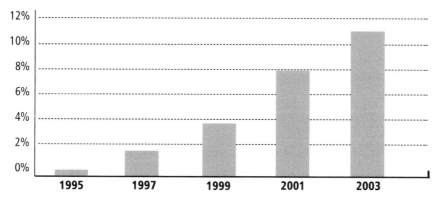

* Less than 1%

Source: The 2003 National Association of REALTORS Profile of Home Buyers and Sellers.

Anyone near or under the age of 30 these days has probably already tried using MP3 technology to download music, cell phones to take digital pictures, and wireless laptops to connect to the Web from anywhere. That puts pressure on the agent who has yet to realize the value and important of technology to these younger buyers. That technology changes at the speed of light makes the challenge even more real: The agent who finally learns how to use a Palm Pilot will probably have to upgrade to a new one within two years (the average lifespan of a technology product, according to the Florida Association of Realtors®' Tech Helpline for members).

As in any type of customer-oriented business, the professional who can't communicate with customers on their own terms is the one who will be most frequently bypassed when it comes time to seal the deal. Some agents have gone into the new technologies kicking and screaming, while others, such as Krigsman, haven't a clue what it was like to work with thick MLS books under their arms and without a cell phone, laptop, and online broker reciprocity system for sharing listing data.

Everyone from the heads of online real estate firms to the technology vendors who develop software and hardware acknowledges that real estate remains a relationship-based business, but it's clear that those agents who opt for the "old ways" of doing business rather than using virtual tours, instant communication tools like cell phones and e-mail, and access to MLS systems that alert customers of new property listings on a regular basis are finding themselves increasingly behind the curve.

RELUCTANCE TO CHANGE

The fact that traditional brokerages have been reluctant to change their ways has opened the door to a slew of new business models within the industry. One of the most daunting for full-service, traditional brokers is the Internet model, which uses licensed agents to sell real estate primarily through the World Wide Web. In the late 1990s a number of these firms surfaced simultaneously, promising to revolutionize the industry. A good number of them fell by the wayside during an online real estate firm shake-out in 2001, but at least two have remained strong and led to change in the industry: eRealty, Inc., of Houston, Texas, and zipRealty, Inc., of Emeryville, California.

Both based on the Web, these companies operate in a more virtual environment and offer complete real estate services for less than the typical 6 to 7 percent commission that most agents demand. For example, zipRealty, Inc., says that it provides home sellers and buyers with an innovative real estate solution. By using the efficiencies of the Internet, the company claims to have streamlined the real estate process and thus is able to pass "significant savings" on to its clients.

zipRealty streamlines the process of buying and selling houses by handling the bulk of the transaction via the Internet. The company offers to list homes at a "competitive fee," usually 1 percent going rate for an area. On a $450,000 home, for example, the savings for the home seller can be as much as $7,000. eRealty offers similar discounts and also runs its business through the Web, with transactions being handled by licensed agents.

In December 2003, eReality stopped offering 1 percent rebates and began negotiating commissions on a case-by-case basis. Russell Capper, the company's president and CEO, says that the company's founders in 1997 homed in on three principles in forming the company. They conducted a deep analysis and uncovered some serious cracks in the traditional residential brokerage methods. He says the company was founded on three basic ideas:

1. There was a tremendous opportunity for improving this very important transaction and buying decision. "It was just so obvious that many steps along the way could be improved immensely by integrating Internet technology," says Capper.

2. It was forecasted and anticipated that many, many consumers would prefer to use technology—the Internet and the Web—in this transaction, which is the most important consumer transaction that most Americans ever experience, and that they wanted to use the Internet in a big way.

3. They observed that the big companies—meaning, the large franchisers operating in the industry—were reluctant to change and
were unwilling to provide their agents, brokers, and franchisees
with improved systems and processes that could address the new
consumer.

Seven years later, Capper says that the first two points have proved to
be true. "We can do the transaction, make the consumer happy, and
spend much less time, effort, and money, so we experience the productivity significantly," he says. "And we all know that consumers would prefer to do it this way—it's a no-brainer."

What wasn't so readily apparent to eRealty's founders, says Capper,
was just how reluctant those large franchisers would be, even today.
"They're still refusing to take an active role in integrating Internet technology, and—as evidenced by the recent debate over technologies like
IDX and VOWs—are actually trying to stop it and slow it down."

SLOW ADOPTION

When RE/MAX International cofounder Dave Liniger saw technology coming down the pike about ten years ago, he made several comments to the
press to the effect that what most real estate agents need is a customer, not
technology. "The vast majority of the real estate agents out there didn't
have enough buyers and sellers to keep themselves busy," says Liniger. "At
the time, the only agents who really needed technology were the top producers, who were handling twenty or thirty transactions and needed tools
like desktop publishing, e-mail, and voicemail to handle the volume of
customers."

Back then it was all about time management, says Liniger.
Technology, it seems, was the perfect solution to the fact that there were
only twenty-four hours in a day and that, at some point, everyone has to
sleep. "It was the same thing as having an assistant or secretary," Liniger
says.

Over the last decade, Liniger says, his views have changed right along with technology, which today provides value to all agents—even the ones who are doing one transaction a month (again, the average production in the industry). That's because the number of consumers who access the Internet has grown over the last few years. A 2003 UCLA study, "Surveying the Digital Divide," found that 72.3 percent of consumers have gone online, up from 66.9 percent in 2000. The hours those consumers spend online jumped from 9.4 per week in 2000 to 11.1 per week in 2002, while the total number of consumers who access the Internet from home grew from 46.9 percent in 2000 to 59.4 percent in 2002.

The fact that eyeballs are constantly surfing the Net—something that wasn't happening ten years ago when Liniger first commented that technology could help only top-producing agents—has opened doors for less productive agents who are trying to build their businesses. "For starters, it's now possible to create customer leads online," says Liniger. "The Internet explosion in particular has become the most popular form of advertising. When it comes to lead generation, technology is very necessary, and of course the busier the individual is, the more valuable e-mail, voicemail, desktop publishing, and various agent productivity software programs are."

To put it simply, Liniger now calls technology a "godsend" for an industry comprised mostly of solo practitioners who juggle myriad tasks for a variety of customers on a regular basis.

Liniger recalls a time in the not-too-distant past when established brokers were afraid that the Internet would somehow separate them from their customers, thus removing the agent from the very process that provided his livelihood. More important, they feared that their only real nemesis at the time—the for sale by owner or FSBO property—would become easier to sell and market thanks to the Internet and inexpensive desktop publishing tools that anyone could use.

"Many brokers were afraid that technology would make it so much easier for FSBOs to sell their houses that they would no longer need the real estate agent," says Liniger, adding that RE/MAX was among the first national franchises to set up a Web site. "We thought the notion was just nonsense. This is one of the most complex business transactions an individual makes in their lifetime, and it's not the same thing as going to Amazon.com and buying your favorite book for 30 percent off."

Again, Liniger comes back to the all-important relationship issue. Recall the client in Chapter 2 who called Mary Zentz no less than four times a day? Such personal connections are impossible without a live agent on the other end of the line, ready to serve. The fact that agents like Zentz are on call to solve problems, answer questions, and offer expertise on a round-the-clock basis is what makes agents so key to the process.

But resisting change is, once again, simply human nature. Liniger recalls a time when answering services were starting to be phased out in favor of answering machines and voicemail systems. Agents were reluctant to force their customers to talk to a machine instead of a real person.

"In reality, we didn't want them talking to a human being—particularly at an answering service, which is staffed by fairly uneducated people working for low wages and giving out wrong information or not answering the phone quickly enough," says Liniger. "Voicemail is now a business standard, which proves that technological innovations as a whole are not a threat but a tool when properly used. It's made all agents more professional and given them the ability to do more transaction sides per year."

IT'S SIMPLE: CONSUMERS WANT IT

In 1996, a real estate manager from one of the world's largest software development firms referred to the residential real estate brokerage industry as "one of the most inefficient industries in the United States," and one that his firm hoped to exploit. He went on to say that "many surplus and wheel-spinning agents will be out of business in a few years." While his firm may dominate the operating system market, it still has yet to capture the real estate market through its own real estate portal. Competitors homestore.com with its REALTOR.com service and Yahoo! Real Estate haven't made much of a dent either. Nevertheless, the idea that a technology behemoth could stake a claim in an industry started by mom-and-pop firms and dependent on face-to-face, personal contact made many agents squirm—particularly the ones who resist technology.

A 2002 study from the Fisher College of Business in Columbus, Ohio, dispelled the dire predictions that the traditional agent-based real estate industry would be eroded by the growth of real estate Web sites. During the mid-1990s, some people believed that the real estate industry would decline with the rise of Internet sites that offered the same services that real estate brokers and agents have provided for decades, according to Waleed Muhanna, associate professor of information systems at Fisher College, who says that the real estate industry has actually grown over the last ten years, not shrunk.[1]

Another prediction that has not materialized, despite the growing number of Internet real estate sites and the unprecedented amount of free information available to home buyers and sellers, is that advances in information technology, specifically the rise of the Internet, will encourage FSBO sales, which, according to industry statistics, historically account for 16 to 20 percent of the market (the percentages are often much higher in hot sellers' markets). However, NAR studies in 2001 and 2002 in fact found the opposite to be true: FSBOs stood at 18 percent of the market in 1997 but slipped to 16 percent in 1999 and 13 percent in 2001 as sales continued to rise.

"Moreover, the once-crowded field of the online real estate sector has considerably thinned out as a result of consolidation and closings," says Muhanna. "At the top of the list of upstarts that failed are e-brokerage companies such as Owners.com, which merged with Homebytes.com in October 2000 and whose primary business model sought to bypass the traditional broker by catering to the FSBO market. The list of survivors is made up of online companies (e.g., homestore.com) that sought to fully embrace the real estate agent rather than cut out the agent as a middleman."

According to Muhanna, conventional wisdom has it that home buy-

---

[1] Waleed A. Muhanna and James R. Wolf, "The Impact of E-Commerce on the Real Estate Industry: Baen and Guttery Revisited," *Journal of Real Estate Portfolio Management,* vol. 8, no. 2, 2002, pp. 141–152.

ers and sellers with access to the information available via the Internet will have no need for traditional "infomediaries" and that the real estate agent, as an intermediary, would be bypassed in favor of sites designed to match buyers and sellers directly. He adds that the Internet was expected to result in the downsizing of the real estate industry, but points out that there are clear reasons why that hasn't actually happened, and why it's not likely to occur as a result of the Internet alone. One key reason is that the transaction cost theory, which forms the basis of the disintermediation hypothesis and, hence, the grim predictions about the Internet's impact, was not applied appropriately. In other words, the folks who were predicting the slow death of the real estate agent and broker system forgot that the business is largely based on personal relationships between home buyers, sellers, and their agents, not on how quickly and efficiently the transaction can get completed.

"By focusing exclusively on the relationship between producers and consumers, proponents of the disintermediation hypothesis overlook the effects of information technology on other relationships, such as that between the consumer and the intermediary," Muhanna says. "Just because property sellers can potentially reach buyers directly though the Internet, that does not necessarily mean that either party will do away with the services of an intermediary. The intermediaries—the real estate agents, perhaps acting collectively—themselves can exploit the new medium to become more productive and enhance the overall efficiency of the transaction."

Muhanna also says that the nature of competition in the industry may also explain the inability of many Internet real estate firms to make inroads into the home buying/selling market despite offering consumers hefty discounts. It also helps explain why the introduction of Web technology is not likely to make the real estate brokerage market fully contestable, says Muhanna, "nor dramatically disrupt the dynamics of competition in the industry, as many seem to suggest."

Going Virtual

One of the key breakthroughs that the Internet has created for real estate was the online virtual tour. Created by the listing agents or outsourced to technology providers who create and host the tours, this innovation allows consumers to preview a home's interior, exterior, and floor plan online. Dean Rouso started uploading virtual tours of listed properties on his web site in 1999, the same year he noticed an increasing number of home buyers heading to the Web to do home searches. At the same time, this broker associate with Dean Rouso Home Team, Coldwell Banker Residential Brokerage in LaGrange, Illinois, also saw more sellers getting wise to the fact that putting their homes at the buyer's fingertips through the use of a virtual tour meant more exposure, thus yielding a better selection of buyers and a higher sale price.

Rouso's early insights were dead on. According to West Lake, California–based homestore.com's (owner of REALTOR.com) own internal research, property listings on the firm's Web site that feature virtual tours receive 38 percent more views than those without. In addition, Realtor.com's 2002 internal logs report that tours receive an average of thirteen hits per day and scenes average four views per day.

As an early adopter of virtual tours as marketing tools, Rouso says that he knew back in 1999 that if his virtual tours could show his agency's listings in a favorable light, then more sellers would come. "To draw buyers to properties and also gain a competitive edge with sellers who were interviewing with several different agents, I needed to add virtual tours to my package," says Rouso. "I immediately included them in my marketing plan."

The numbers of consumers flocking to the Web to view homes online are expected to grow in the future, so if you're not already using virtual tours in your own business, you may want to start. A 2003 recent study from the California Association of Realtors® (CAR) found that home buyers are becoming more Web-savvy and are investing a significant amount of time investigating the housing market and financing options before they contact a real estate agent. A full 78 percent of Internet home buyers reportedly found their agent on the Internet—not as a result of farm-ing, referrals, advertising, or sign calls—and 23 percent of Internet home buyers found the type of house they wanted on the Internet, according to CAR's study.

Plus, the agent who shells out the $75 to $150 it takes to produce and post a virtual tour through a service like IPIX increases the likelihood of a home shopper's viewing that listing by 40 percent, according to indus-try statistics. So while that large software firm's big-talking executive was clearly incorrect about his dire predictions for the industry, it's clear that smart agents have taken what could have been a threat to their existence and turned it into a useful tool. Isn't it time you joined the party?

FROM PLATFORMS TO GADGETS

When Krigsman got into the real estate business, one of his first invest-ments was a $35,000 Web site. Sounds like a lot of money? Well, the way Krigsman viewed it, the price would be capitalized over several years, and a site that went beyond the basics would pay off handsomely over time. He also felt that a high-quality site would appeal to high-quality consumers, and it has. "It's really a niche Web site that caters to the mid- to high-end urban property buyers and works in tandem with the corporate Web site to showcase each listing," says Krigsman. "It connects seamlessly with that site, so I don't have to reinvent the technology to create listings. The result: instant credibility. Even before I've met my clients, they feel that they know me."

Not all tech tools have worked out for Krigsman. Among the most disappointing have been the several GPS systems that he's purchased for his car, hoping to use them to get around without having to use maps and scribbled directions. "I've gone through four of them and none of them lived up to their promises," Krigsman laments. "They're too slow, clunky, inaccurate, and hard to see." Determined to make technology work for him, he recently bought another that connects to his laptop, but he says that he doesn't have much hope for it.

What Krigsman does rely on heavily is his local online MLS system. The fact that over the last few years buyers have gained access to the listing data through their own computers—via his and other brokers' Web sites—has drastically cut down on the amount of time he has to spend with customers. Before technology came along, he estimates that agents spent 75 percent of their time in the car, showing properties. "That time has collapsed, since buyers already know the details on the listing inventory," says Krigsman. "Our role has changed, and those agents who don't realize this and take advantage of it just won't be in business."

What the online MLS has also done is raise many a hackle in an industry whose cornerstone was brokers and agents who held all of the cards with their MLS books. In 2001, NAR brought the entire industry into the new millennium when it mandated that all MLS offices be IDX (Internet Data Exchange) compliant by January 2002. For most of that year, MLSs struggled to get up to speed, while many individual brokers and agents tried to comprehend why they would suddenly have to allow their competitors to post all of an area's listings on their Web sites. Brokers were given the option of "opting out" of the system, which meant that their listings wouldn't be displayed on their competitors' sites.

The issue got stickier with the advent of virtual office Web sites, or VOWs, which essentially circumvented the need to offer opting out by making all of the listing data available to those consumers with whom the broker or agent had an "existing client relationship." That relationship was established via a registration process that prompted consumers to give up a bit of personal data before they could gain access to the VOW. One of the system's biggest users was online real estate firm eRealty, Inc. (see Figure 3-2).

After about 18 months of debate over how the listing data should be shared online, just how much of it consumers could access, and how "legal" it was for companies like eRealty to provide such data to consumers nationwide through a number of MLS systems, NAR came up with a policy at its 2003 midyear meeting, and approved the display of MLS real estate listings on the Internet.

Figure 3-2.

WHAT'S THE DIFFERENCE?

Your broker may know the acronyms used to describe those nifty tools that allow consumers to search listings online, but do you? Here's a primer:

Virtual office Web site. A VOW is the "equivalent of a brick and mortar office where potential purchasers enter, describe the property being sought, provide contact information, and receive listing information responsive to their stated needs," according to NAR. The acronym VOW refers to a participant's (read: the broker who has the information posted on it) Web site, or a feature of a participant's Web site, through which the participant provides real estate brokerage services to consumers with whom the participant has first established a broker-consumer relationship. Put simply, VOWs require that users "register" by providing a certain amount of personal information and property search criteria before they are allowed to search the MLS database.

Internet data exchange (IDX). This is NAR's answer to the broker reciprocity concept. Through this system, MLSs provide their brokers with technology to help them display not only their own listings online, but also those of competing brokers. For consumers, this means complete access to properties for sale from a single broker's site, which in turn promises to produce greater numbers of leads and a larger pool of consumers to whom brokers can market their services. IDX was adopted in 2001 by NAR, and all MLSs were mandated to implement the system by January 2002.

Broker reciprocity. Broker reciprocity is basically the underlying concept behind both VOWs and IDX. It's a business program in which brokers grant each other permission to display their listings on each other's Web sites. Brokers who participate in the program can display all active listings of all members participating in the program. If a broker chooses not to participate, no other broker will be permitted to display that broker's listings.

NAR's new policy governing the display of real estate listings stated that by 2004, brokers who participate in the nation's approximately 900 MLSs would be "allowed to display the property listings so that they can be accessed by consumers on Web sites that provide on-line brokerage services, which are known as VOWs." The NAR board of directors approved the policy, which is the result of over a year of research and deliberation by two NAR work groups.

According to NAR, customers who deal with brokers who participate in an MLS service and operate a VOW will be able to view MLS listings, which typically contain a great deal more detailed information about properties than the online advertisements currently displayed on most real estate sites. "The new policy on VOWs will make it possible for real estate consumers across America to see virtually the same information about residential property that professionals use," says NAR president Cathy Whatley. "Under this new policy, Realtors® will remain at the forefront of the real estate transaction and more consumers will have access to more information than ever before."

The new rule also states that sellers and the brokers representing them will have the right to withhold their listings from display on others' VOWs—either on a blanket or a selective basis—despite the fact that the properties may be available for sale through an MLS. Before consumers can access listings on a VOW, they first must become bona fide customers of the brokerage operating the VOW and sign a "terms of use agreement."

That the NAR had finally laid down the law on how listings could be shown and viewed online was music to the ears of some, but spelled the death knell of "real estate as we know it" for others. Major national brokers spoke out on both sides of the issue prior to the decision, with some convinced that VOWs offer entirely too much information to the consumer, essentially "giving it all away"—something that a number of traditional real estate agents would rather not do.

But if you look at the true value that the agent brings to the table, says Interealty's Foreman, you'll see that it isn't so much the information as the way the agent helps consumers interpret the information and adds her own knowledge to the mix that counts the most. Rather than looking at the online MLS as an "opening of a can of worms," he says, agents should see such technological advancements as a way to be more efficient for their customers.

"I can't think of any real estate agents who wouldn't like a customer coming to them already having pinpointed and looked at three houses online," says Foreman. "They found them online and did their homework, and now they need help in actually buying the house or deciding among the three. It sure beats spending three days or more in the car driving from house to house to just get the preliminary search out of the way."

CATCHING ON

So, we know that consumers are using the Web, but how are agents doing at keeping up with the Internet and all of the technologies being thrown at them? According to NAR's Center for Realtor Technology (CRT), agents are using the Internet and Web-based technologies in the course of business. The percentage of agents who believe that having a Web site and using the Internet has changed the way they do business has increased to 64 percent in 2003 from 50 percent in 2002 (see Figure 3-3).

And while the cost of Web sites is perceived to be high, over 60 percent of agents have a personal Web site, either their own or through their brokerage. Mark Lesswing, NAR vice president and director of the CRT, says, "The changes in technology usage from 2002 to 2003 suggest an increased reliance on the Internet and new consolidated technologies in the conduct of Realtor business over time."

The CRT survey, along with similar research conducted in 2002, also highlights changes in Realtors' use of searchable listings, e-mail, and other emerging technologies over the last two years. Usage and availability of IDX technology are increasing, especially among larger firms. "The MLS is the dominant source of listings for the Realtor," Lesswing says. "The market for listing search tools seems to be growing, together with the use of electronic, searchable property listings. Over the last year, use of wireless Internet and wireless e-mail has also increased by 6 percent and 4 percent, respectively."

Figure 3-3.

REAL ESTATE TECH TRENDS

Charged with investigating emerging real estate technologies, NAR's Center for Realtor Technology surveys the real estate industry every year to find out what technology innovations and tools agents are using. In its 2003 survey, NARCRT reported the following technology trends within the industry:

Pager use is in decline and PDA use is increasing. Nine percent fewer agents are using pagers compared to 2002, while 8 percent more are using PDAs.

Web sites are perceived to be expensive. Nine percent of agents say the reason they don't have Web sites is because they're too costly.

IDX availability and usage are increasing. Twenty-three percent of agents now have access to IDX, versus 5 percent in 2002.

The MLS is the dominant source of listings for 65 percent of the survey respondents.

The market for listing search tools appears to be growing. Today, more than 50 percent of agents have Web sites with searchable listings.

Realtors at large firms are more likely to have a Web site. Seventy-two percent of agents at firms with more than 100 agents have Web sites, compared to just 52 percent for those working for firms with one to five agents.

Realtors at large firms are more likely to be using IDX. Sixty percent of agents at firms with over 100 agents are using IDX, versus 52 percent at those offices with one to five agents.

Large firms continue to enjoy greater use and availability of technology. For example, 80 percent of agents working for firms with over 100 agents are currently using Web sites with property listings, versus 39 percent for firms with one to five agents.

The survey also showed that Realtors use a wide range of technologies in their business, with mobile phones or pagers now being used by 98 percent or more, up 1 percent from 2002. Use of computers by the survey group now approaches 100 percent, with members using a combination of home and office desktop and laptop computers. Electronic mail has become more common, with 94 percent of respondents using e-mail for business, especially to stay in touch with clients. Use of digital cameras has reached the 85 percent level.

One particularly valuable tech tool that agents rely on these days is the online or electronic comparative market analysis (CMA) report. Where agents once had to dig through data on sold houses in a particular neighborhood to determine a fair market value for a customer's home, they can now punch a few key pieces of data into a service like MLSNow and retrieve a professional report within a few minutes. The CMA has already served as a reference point for agents trying to determine the right price for a home or property long before they even sit down at a listing appointment with the consumer, so allowing technology to handle it in a deft manner is a big boost for agents.

The movement is important to agents like Mary Zentz, who ten years ago didn't even know what the World Wide Web was. Today, she uses a combination of tech tools that includes a personal Web site; a contact management database; hardware like laptops, personal digital assistants, digital cameras, and cell phones, and—perhaps most important—an automatic update program that keeps her entire database informed about new listings and updates to the MLS. The funny thing, says Zentz, is that many of those contacts opt to receive similar information from a dozen or so different agents, thinking that one of them might have different information from the others.

"Automatic updates really minimize the peaks and valleys that happen in the real estate business from month to month, but it's funny to see how consumers use them and react to them," says Zentz. "Somehow, they think that different agents have different information, but it doesn't work that way."

FIXING MISTAKES

If Jim Secord had a dollar for every agent who calls himself or herself "tech-savvy," but who spends thousands of dollars to establish an online presence and then never properly promotes it, he'd probably be a rich man. A quick browse of the World Wide Web reveals a ton of real estate Web sites wallowing in mediocrity. Most of them look the same, and very few of them deliver anything of real value to consumers. Worse yet, the agents behind the sites do little to promote their online presence, thus rendering their big investment null and void. "They think that just because they have a Web site, customers will come to them," says Secord, vice president of technology at Interealty Corp. "What agents need to do is get that Web address on their business cards, for-sale signs, newspaper ads, and listing flyers."

Ignoring the "push" marketing aspect of the Web (in which companies push information out to consumers instead of waiting for consumers to come to them) is just one of several major tech no-nos that agents commit on a daily basis, says Secord. Another major faux pas is the lack of expediency in dealing with e-mail. He says that a recent Interealty survey revealed that the optimal or "hot" time for returning an e-mail messages is during the first two to four hours after it's been sent. The agents' "hot" time is decidedly different, says Secord.

"There's a major misunderstanding that if they check e-mails every two or three days, they are checking their e-mail, but the reality is that the opportunity will be long gone by that point," says Secord. "Using e-mail effectively means checking it frequently and treating it like a phone call. You wouldn't wait two or three days to return a phone call, would you?"

Quick e-mail response—something that can now be achieved even on the road, thanks to new wireless handhelds like the Blackberry—is particularly critical in this age of IDX and VOWs, where the consumer has access to a number of agents and their listings. "Someone who is looking at five or six different properties will probably dash off a note to each of the agents involved," says Secord. "The agent who responds first will probably get the business."

When it comes to technology, Interealty's Foreman says there are entirely too many agents working in the field who purchase the latest gadgets and software, only to let them sit on the shelf and gather dust. Instead of wasting money on the latest and greatest technology being offered by your local computer or office superstore, Foreman suggests evaluating the products first.

Most prone to overbuying, he says, are the 20 percent of agents that enter the market each year. Eager to get going and lacking any type of direction, they head down to the local computer store and load up on the latest PDAs, laptops, desktops, phones, and software, without knowing what they really need to run their businesses. To them, Foreman suggests a thorough evaluation prior to buying. Ask yourself: What am I really going to use this for? Why is it better than what I already have? Will this pay off for me over time? Are other agents using it, and if so, is it useful for them?

"There is so much stuff that just ends up sitting on the shelf," says Foreman. "Before making any purchases, agents need to figure out what products they'll be able to best leverage for their success, and more often than not that new Palm Pilot or contact management software ends up gathering dust because the agent didn't take the time to understand the benefits of it, or because there just weren't enough benefits to have an impact on them."

FINDING TECH HELP

If technology itself poses a challenge for real estate agents, then supporting that technology and keeping it running smoothly just throws another kink into the process. After a busy day of prospecting in the community, for example, agents often drive back to their offices to input a pile of new prospect information into their favorite client management software program. They boot up the computer, click on the program's desktop icon, and wait for the program to come up, but their hearts drop when an ugly blue-screen error message looks them in the face and tells them that a critical file is missing. Without it, the program can't open.

The agent's first instinct will probably be to reach for the owner's manual or make a call to the vendor's tech support line, but the first of these options can be frustrating and the second downright time-consuming and expensive. Luckily for the agent, there are myriad other tech support options available through computer technicians and consultants and your local, state, and regional Realtor associations—many of which are less expensive and quicker.

Today's software vendors are a wizened bunch that realize just how much people are willing to pay for good tech support. If shelling out hundreds of dollars to solve problems over the phone for the next twelve months isn't what you had in mind, then you might want to open your Yellow Pages or ask around for a good local tech consultant or guru, who will probably charge a flat fee or an hourly rate to come to your home or office to solve the program.

"The majority of real estate professionals are not focused on being technologically savvy," says Greg Herder, CEO at Hobbs/Herder Training in Newport Beach, California, a developer of the proprietary Web site control and e-mail marketing system MegaAgent, for which Hobbs/Herder provides technical support at no charge. "So technical support and assistance are paramount to making the most of what [technology] products and systems have to offer."

The Artasm Group, Inc., of Green Bay, Wisconsin, works often with real estate agents in need of tech support through a "Help Desk" manned by computer technicians and accessible either by telephone or in person. Common complaints that company CEO Brian Katsetos hears are, "I can't access the network" and "I can't open a program."

"Our computer technicians will research the problem and give the agent a solution on how to fix the issue—or will fix it for them—depending on the user's skill level," says Katsetos. The company charges $30 to $125 an hour, depending on the complexity and type of problem

Success Computer Consulting, Inc., in Minneapolis also caters to real estate agents who need assistance with product selection, installation, and training and help desk support, the latter of which is the firm's "most valuable service," according to Erik Thorsell, president, who says that the company can solve almost every problem right from its office, via the

Internet. Requests range from fixing a computer to helping to create a spreadsheet formula. Rates vary depending on the service required, he says, but generally run from $100 to $175 per hour.

MAKING THE TACKLE

When Paul Chadwick got into residential real estate in 2002, his broker urged him to learn all he could about e-marketing—a technology-based way to reach out to potential home buyers and sellers through the Internet, e-mail, a Web site and other electronic means. Within a few months, this broker associate with Baird & Warner in Geneva, Illinois, had already closed three sales and earned $18,000 in commissions as a direct result of his e-marketing efforts.

Following his broker's advice, Chadwick took advantage of the free courses that the Multiple Listing Service of Illinois (MLSNI) offered its members in basic and advanced Fusion and RE/Xplorer. "New Realtors have one asset—time," says Chadwick. "I put mine to good use, taking every single class that they offered."

The first e-marketing tool Chadwick used was RE/Xplorer, a program designed for clients who aren't Internet-savvy, but who still want up-to-date information on properties. "They give me their wish list, and I mail them a hard copy of possible properties every week," says Chadwick. Fusion takes that same process into the Internet age, updating potential buyers every few hours via e-mail—with a message that includes Chadwick's contact information and photo—directly from MLSNI.

"I key in the buyers' criteria, then Fusion automatically sends them an e-mail message when there's a match," says Chadwick, adding that a real estate agent's lack of control over the Fusion program is challenging, as are some Internet providers' e-mail addresses, which sometimes spit back the messages as undeliverable.

To create and manage his recipient list, Chadwick uses a basic spreadsheet document saved on his computer. Both RE/Xplorer and Fusion have their own built-in contact managers, so he stores alphabetized client lists in both. In the future, he says, he may add Top Producer and a Web site to his e-marketing stable.

What Chadwick doesn't ever do is send out mass e-mails to his valued contacts, primarily because he says the Internet is so cluttered with spam that the last thing he wants to do is add to the problem. "Early on, I outline to these people exactly what I'm going to send them, and it doesn't include garbage e-mail that they don't need," says Chadwick. "It irritates me to receive unsolicited e-mail, so I know it irritates them, too."

AROUND THE NEXT CORNER

As vice president of Coldwell Banker Residential Brokerage in Beverly, Massachusetts, Jay Burnham may have twenty-one years of real estate experience under his belt, but he still insists on staying on top of the latest technology trends. These efforts have paid off handsomely: In 2002, a full 40 percent of his $14.6 million in property sales came from working with clients who came to him via his personal Web site.

"My site has grown from zero hits to over 150,000 in the last two years," says Burnham. "Clearly, technology is a critical component of the real estate industry, on both the company and agent levels."

This is just one example of how technology is changing the way agents and brokers nationwide do business. Still largely based on close, personal relationships with buyers and sellers, the home buying and selling process has been accelerated by the advent of the mobile phone, digital camera, desktop and laptop computers, and personal digital assistants (PDAs). According to the National Association of Realtors' Center for Realtor Technology (NARCRT) 2003 Technology and the Realtor survey, agents nationwide are using emerging technologies for marketing, sales, organization, and communication.

The use of Web sites, searchable listings, and e-mail is high, as is the number of agents who believe that the Internet has changed the way they do business. NARCRT reports that 94 percent of agents currently use e-mail for business, while over 60 percent have a personal Web site and 20 percent rely on their brokers' site for an online presence.

Of course, everyone already knows about e-mail and Web sites. What you really want to know is, what's around the next corner that will affect your business? Here are four key technological innovations that all agents should be bracing for in the near future:

The Wireless Advantage

Once thought of as too expensive for the average professional to afford, wireless technologies have come down to earth and today can be had for just $200 for a wireless network card that plugs right into a laptop and a $30 to $40 monthly subscription fee.

Darren G. Ross, director of electronic commerce for Stewart Title in Houston, Texas, says that the agent's mobile lifestyle dictates the need for connectivity away from a desktop computer.

At the heart of the wireless trend is WI-FI, a wireless local area network (LAN) that allows agents to hook up to their local MLS system, send and receive e-mail, or download virtual tours from their cars, customers' homes, and other remote locations.

Ross calls this advance invaluable for real estate agents. "The average real estate professional's primary goal is to obtain and sell listings—something that can't be accomplished by sitting behind a desk all day," he says. "Wireless technologies will enable agents to quickly and easily access information and stay in communication with their customers and business partners from anywhere."

Stephen Canale, an Ann Arbor, Michigan–based speaker, trainer, and author on technology, marketing, and sales says that the agent who can sit in a client's home and conduct an MLS search will avoid deal-killing statements like "I'll go back to my office, look it up, and e-mail it to you later."

More Listings Online

Online listings through IDX, VOWs, and the standard MLS systems are all the rage right now and are gaining ground as more consumers head to the

Web to conduct home searches. "For agents, the trend has nothing to do with technological prowess," says Canale, "and everything to do with differentiating yourself in the marketplace."

Yet according to NARCRT's 2003 survey, agents aren't tapping the possibilities of online listings. Survey results revealed an increase in IDX availability from 2002 to 2003, but also suggested that agents are not fully aware of the technology's possibilities. Roughly half of the agents reported using a Web site with searchable listings. "This is the type of service that more and more consumers want, and the fact that many agents aren't taking advantage of it really gives a leg up to those who are," says Canale.

Where agents win is by providing online listings, virtual tours, and property information, thus passing some of the more mundane research onto their clients, who are hungry for it anyway.

Secord concurs, but says that the real estate industry as a whole continues to struggle with the issue of how to properly manage the online data that at one time were relegated to the pages of a paper-based MLS book. "This is a huge issue for agents and brokers right now," says Secord, "and one that will continue to develop as consumers demand even more information."

The Paperless Transaction

To call the real estate transaction process "paper intensive" would be an understatement. The financing, inspections, and disclosure paperwork alone is enough to fill a thick file that puts a strain on even the strongest biceps. Relief may be in sight, says Ross, who predicts a time when a good portion of that paperwork is delivered, signed, and returned via a secure Internet connection.

"Transaction management systems (TMSs) are the next big wave of technology tools for the tech-savvy agent," says Ross. "These systems provide a secure, Internet-based platform and virtual transaction folder (VTF) for all parties associated with a real estate transaction. More importantly, these systems actually improve the workflow between the parties by automating the necessary tasks associated with the transaction process and eliminating or reducing the need to do these manually."

Through such systems, Ross says, the listing agent, selling agent, mortgage lender, title company, closing officer, buyer, and seller all gain access to a single, information-packed application that includes the status of services ordered as well as online documents like good faith estimates and HUD/closing statements. Through it, Ross says, communication and collaboration between all parties will be improved, as will the consumer's real estate closing experience.

"It's all about customer service. By providing customers with instantaneous access to up-to-date information on every aspect of their transaction(s), you eliminate the necessity for and inconvenience of having to make multitudes of phone calls, faxes, e-mails, etc.," says Ross. "Transaction management systems enable real estate professionals to provide a proactive, rather than reactive, real estate transaction process. This saves time and money for everyone while providing better customer service."

Canale adds that the movement to paperless transactions is already underway, with companies using software like Adobe Acrobat and ScanSoft PaperPort to move "at least some of the paper-intensive process" onto their computers. "Combined, Adobe and ScanSoft create almost an unbeatable tool not only for storing and organizing documents internally," says Canale, "but also for sharing them with customers and clients."

Like wireless smart phones, Canale says, early paperless office technologies had "overpromised and underdelivered," but he says that they have now caught up to the promise.

More Gadgets Ahead

If you're an agent or broker who enjoys testing out the latest productivity tools and gadgets, you're in luck. Rolling off the assembly lines on a constant basis are new gadgets that promise to make their users' work and personal lives easier and more efficient. In the future, look for gadgets that handle more than just one function. With the increased proliferation of multifunction electronic devices such as PDAs—which can serve as access to wireless Internet/e-mail, contact lists, and calendars/appointments; calculators; and word processors—Ross says, agents will be able to reduce the number of single-function electronic devices that they once had to carry around.

Another wireless innovation that agents can expect to see, says Canale, is "smart phones" that can send and receive e-mail, serve as PDAs, and also take phone calls. "They have been played up for several years now, but haven't been too impressive," says Canale. "Now they're starting to really deliver."

Also expect to see more digital cameras, multifunction cell phones (like those that come with built-in digital cameras), PDAs, wireless devices (like the Blackberry), and other gadgets coming off the assembly lines. As the gadgets evolve, they'll become faster, smaller, and more efficient, while also incorporating more wireless technology.

But remember, says Secord, that the latest, greatest gadgets may not always meet expectations and could end up gathering dust on the shelf. And he adds, "We see a lot of agents invest in technology and never use it." To avoid wasting time and money, Secord advises agents to evaluate the devices and pick only those that will provide the most benefit.

YOUR CUSTOMER DATABASE

One of the most important technology tools that agents can have in their arsenal is an updated database of contact information about their current, potential, and past customers. "The worst thing an agent can do is not keep an updated electronic database," says Desiree Savory, owner of Houston-based Technography Solutions, which offers personal and group computer software coaching to real estate agents and brokers.

"Without an updated database, it is virtually impossible to be effective and to follow through with clients and customers," says Savory. She cites a recent NAR study that found that 74 percent of home buyers indicate after closing that they would use their agent again. "Years later, however, only 9 percent actually do."

What does that mean? Well, for starters, it means that agents are not keeping in contact with their clients after the sale. It's kind of like the carpet cleaner who knows that a home's carpets should be cleaned once a year, but who doesn't send out a yearly postcard or e-mail reminder to his past customers. By keeping in touch with clients who are obviously going to need your services again in the future, professionals from all walks of life can ensure repeat business and referrals.

Managing that information takes a good database management software program. Agents who are new to the database arena have several contact management alternatives. Not every program is a good fit for every agent, so Savory advises doing a quick poll in your office or with your colleagues in the area to see what they're using and to find out what's working and what they've tried that hasn't worked. From there, you can figure out which program will suit you best. Many agents use programs from Top Producer (designed specifically for the industry), while others use ACT!, Goldmine, and even Microsoft Outlook to keep a handle on their databases.

Once you've figured out which software program to use, Savory says, consistency is the key to keeping it current and useful. "No matter how large, small, or deep it is," says Savory, "we've all heard the phrase 'garbage in, garbage out.'" (In other words, if you don't update the contact management information in a consistent manner, it will quickly become useless to you as an agent.)

Savory says that the absolute minimum information that an agent should keep on clients is name, address, all contact phone numbers, all e-mail addresses, present and future home information, and family birthdays and anniversaries. Enter the data accurately the first time, she says, and maintain it. When a client gets married or moves to a new company, for example, it's time to enter an anniversary or new business address.

To populate your database, Savory suggests collecting information from everyone you meet (both during the course of business and otherwise) or from people who are referred to you. Many in the industry would call this an agent's "sphere of influence"—those individuals who are already familiar with you. "This is an important ingredient because of the increasing frequency of spam that e-mail recipients are subjected to," says Savory. "Having your e-mail presence in their inbox will ensure that yours will not be one of the many that are automatically deleted."

Once the database is in place and being constantly updated, what's an agent to do with it? According to Savory, such a database provides the foundation for agents' distribution lists that focus on client and customer needs. A monthly e-mail with quick, relevant, and crisp information, for example, keeps your recipients in touch and up to date with current data. A postcard in the mail to let them know that you just listed or sold a home lets them know that you're active and working hard, while a card on an anniversary or birthday shows that you care. It's a matter of simply reaching out and letting your clients know that you're still around, that you still care, and that you'll be there for them the next time they need to make an important real estate decision.

THE TIME IS NOW

If you happen to be an agent who is still unsure about just what role technology will play in your career's future, get over it. The fact is, your customers aren't confused at all. They know that they want to visit Web sites that are jam-packed with useful information, they know that they love the listings that feature virtual tours, and they know that they want to contact you via e-mail, cell phone, or pager when they find the right one. Buyers and sellers are equally tech-savvy: Sellers want you to come out and snap digital photos of their homes, then upload them to the most popular real estate Web sites as quickly as possible, while buyers like agents who tote around PDAs that can handle MLS data for them to view while they're out on Sunday afternoon looking at homes.

Canale, who works often with real estate agents and brokers, says that the value that an agent places on technology is more a function of where that agent plans to be in ten years than anything else. To put it simply, those successful agents who are coasting to the end of their careers and who have already survived decades in the business without it can probably get by with the basics, like a cell phone and some knowledge of properties online. For the real estate agent who wants to be highly competitive or even dominant over the next five to ten years, however, technology is undoubtedly one of the most critical functions to focus on.

Those old-timers who choose to live without technology, says Canale, will lose the ability to gain productivity at a rate of 5 to 10 percent annually, or 50 percent over ten years' time. "They will also lose business because they won't be as appealing to consumers. That's where agents really miss the boat," says Canale. "It's because those who don't embrace technology tend to attract only consumers who are also not embracing technology. The agents don't realize that there are other consumers out there that might do business with them if they had other capabilities."

And if you still need more reasons to jump on the tech train, Canale says, consider the fact that technology provides the perfect tool for differentiating yourself in a competitive marketplace. Anyone can create marketing campaigns, hire good staff, and purchase and implement systems for providing good customer service, but few agents can effectively integrate technology into their relationship-centric industry. "Technology is one of the few tools that agents can use right now to differentiate themselves and be more productive," says Canale. "For that percentage of agents who are doing it, nothing is more important."

SIX THINGS TO REMEMBER FROM CHAPTER 3

❑ Ten years ago many real estate agents and brokers were fearful that technology would somehow disintermediate them from the home buying and selling process.

❑ So far, those fears have been unfounded, although technology has dramatically altered the way agents conduct business, communicate with clients, and market properties to the masses.

❑ Younger agents tend to embrace technology more readily and as such are more apt to work with those tech-savvy home buyers and sellers who want to communicate and do business with agents on their own terms.

❑ Tech tools like the Internet, Web sites, IDX, VOWs, and broker reciprocity have created new opportunities for agents, while gadgets like PDAs, cell phones, and digital cameras have greatly facilitated the business process.

❑ Not all technology tools are useful or necessary for every real estate agent, and some just end up gathering dust in the corner. To avoid wasting money, agents should carefully evaluate the benefits and features of each new tech tool or option before buying.

❑ The agent who wants to succeed over the next five to ten years and make 50 percent or more gains in productivity must embrace technology and integrate it into day-to-day operations.

PART 2

PRICING PRESSURES

CHAPTER 4

The Commission
Compression Factor

CHIPPING AWAY

If there's one thing that every real estate agent dislikes, it's dealing with a hard negotiator who for whatever reason feels that the standard 6 or 7 percent commission rate for selling a home is somehow unwarranted or unearned. What few customers realize is that a 6 percent commission split on a $150,000 home can take months to earn, and is shaved down to about $1,575 once the showing agent, the broker of record, any referral sources, and the tax man take their share of the winnings (see Figure 4-1).

First, split that seemingly large $9,000 check in half, with $4,500 going to the showing agent. Then, cough up half of the check for the listing agent's broker (this percentage varies and is sometimes as low as zero for an agent working on a 100 percent commission split for companies like RE/MAX and Keller Williams) and 30 percent (give or take a few percentage points) for taxes, and the agent takes home about $196 a week, based on a sixty-day closing process. The amount doesn't factor in any overhead (which is usually minimal for agents), advertising costs that the agent might have to pick up, or referral fees that the agent might have to shell out to, say, an agent from outside the state who referred that customer.

Figure 4-1.

HOW IT BREAKS DOWN

The billboards scream out "We'll Sell Your Home for 2 Percent" and "Down With Full Commissions," but most consumers don't realize just how financially insignificant their single home sale is to a top-producing agent. Here's an example of how the commission on a $250,000 home breaks down, assuming that the agent handled the listing side of the transaction at 6 percent commission, and that he splits his commission 80/20 with his broker:

Home sales price: $250,000

6 percent commission: $15,000

Selling agent's portion: $7,500

Listing agent's portion: $7,500

Broker's portion of the listing agent's half: $1,500

Listing agent's gross profit: $6,000

Taxes and overhead (estimated at 40 percent): $2,400

Agent's take-home pay for that sale, (which probably took at least 60 days to earn): $3,600

Of course, agents don't talk much about their net finances, but instead focus on how they've sold "$10 million in properties this year," which to the uninitiated sounds like they're making $600,000 a year, based on an average commission rate of 6 percent, which is typical in most markets even though commissions are negotiable. Combine the fact that consumers are usually focused on that $9,000 chunk of change that they have to fork over for the sale of that $150,000 home with the fact that consumers are exposed to more information and alternative ways to sell their homes, and the result is a customer who wants to whittle that $9,000 down by negotiating a commission less than the 6 to 7 percent "norm."

It seems that agents are giving in to the pressure. A recent National

Association of Realtors® report revealed that 30 percent of agents discount more than 50 percent of their commissions. In its own report, the Council of Residential Specialists found that the pressure on real estate fees is downright pervasive. When asked if they were seeing pressure on their fee structure, an overwhelming 85 percent of agents answered affirmatively. More specifically, when respondents could select multiple answers, 79 percent are being asked by customers for "lower fees," and 43 percent are being asked for "other concessions," such as paying out of their commission to resolve minor inspection issues.

Who can help them when consumers are trying to negotiate those rates downward? With business publications printing articles nationwide targeted at home buyers that suggest that the buyers ask prospective agents if they are "willing to take a lower commission on the sale" and tell readers that for a $150,000 home, "every point less that you can negotiate on a commission saves you $1,500," it's hard to ignore the trend.

Where agents *are* fighting back is in their attempt to "boycott" listings where at least the showing agent side doesn't live up to what the market demands. Take the agent who takes a listing at 4 percent, for example. If the going rate in the area is 6 percent, then that agent knows that she'd better offer 3 percent to the selling agent if she wants to sell the home. It's basically a full-service agent's way of saying he's not going to work for peanuts, even if the listing agent does.

The pressure is coming from all sides, according to the CRS. In its report, the group found that 52 percent of agents are being asked by their professional real estate peers for "higher referral fees." In response to those pressures, 66 percent are "sticking to their fee schedule and emphasizing their expertise," and 13 percent are "providing specific fees for specific services" (i.e., providing a menu of services; see Chapter 6). Additionally, 25 percent are "charging add-on fees or transaction fees" to meet increased demands.

"The demand for referral fees is probably an agent's biggest challenge right now," says Daryl Jesperson, CEO at RE/MAX International Inc. in Greenwood Village, Colorado. "It's coming at agents from all sides, and it looks like incremental business at first blush."

HOW COMMISSIONS WORK

In most regions of the country there is a "customary" commission percentage that most agents expect to earn. Nationwide, it ranges from 5 to 7 percent, depending usually on how hot the housing market is (in California, for example, agents fight tooth and nail to get listings, often taking significant commission cuts in exchange for the added listing inventory). The commission amount is completely negotiable, yet for years most consumers just stuck with what was put on the table as the "standard" commission. Agents need to know that, according to real estate license law in all states, commission rates are negotiable. In fact, some state regulatory bodies (such as the Department of Banking and Insurance) don't even allow commission rates to be preprinted on real estate contracts.

You probably already know how commissions work, but for those of you who don't, here's a quick primer on how the money breaks down. Real estate agents are paid on a commission basis at the successful conclusion of a real estate transaction. The commission rate is a negotiated percentage of the sales price of a home, and the commission is paid to the agents of the buyer and the seller. Using an example of a 6 percent commission rate, the 3 percent listing commission is divided between the listing agent and the broker on a basis that ranges from 50/50 to 100/0. The 3 percent selling commission is divided in a similar fashion, with the selling agent splitting it with the broker.

These splits vary from company to company, based on the parent firm's business model. In a 100 percent environment, agents usually pay for everything from their own paper clips to the rent on their office space. In a 50/50 or 60/40 office, agents can usually rely on their brokers to provide the overhead needed to run their offices and a comfortable place for clients and agents to meet and to conduct business. In such settings, the broker typically picks up the overhead to maintain the premises, including telephone services, computer expenses, utilities, insurance, taxes, MLS membership (agents usually pay their individual MLS fees), advertising costs, sign expenses . . . the list goes on.

Agents working in offices where the broker shoulders much of the financial burden typically do not incur high overhead expenses. They do, however, pay for their own license fees, educational expenses (agents must take accredited real estate courses on a regular basis, depending on which state they're licensed in; see Chapter 8 for more details), and keep their cars properly maintained and running.

Because the broker is most often an agent of the seller, the seller usually pays the commission to that broker, who is the owner's representative and whose charge is to get the highest price possible for the client. A buyer's agent, on the other hand, usually does not list property and instead works in the interest of the buyer, helping her to get the best possible price for the home she wishes to acquire. The concept is a fairly new one. Years ago agents were obligated solely to the sellers, but these days buyers' agents work exclusively for the buyer and have the buyer's best interest in mind throughout the process. Whether an agent chooses to work primarily with sellers, buyers, or both is purely a personal decision, but those who opt for the buyer route should know that, according to NAR, when a buyer's agent is used, prospective buyers found homes one week faster and examined three more properties than buyers who did not use a buyer's agent.

DRIVING FORCES

Rising prices in a seller's market, coupled with pressure from discount brokers, have forced full-service real estate agents to rethink the way they position themselves in the marketplace when it comes to fees and commissions. NAR reports that housing inventory has been relatively low for the past three years, with a total of 2.5 million homes for sale in mid-2003. That's a 5.1-month supply, which means that it would take that much time to sell the total inventory available.

Some areas boasted higher numbers (the Triad area of North Carolina and Houston, for example, were both hovering in the eleven-month range in mid-2003), while areas of California were down to a svelte two or three months. Overall, however, NAR reports that the range of inventory for the last couple of years has been between 4.5 and 5 months, compared to the 1990–1991 recession time frame, when the nationwide number was at about nine months' supply.

Steve Murray, editor of REAL Trends, a publishing and analysis company that studies the residential real estate market nationally, says that the average commission rate in 2002 was 5.1 percent. In 1991, it was 6.1 percent. Among the fifty largest brokerage firms, with aggregate homes sales volumes of $1.73 billion and higher, REAL Trends reported that commissions averaged slightly less than the national rate, 5.04 percent. Among major brand-name firms, ERA's commissions averaged the highest (5.68 percent, according to the study), and RE/MAX's commissions averaged the lowest (4.88 percent).

Murray calls the decade-long downward trend "very steady and very gradual" and says that it's being driven partly by the increase in housing prices and partly by the change in generational attitudes. "The younger generation [those individuals under 35] tend to trust the institution of professional real estate less than their parents and want to haggle more than their parents," Murray says.

That means that, once again, it's the consumer who is largely driving change in the real estate market and stoking the commission compression trend, particularly in hot markets where demand has outstripped supply and real estate agents scramble to fill their listing inventory. And while it's ultimately up to the individual agents to decide whether they want to drop their prices or not, the very thought of dropping rates at the customer's whim sends chills up one Buffalo, New York–based broker's spine. This broker has some genuine concerns about discounter real estate brokers who devalue their services and alter the agent-customer relationship from service-oriented to price-oriented.

To put it simply, he says it commoditizes the industry. To combat the trend, this broker took a "join 'em" stance and created a fee-for-service entity (see more details on menu options in Chapter 6) to complement his full-service firm. He also utilizes a system that gives consumers three different commission plans, depending on their individual abilities and needs during the home-selling process. "Instead of constantly reducing the discussing to 'will you do this for this amount?' we help agents focus the seller on what they're getting for the commission," he says. "My agents provide the choices, and allow their customers to make the ultimate choice."

Virginia "Ginny" Lomagno, managing broker of fifty-two agents in two St. Petersburg, Florida, Coldwell Banker Residential Real Estate offices, has been in the real estate business for twenty-six years and says that bargain hunting is simply human nature. She says that discount brokers have been around for the entire time she's been in real estate, and that they haven't significantly affected her company, which posts increased sales volume year after year. She simply tells her agents that if they offer value, and if their customers want quality service, representation, and results, then the customers will pay the going commission rate.

The problem, she says, is that all a discount broker can really offer is a discounted commission, which usually also means limited services, whereas a full-service firm like Coldwell Banker provides the technology, the tools, and the brand name to expose properties to the greatest number of buyers, which results in a quicker sale. "I help agents show the customer just where our value lies," she says. "And if the customer still doesn't recognize the value that we bring to the table, then the commission is irrelevant anyway. Our customers are primarily concerned with prompt results and an acceptable bottom line. There will always be people who look for a discount, but we service customers who want quality."

Commission compression is prevalent in Curry Jameson's northern Nevada market. In the real estate business for twenty-eight years, Jameson, the president of Realty Executives of Northern Nevada, says that his market is characterized by rising prices and low listing inventory—two trends that tend to drive down commissions. After all, if listing inventory is hard to come by and home prices are going up anyway, why not knock your commission down a percentage point or two, right?

"We have a situation here where we don't have a lot of inventory and we have a huge demand from our incoming market, which is primarily the Northwest and northern California," says Jameson, who adds that commission compression is enhanced by the ease of selling property fairly quickly and the knowledge base that today's consumer has about the home selling process. "All fees are negotiable anyway, but there is certainly additional pressure coming from firms with discount business models and fee structures, particularly in those areas of the country where we've seen a big advertising push by those companies."

Jameson says that his own agents try to avoid succumbing to the pressure by positioning their services and experience in a desirable light, and sometimes even discussing the issue of commission compression itself with the home seller. "I show them how to explain full-service and semi-full-service versus no service at all," says Jameson. "By doing this, they've stayed on track with a fee basis that provides the best full service for consumers, no matter the market."

REFERRAL FEE, PLEASE

Just when you thought there were enough people standing at the closing table with a hand out, waiting for a chunk of your precious commission check, the online referral fee system has become one of the newest models in real estate. With this model, an online firm uses MLS data to entice home buyers and sellers to provide personal data like names and telephone numbers. The company then sells the "leads" to real estate agents for a flat fee or a commission cut. These online referral fee firms have received mixed reviews from agents—with some complaining that the companies gave out leads to more than one agent—and should be approached with caution.

There are literally hundreds of referral firms operating in the market, attempting to act as intermediaries between customers and agents. We'll look at two in particular that advertise their services to agents. All Florida Referral Network promises cybersurfers that they can "earn Florida real estate commissions at home" and says that there are an "extremely large number of individuals" who have earned real estate licenses, but cannot devote themselves full time to their real estate careers. For them, the company offers a position of referral agent. "You can now financially benefit by generating lucrative Florida real estate commissions," the company's Web site states. "All Florida Referral Network, Inc. can offer you the opportunity to keep your real estate license active and share in the earning of real estate commissions without committing a tremendous amount of your valuable time and energy."

How does the firm do it? By hiring referral agents who have real estate licenses to provide referral leads to the All Florida Referral Network. The firm then places the lead with a qualified full-time real estate agent (presumably an individual from the company's brokerage, All Florida Realty Services) who services the client in a "professional manner."

Another referral company is Service Magic, which uses a similar model and lists "Find a Real Estate Agent" as one of its top ten requests, among dozens of other referral offerings that the company specializes in. The Golden, Colorado–based firm charges agents a flat fee to register with the service, with the idea that when a home buyer or seller comes to the site to enter search criteria, the company will then "sell" (as of August 2003, the fees posted on the company's web site were $30 for a customer who is buying a home, $40 for a customer who is selling a home, or $60 for a customer who is both buying and selling a home in the same area) that lead to an agent in the appropriate region. It's then up to the agent to turn the lead into a sale.

Also cutting into the commission pool are for sale by owner, or FSBO (pronounced fizz-bo), properties that owners are selling on their own with the limited help of real estate attorneys and title companies. Some veteran agents will tell you that the FSBO market was never within reach to begin with, and that there will always be a certain percentage of homeowners who can, and who will, sell their own homes with just a sign in the yard or a Web site posting. NAR reports that among repeat home buyers who intended to sell their previous home, 83 percent did so using a real estate professional. This includes the nearly 4 percent of buyers who first tried to sell their home themselves but then used an agent. This continued an upward trend that began in 1999, when only 77 percent of sellers used an agent.

Roughly 14 percent of home sellers sell their homes without the assistance of a real estate agent, according to NAR. That number includes the 1 percent of buyers who first listed their home with an agent and then sold the home themselves. Among those who sold their home without using an agent, 35 percent sold their home to a friend or someone whom they knew prior to the sale. Whether a seller uses a real estate agent or not also has something to do with geographical location, and is perhaps somewhat based on a herd mentality. (If my neighbor can sell his own house, why can't I?) NAR says that sellers in the Midwest were the least likely to use an agent to sell their home. In 2003, 79 percent of sellers in the Midwest used an agent, compared to 83 percent in the South, 82 percent in the Northeast, and 84 percent in the West. In the Midwest, 17 percent of sellers sold their home without the assistance of an agent, compared to approximately 13 percent of sellers in the other three Census regions.

It's no big secret that technology and new user-friendly marketing tools have made it even easier for owners to do it themselves. Add in the fact that companies like ForSaleByOwner.com (which in late 2003 acquired three "for sale by owner" real estate Web sites, www.fisbo.com, www.salebyowner.com, and www.byownersales.com, to peddle the parent firm's listings data and resources to customers) and Buy Owner charge a small fee for a marketing kit and a listing on their nationally advertised Web sites, and you can see how the draw might be compelling for those homeowners who have the time and initiative to hold open houses, manage the legalities of the sale, and see the transaction through to the closing table on their own.

The FSBO trend is especially prevalent in areas where demand for housing is high. In a market where a home with the right price takes just a week to sell via the MLS, it's not out of the question to think that a home could sell within a few weeks or so, or less, without the system. So what's an agent to do? Well, in the olden days they would capture phone numbers off of those FSBO signs and classified ads, then call up asking if what that buyer didn't really want was a good agent to handle the sale. Sometimes an owner will put a sign in the yard, then throw in the towel and sign a listing agreement with an agent after realizing how complicated and time-consuming the sale process really is.

Where agents can prove their value to FSBOs is not so much in lower commissions or MLS listings, but in the experience, knowledge, and wide range of services that they can either provide or hook the seller up with.

That includes pricing the home correctly, screening buyers to gauge how serious they are about making the purchase, showing the home from an impartial perspective, and supervising inspections once the contract is signed.

HOT MARKETS = MORE PRESSURE

Where there are hot markets, there is very intensive commission compression. In the Northeast, for example, 7 percent commissions are the norm. Out west in California, however, agents fight tooth and nail to take listings for as low as 3 or 4 percent just to boost their listing inventory and give buyers a reason to call their offices or visit their Web sites. In regions like Houston and Charlotte, North Carolina, however, inventory levels topped out at around eleven months in mid-2003, thus creating a "buyer's market," and much less competition for listings. In such markets, the going commission rates tend to stick much better. Like most economic forces, real estate is highly cyclical, so the dynamics change from month to month in many markets.

In a 2002 study of commission rates, REAL Trends found that average commission rates vary significantly from region to region, and even from firm to firm. In 2002, for example, commissions were highest in the midwestern states, where they averaged 5.62 percent. They were lowest in the mid-Atlantic states, at 4.78 percent. In New England, the average commission was 5.2 percent, while the southeastern states averaged 5.5 percent. The far west came in at 4.92 percent, while the Southeast and mountain states averaged 5.16 percent.

In Mission Viejo, California, David and Jan Pingree, broker Realtors® with Regency Real Estate, say that they're feeling commission compression from all sides. They've been in the business for sixteen years, and they posted about $3.5 million in sales in 2002. Particularly intrusive, they say, are the relocation companies, which have pushed their referral fees up to 35 percent of the sale, when they used to charge 25 or 30 percent. Like Jesperson noted earlier in the chapter, everyone seems to want an even bigger piece of that pie in mom's kitchen window.

David Pingree says that the added strain hasn't hurt his business much, though he says that the newer players in his ninety-agent office are buckling under it. Compounding the problem is the fact that properties in his area priced below $500,000 are listed at 2.5 percent for the selling agent instead of the customary 3 percent, so it's easy to see how an agent's take can quickly get whittled down to a minimal amount.

"We're actually seeing very few 3 percent listings, which means that we as an industry have cut our own throats by taking discounted listings and passing the cut along to the selling agent as well," says Pingree, who recalls a time in the not too distant past when only the listing agent took the commission hit, so as to entice selling agents to show the property. "Now, thanks to the low inventory, agents are putting their listings in at 2.5 percent and everyone is still showing them," says Pingree. "As you work your way up above the $500,000 price range, there are more at 3 percent because there's more inventory and more competition in that range."

Pingree blames not only the low inventory (in some price ranges, there's a one month's supply or less in his area) for causing the problem, but also the fact that agents are willing to discount their commissions, often taking a 5 percent commission and splitting it 50/50 with the selling agent. (The conventional wisdom in real estate is that without inventory, you can't attract buyers. The success of the buyer's agent movement has dispelled this myth, although most real estate offices still live by it.)

"The sellers are really in the driver's seat at this point," says Pingree, adding that he typically avoids showing listings that come up in the MLS with a selling percentage of 2 or 2.25 percent. Pingree says that pressure is also coming from the Internet and flat- or reduced-fee brokers (see more on these real estate firms in Chapter 5), which have forced full-service brokers to rethink not only their commission fees, but also the way in which they conduct business.

Exacerbating the problem is the fact that the cat is out of the bag, and sellers—at least in Pingree's region—know that agents are hungry enough to drop their commissions a percentage point just to get the listing. When they are working with a referral client—one whose referring company is presumably commanding 25 to 30 percent of Pingree's take—they try to get the full 6 percent commission. For other listings, they offer the selling agent 3 percent, despite the total commission, to avoid hurting the seller's position in the market.

To agents operating in a comparable selling environment, Pingree advises stressing service and establishing rapport with customers in order to avoid commoditizing your services by marketing them on price alone. If that fails, realize that you can command only what the market will bear. If you're going to a listing appointment, for example, and three other agents are willing to list the home at 5 percent while you're asking 6 percent, then you'll probably be forced to accept the reduced fees if you want that listing.

LEARNING TO DEAL

Cutting your commission rate sounds simple enough, right? After all, what's one tiny percentage point on a $500,000 home sale? Well, it's not much to the individual agent, but the implications could be serious in the long term for the industry as a whole. Look at it this way: You're listing that home, which means you'll see a $2,500 difference in your side of the deal. On a broader scale, however, your move could open the door for many other homeowners to try to drive down prices to a level that they know certain agents in the marketplace are willing to work for. Word gets around quickly, and some would say that you're also succumbing to the idea that real estate agents and their brokers make entirely too much money, that commission rates are inflated, and that agents should be willing to take what they can get in order to get a listing.

David Jenks, vice president of research and development for Keller Williams, says that the field is divided unevenly between the experienced, confident agents who go on every listing appointment knowing that they'll get the listing at the right rate (20 percent of the agents in the industry) and those who go in less than confident, leaving the door open to hard negotiations (the other 80 percent). Jenks says the proof is in NAR's 2003 Profile of Homebuyers and Sellers: Two-thirds of all home buyers who used an agent interviewed only one agent, and nearly all of the remaining one-third interviewed only two or three agents.

"That means that the 20 percent of agents who have a sphere of influence and referral-based business are not out there competing on price," Jenks reasons. "In our experience working with top agents, we've found that they usually get a call to list a home, give out the customary price, and sign up the customer with little or no haggling on price."

The problem for the other 80 percent of agents is that they're out in the field competing for the one-third of property owners who are interviewing multiple agents, hoping to find one who will chop the commission down. A self-proclaimed numbers guy, Jenks says that he's studied commission trends over the last twenty years and noticed a slow, steady erosion over that time. Two decades ago, he says, the average total commission was about 6.1 percent (some areas were as high as 7 percent, while others were around 6 percent).

But while the commission rate has since come down to 5.4 percent nationwide, the average sale price in the United States has tripled, leaving the doors of opportunity wide open for real estate agents. "When you multiply the 2.7 percent change (5.8 percent divided between the listing and selling agents) by an average sales price of three times what it was twenty years ago, it's clear that the available commission today for agents is nearly four times what it once was," says Jenks. "Factor in home sales—which have increased in volume over the last two decades—and my estimation is that available commissions have risen from about $200 billion in 1983 to a current $1.2 trillion."

But don't let those extra zeroes blind you to the fact that the cost of doing business has certainly increased during the same time period. In speaking to an agent whose average home sales price in the Los Angeles area is over $3.5 million, Jenks says he learned that she shells out an average of $10,000 to $15,000 for marketing and advertising on every property that she lists.

"The cost of doing business in the real estate industry has cranked up at a rate nearly that of the home sale prices themselves," says Jenks, adding that these days, it's very difficult for an agent to net (take home) more than 30 to 40 percent of the commission from his side of the sale (be it listing, selling, or both). He refers back to the formula for figuring commissions and says the bottom-line number for the typical agent is 1 percent of the home's selling price (or $10,000 on one of those $1 million homes).

So the successful agents are doing one of two things: volume or high-end homes. To put it simply, either they're listing and selling much more than the industry average of one home per month, or they're specializing in higher-end homes that fetch higher commissions and make their jobs worthwhile.

BEATING THE ODDS

For those agents who are feeling the commission compression firsthand, dealing with it requires good negotiating tactics, knowing how to take the emphasis off of price, and, perhaps most importantly, knowing when to walk away from a deal that's not in your best interest to pursue. There are books galore available on negotiating skills (you'll find a few listed in the appendix of this book) and walking away from unfavorable deals, so I'll focus on a newfound strategy that many agents are unaware of: learning your value proposition—which is basically the knowledge, expertise, and consultative skills that you bring to the table—and knowing how to maximize it.

Your value proposition should focus tightly on maximizing the value-added services that you bring to the table that no other agent, broker, cut-rate broker, or online real estate firm can bring. For some agents, that means being intimately aware of the communities they work in, including property values, conditions, and even where the sinkholes are. For others, it's knowing about specific buyer or seller groups, such as teachers and policemen, who otherwise wouldn't be able to find adequate financing and help to get into their first homes (see Figure 4-2).

And sometimes it just means spelling things out in black and white for buyers who ignorantly think that real estate agents are completely focused on money. Mary Zentz, a Realtor associate with RE/MAX

Figure 4-2.

METHOD USED TO SELL HOME
(Precentage Distribution)

	1991	1993	1995	1997	1999	2001	2003
Real Estate Agent	77%	82%	81%	80%	77%	79%	83%
FSBO	19	17	15	18	16	13	14
Sold to homebuying company	4	1	2	1	2	1	1
Other	*	*	2	1	5	7	3

In 2003 Only	Northeast	Midwest	Southwest	West
Real estate agent	82%	79%	83%	84%
FSBO knew buyer	5	6	5	4
FSBO did not know buyer	8	11	8	9
Sold to homebuying company	*	*	2	*
Other	6	4	3	3

* Less than 1%

Source: The 2003 National Association of REALTORS Profile of Home Buyers and Sellers. Used with permission.

Suburban in Chicago, ran into one in 2003. He called regularly on one of her listings, checking to see if it's price had been reduced. Out of the blue he decided to make an offer on the property, which eventually wound up in a dual-offer situation, with Zentz presenting not only her buyer's offer, but also one from another selling agent.

Then came a bombshell: Zentz's buyer was interested in working with listing agents in hopes that they would give up their "selling" half of the commission so that he could get the home at a lower price. Zentz told him that she didn't work that way, and he insisted on talking to her boss about it. "I am my boss, and I don't have to talk to anyone about it," Zentz told him. "By law, I couldn't tell him that the other offer was better anyway. He was going on the assumption that no one would have paid that kind of money for the house. He was wrong."

Where the buyer went wrong was in assuming that Zentz was solely money-oriented. "I have to look at myself in the mirror twice a day when I brush my teeth, and I want to be able to sleep at night," Zentz says. "While I knew it would be nice to have an extra $2,000 in my pocket (her share of the selling commission), was I willing to give up $8,000 to salvage $2,000? Not particularly." That's because like all agents, Zentz works hard for what she earns and thus resents it when someone tells her that what he's offering is better than nothing. "Especially when the seller had already fairly decided what I, as a dual agent, and all other buyer's agents deserved in that case," she adds.

Besides, a buyer who is so eager to chip away at your commission on the front end will probably raise even more hackles down the road, like when it comes to "helping" to pay for repairs and credits. "Once you open your pockets, people expect you to continue opening them," Zentz says. "Worse yet, they'll refer people to you who want you to do the same. This guy should have been dealing with a discount broker who rebated him money at the closing table, or some other nontraditional setup."

The following day, Zentz says, the same buyer paid $50,000 more for a home located one block away. Such actions are often clear indicators of just how much the buyer wants the home. If they want it only at their price with their terms, says Zentz, then they're not committed to that house. "It's typically best for the seller to have a buyer who is totally committed and really wants their home," she says.

Matt Deasy, a general manager who oversees six offices and 330 agents at Windermere Real Estate East Inc., in Bellevue, Washington, says buyers often approach the firm's listing agents with requests for discount commissions because they're not working with a buyer's agent. Deasy says he's trained agents to give simple, two-letter answers to that question: "No." The reason is simple: Buyers need buyer representation.

"In addition, protecting the integrity of the agent's fee structure is essential to the maintenance of a truly professional agent base," says Deasy, who adds that because his firm has a large market share in its area of the country, its actions tend to set precedents for the rest of the industry. In other words, if Windermere were to succumb to commission compression, the effects could trickle through the entire industry.

"The reality of it is that if a buyer is going to buy only a house on which a listed agent is willing to give her part of the commission (and that does not define most buyers), the agent needs to learn how to draw the line there," says Deasy. "Our job as managers is to get agents to think through how they want to handle this issue when they are not actually in a specific transaction, then proceed accordingly when the situation really does come up."

Ask J. Lennox Scott, chairman and CEO at John L. Scott Real Estate in Seattle, what he thinks about the commission compression coming from the customer side of the equation, and his answer comes quickly. It's not widespread in the Northwest, he says, and combating it means finding the definitive value that the agent brings to the transaction and putting that in front of the customer.

"It comes down to each agent's confidence and how their company is supporting them with marketing programs and technology," says Scott.

SURPRISE, SURPRISE

So, you know that commission compression is an issue for agents working in the field, but did you know that it also affects your broker, who really isn't making much money to begin with? That's right; the majority of the income generated in the industry comes from the agent side, not from the brokerage itself. According to "Future of Real Estate Brokerage," a study commissioned by the NAR, as the number of real estate transactions has increased over the years, brokerages are not reporting a comparable rise in profitability.

One broker-owner of a Texas-based real estate firm is among those grappling with eroding margins in an increasingly competitive business environment. With one office and twenty-six agents, the broker uses a few different commission splits that range from 55 percent for the agent to 82.5 percent for the agent, depending on the individual agent's production over the prior twelve months. New agents start at the 55 or 60 percent range, while more experienced agents earn higher rates, based on performance.

He says his company instituted the graduated plan in early 2002, after competitive pressures in the marketplace—mainly from those brokerages offering 100 percent commissions—forced him to rethink his firm's compensation plan. (According to NAR, compensation of agents working on 100 percent commission [known as the "agent service bureau model"] was more than 50 percent higher than that of agents earning commission splits, as of 2001.) And while he obviously succumbed to the pressure, the broker says a full-service firm like his has overhead like advertising, technology costs, rent and utilities to maintain that those 100 percent shops do not, thus warranting the higher split for the broker.

"There's a real partnership here in that our office offers services to both the agents and their clients," he says. "We strive to keep that mentality all the way through our organization, despite the individual agent's performance." So far, the brokers' willingness to create a sort of "hybrid" commission structure—not 50/50, but not quite 100 percent either—hasn't paid off for the company. One year into it, he says, "profitwise, it wasn't necessarily a good move" for the company. After the second year of using the program he expects to have a better picture of just how well it is, or isn't, working.

"The trade-off was that we knew that for it to work, the numbers (sales volume) would have to be higher than what they were before," he explains. "For the first year, we were giving away what probably worked out to be about 5 percent of the company dollars. That doesn't sound like a lot, but when you already give away 4 additional percent, it compounds to create a pretty big swing in profits."

This broker has good company in the industry. Darla Scott, president of Management Masters in Philadelphia, often works with real estate brokers to provide commission plan analysis and profitable new designs, as well as recruiting and retention strategies. She says the Texas broker's situation is not unusual in an industry where the majority of the money flows to the independent contractors who work for the brokerage.

The increase in the 100 percent concept companies is also making it harder on the traditional brokerage firms, especially in states where those firms have gained significant market share, she says. In order to keep their productive sales associates and attract new ones, brokers are being forced to give higher and higher commission splits, while still providing the services of the traditional broker. But Scott says 100 percent concept companies aren't faring much better. "Because their profits remain fairly flat no matter how well the individual sales associates perform, they usually have to supplement their income (and sometimes the expenses of the company) by continuing to list and sell homes," says Scott. "To increase their profitability, most of them now provide a variety of traditional commission plans and 'deferred payment plans.'"

To put it simply, there seems to be no way for the brokerages themselves to win. "The traditional companies and the 100 percent concept companies are not that far apart when it comes to bottom-line profit," says Scott. "There is precious little profit left to run a real estate company, unless you have the volume of transactions to warrant having mortgage, title, and insurance operations, which are profitable."

Scott says some of the fault lies at the feet of the brokers themselves. Many traditional brokers are stuck in outmoded commission models, and the 100 percent concept brokers are afraid to raise their management and desk space fees for fear of losing their sales associates. "As a professional consultant specializing in commission plan analysis and design, I find that many real estate companies don't want to take the time and money to analyze their expense and revenue situation in order to determine their true breakeven point and create a plan that is fair to agents and owners alike," says Scott. "The quick-fix commission plans, sales associate commission exceptions, and hiring incentives that are being offered are short-term gain for long-term pain."

One alternative that most brokers dream of but would never implement, for fear of losing the entrepreneurial spirit of their independent contractors, is the salaried agent. The Texas broker says he's toyed with the idea, but admits that he'd never be the first in his area to institute such a plan. Scott, however, says that there are situations that warrant salaried agents, particularly now, when the industry is trying to attract younger agents.

"In order to compete with other industries that typically offer a salary plus commission and benefits," says Scott, "a broker owner might consider a salary and smaller commission split on sales for the first six months to a year, giving the new hire the opportunity to make the transition to the straight commission method."

The moral of the story is this: If your broker's cut of the pie is leaving your pockets empty, you have alternatives. But also remember that your broker is probably doing some nail-biting too, wondering how to eke out a profit in a business where the majority of the profits flow to the individual agents, not to the companies they're representing. The days when the 50/50 split were the norm are long gone, and for top-producing, established agents there are 100 percent brokerages that offer bare-bones service but maximum income potential. For mid-level agents there are splits that range from 50/50 to 80/20 and offer more support, marketing, technology and overhead. For beginners there are options that include low up-front costs to get you through to that first, all-important trip to the closing table.

MORE THAN JUST DOLLARS AND CENTS

Julie Greenwood knows that agents who hang their licenses with her company aren't looking for high commission splits. "Good, professional agents don't go somewhere just for the split," says Greenwood, broker-owner at Greenwood-King Properties, Inc., in Houston. "I can't really say we've ever had an agent join us just for our commission plan." What good agents want, says Greenwood, is a company with a good reputation in the marketplace and an established infrastructure that includes marketing, management, advertising, and brand support. "Agents should be looking at the whole picture," she says. "They should seek out a market leader who can provide them with all of the services that they need in order to operate successfully."

At Greenwood-King, those services include a direct mail program, a team of professionals who show the company's listings, a public relations professional, and a full-time graphics designer who creates marketing materials for the company and its agents.

It also includes an in-house advertising agency, full-color brochures, and a two-page ad in the *Houston Chronicle* every week.

Scott says that the key factors that an agent should be looking for in a brokerage are (in order of importance) company reputation (including that of the owners, management, and agents), administrative support services, commission plans, technology and training, and market share (see Figure 4-3). And while it's easy enough to be lured in by companies that dole out 100 percent commissions, Greenwood warns agents to be wary of companies that "give everything away," only to find themselves unable to provide their agents with basic services and consistency.

"Agents have to focus on all of the services and support that a brokerage can provide, and not just get lured into changing or choosing companies based on the commission plan," Greenwood adds. "When I was an agent and thinking about changing companies, I never asked about the commission plan. It wasn't what it was about."

Figure 4-3.

IN ORDER OF IMPORTANCE

Darla Scott, president of Management Masters, LLC, in Philadelphia, has compiled thousands of written real estate agent surveys over the last few years. In doing so, she's found that the key factors that agents consider when choosing a wall to hang their license on haven't changed much. Here they are, in order of importance:

1. Company reputation (owners, management, agents, and so on)

2. Administrative support services

3. Commission structure

4. Technologies and technology training

5. Market share

THINKING OUTSIDE THE BOX

Real estate has always been known as the industry where agents go without company-sponsored benefits, insurance, or retirement plans. In exchange, they pocket what most people think are hefty commission checks. We all know that for the average agent, this isn't true, and lately a new crop of real estate firms seem to be catching on to agents' basic financial and personal needs. One that appears to be focused on the "retirement income" side is EXIT Realty Corp. Founded in Ontario, Canada, in 1996, the company has been operating in the United States since 1998 and currently has over 6,000 agents working in 345 agencies in 32 states.

To the consumer, EXIT Realty looks like any other real estate company, but to its agents, EXIT Realty is different in that it rewards them with "residual income" when they recruit, then help retain and nurture other productive agents. According to Tami Bonnell, president of EXIT's U.S. operations, agents earn a 10 percent sponsoring bonus, or up to $10,000 annually, for new recruits. She says EXIT Realty's residual system works only on a single level, meaning that agents earn residuals only from those recruits that they "sponsor" and nothing extra from the agents that their recruits bring into the system.

"Agents are rewarded for their own personal efforts only," says Bonnell, adding that EXIT has been compared to a multilevel marketing firm, but that there is a serious flaw in the multilevel marketing (MLM) structure, where most of the income is distributed among the early entrants and those near the top of the MLM structure. "All agents have the same growth opportunities here, regardless of when they joined the company," she says. EXIT Realty's residual program also includes a 5 percent death benefit for beneficiaries, should the agent die unexpectedly, and a 7 percent residual upon retirement.

Agents with enough recruits can make money without selling real estate, though Bonnell says that her company considers anyone who does less than eight transactions a year to be retired, and thus eligible for only the 7 percent residual and not the full 10. Bonnell says that the company's founder, Steve Morris, who was at one time owner of the second

largest RE/MAX franchise in North America, created the residual program because he wanted to provide a better quality of life for Realtors,
who typically have no retirement accounts or benefits. "The individual
agents are every real estate office's biggest asset," says Bonnell, "yet
they're only as good as their last transaction."

TAPPING YOUR POTENTIAL

So you know that the odds that someone will try to chip away at your standard commission rate are very high, and that this isn't a new problem in the
industry but one that's been slowly growing over the last twenty years and
probably isn't going to go away anytime soon. You also know that the
newest of the threats includes referral fee companies that offer you leads in
exchange for a flat fee or a portion of your commission. Whether you
choose to deal with these companies is your business, but it's probably best
to ask around in agent circles about how effective they are and whether
doing business with them violates your state's license law before you
exchange information or fees with them.

Finally, you also know that your broker is in the same boat with you,
trying to fight eroding margins while at the same time keeping customer
service levels (for you and for your buyers and sellers) as high as possible.
It should be comforting to know that as an agent, you definitely sit on the
better side of the fence financially than the broker ever will, and most of
the honest ones will admit that. That doesn't mean that you need to go
seek out a more profitable broker who is guaranteed to be in business for
the next hundred years, but it does mean that you should factor in the
overall health of your broker before trying to squeeze more blood out of
the rock (i.e., asking for a bigger agent split).

There's also some good news for agents. While commissions are slowly eroding, the number of homes sold every year in the United States, and
the prices at which they're being sold, have skyrocketed during the same
time that commissions were cut back by barely one percentage point. No
profession likes to see its per-sale revenues lose ground, but few in real

estate would argue that it's the individual agent and broker who are out in the field working who can make the difference.

"From the agent's standpoint, if you look at the appreciation in value that we have seen in housing over the last five years versus the commission compression, agents are making more for transactions today than they ever have," says Jesperson, who advises agents to focus not on the commission rate (which has, in fact, softened) but on the total pool of commissions that's available in today's home marketplace.

"Look at it that way and you'll find that it's still a very lucrative career," says Jesperson, who expects the commission compression trend to taper off a bit when the hot real estate market of the late 1990s and early 2000s slows to a more normal level. "The fact is, in tighter times, agents tend to get a little more backbone and provide more service, while in really hot markets they're more likely to discount their commissions."

SIX THINGS TO REMEMBER FROM CHAPTER 4

- ❏ Real estate commissions have been on a slide nationwide for the last ten years, thanks to increased competition, an influx of online and cut-rate brokers, and consumers themselves.

- ❏ Full-service real estate agents don't have to compete on price with their cut-rate competitors if they add value to the transaction and become a trusted, loyal adviser to their customers.

- ❏ Where you're located in the United States has a lot to do with the level of commission compression you experience. Hot markets in California are particularly prone to discounting, as are areas where discount brokerages are prevalent.

- ❏ While the real estate industry has evolved, agents' top priorities when it comes to choosing a broker have not; they include company reputation, management, administrative support services, commission structure, technologies and technology training, and market share.

- ❏ When it comes to selecting a broker, agents should look at more than just commission splits and focus on the service and support that those brokers can provide. Those who don't need the extra help would probably do best at a broker that offers 100 percent commissions.

❑   The good news for agents is that as commissions have gone down, both home prices and home sales have skyrocketed, leaving the door open for those enterprising agents who are braced to grab more of the commissions that are available in the marketplace.

CHAPTER 5

Dealing with Discounters

ROLLING BACK PRICES

Discount brokerages are constantly hovering behind Joyce Gomoljak, and she knows it. A Realtor® with Champion Realty in Annapolis, Maryland, Gomoljak has been in the business for six years and sold $4 million in properties in 2002, ranking her squarely in the "six-figure income" slot among agents.

Over the last two years, pressure from discount brokers has gotten so intense that Gomoljak can't even remember most of the company names anymore, probably by choice, since she specializes only in the full-service, full-commission approach to real estate. What she does notice, however, is the way those companies take home listings for "so little money," compared to what full-service brokerages charge, yet deliver so little service in return.

"They'll put the home in the MLS, and that's about it," says Gomoljak. "The more a homeowner asks for from them, the more they charge. If you combine all of their services, compare them with what we provide, and weigh them against the fees that each company charges, it's clear that we give consumers more for less." Gomoljak says the discounters—which include both online-only companies and office-based firms that list and sell homes—do serve a purpose for homeowners who want to handle the sale themselves while getting MLS exposure at the same time.

"If they don't want anyone to manage the process, follow up and screen potential home buyers, and inform them so that they can successfully negotiate contracts, then that's exactly what they'll get for their money," says Gomoljak. "Consumers who use these discounters are shooting in the dark and paying a lot for very little."

When asked to list homes at discount prices, Gomoljak says that she tells her sellers flat out that she pockets just one-quarter of what the seller is being charged (with half going to the selling agent and the other quarter going to Gomoljak's broker). She offers to negotiate a bit on the price, but explains clearly that X is the customary percentage that full-service agents charge to do the job from concept to completion.

The pressure is also affecting buyer's agents, who sign an agreement to receive a certain percentage of the commission before hitting the streets in search of the perfect home for their client. Should a home be listed for less than the going rate in a certain area, the buyer's agent takes home less. "That's something agents really need to discuss with their clients ahead of time," says Gomoljak, who herself has come close to selling a home with a selling agent commission of less than the going rate in the MLS.

DISCOUNTERS ABOUND

A mix of consumer demands, unprecedented property appreciation rates, and a slew of new technology tools have helped to create a marketplace for real estate business models that break the traditional "full-service" mold and offer what industry experts refer to as the "no frills real estate" model. In all fairness, while Gomoljak and other agents' business dealings with discounters have been largely negative, there are nontraditional companies that do provide a respectable level of service in exchange for their lower-than-market fees.

Discount brokers have been around for years, offering to undercut their full-service competitors, but the advent of the Internet and the ability to work virtually (i.e., without a high-profile office location) has helped them proliferate in recent years. The newer players in the market range from online brokers to virtual brokers (with no physical offices for agents) to flat-fee companies that charge, say, $299 for a listing on the local MLS system plus additional fees for more services. Most traditional agents lump all of these into the "discount" category, which is why they are all covered in this chapter. Most of them would argue, however, that they are not discount brokerages, but rather companies that have found a more efficient, effective way to help people buy and sell real estate.

Foxtons, which calls itself the "home of the 2 percent commissions," is one of these companies. This New Jersey company claims to have saved its customers over $75 million in commissions since its inception in 2000, based on total commissions paid on its listings versus total commissions that would have been paid if a 6 percent commission had been charged. Along with a 2 percent fee for listing a piece of property, the company also offers additional services (such as help with showings and open houses) for 3 percent, and charges a total of 3.5 to 4.3 percent for properties that are listed on the MLS (with 2 to 2.5 percent going to the cooperating or "selling" agent).

The consensus among industry experts is that discounters like Foxtons have captured less than 10 percent of the market, but that the number could be growing. Brokers and agents seem to be most threatened by those discounters who cut commissions and force the traditional agents to work harder. In other words, where full-service agents feel the brunt of the discounters' price slicing is not so much on the marketing side of the business as in their own interpersonal dealings with these new entrants.

One agent in Boca Raton, Florida, for example, says that she's fed up with all of the extra work she has to do when one of her buyers chooses a home that's listed either as an FSBO or by a cut-rate broker. In order to get the deal closed, this RE/MAX agent knows that she'll probably have to help draw up the contract, handle the disclosures, schedule inspections, and oversee the entire transaction—all steps that the listing agent working with a seller should handle. She's not alone. Traditional brokers and agents have voiced their concerns about the cut-rate industry for years, and most feel that discounters not only force them to work harder when completing a deal, but also leave their customers to deal with the buyer's agent, who by law is not the right person to assist or advise the seller.

Full-service agents have stood their ground in the fight by refusing to show discounters' listings, complaining about discounters to their state real estate commission, and voicing their concerns about the discounters to the media. Brokers in the state of Texas, for example, lobbied the Texas Real Estate Commission to enforce a minimum level of service requirement that would have severely hampered discounters' ability to operate as no-frills companies, charging fees to list properties in the MLS. In 2003 the Texas Real Estate Commission took a bold step and tried to enact a rule requiring brokers to provide negotiation services. The rule would have resulted in the elimination of limited services brokers' ability to list homes on their MLS systems, making it very difficult for any non-traditional brokerage to operate in the state.

The rule was repealed, but not before it raised some hackles in the discount brokerage community. A company known as Texas Discount Realty immediately brought a lawsuit against TREC for enacting the rule. This company collects a fee to place the seller's listing on the MLS and also offers two other levels of service.

Under Texas statutes, brokers act as fiduciaries or agents of buyers or sellers. If they represent both parties, they do so as intermediaries. According to the Texas Association of Realtors®, the original rule was prompted by the fact that some brokers were telling sellers that they were acting as their agents, even though listing property on an MLS is not a fiduciary or intermediary function.

The new rule would have prohibited basic home listings, where the consumer does much of the work of selling the home. To put it simply, the rule would have required agents to provide home sellers with a full range of brokerage services, whether they wanted them or not. That includes accepting and presenting offers and counteroffers, representing the seller in communications with buyer's agents, and answering the seller's questions about offers and the transaction.

The ruling was put on hold by TREC in January 2003 as the group took a harder look at the issue. In April 2003, the ruling was repealed, with a promise to replace it in the future. A few months later the Texas Association of Realtors asked TREC to revisit the issue, so stay tuned.

ALTERNATIVE METHODS

Because the efforts of full-service brokers to somehow eradicate their cut-rate or flat-fee competitors haven't worked out as planned, most successful agents have learned to live with and deal with their lower-priced competitors—as any business would. In New Jersey, for example, Foxtons sells 150 to 200 homes a week, 80 percent of which are sold at a 2 percent commission. For that price, homeowners get a virtual tour on the company's Web site, newspaper advertisements and general advertising for the business, and the services of one of Foxtons' ten agents in the Bergen/Passaic county area. The downside is that sellers have to show the home themselves. Foxtons will show the home for a 3 percent commission and include an MLS listing for a 4 percent commission.

The company's business model is based on exposure, advertising of its listings, and the $12 million a year it spends on advertising the company's listings to the public via television, radio, billboards, the Internet, and newspapers. It credits itself with helping to make real estate commissions more flexible, although some real estate experts are skeptical about such firms' ability to make a dent in the market. Steve Murray of REAL Trends says that while a company like Foxtons has a place in the market, it caters mainly to consumers whose inclination is to seek to pay less than market for real estate services.

"This segment of the market could be larger than the shares currently held by the nation's largest existing brands, in the area of 12 to 15 percent. Whether Foxtons or others offering these kinds of services and prices can capture that large a share of this segment remains to be seen," Murray says. "It also remains to be seen whether they can deliver a consistent profit if they do succeed in building sufficient share."

TAKING A BITE

Most real estate agents and brokers pooh-pooh the idea that someone out there can possibly replace them for $299, or for a mere 1.5 percent of a home's selling price. The problem is, consumers don't always know the difference between a discounter or "nontraditional" broker and a broker who works for a full commission. In my area, HomeDiscovere.com has been sending out regular postcards touting its 2 percent real estate commission. Its mailings include bullet points that say, "Expert Salaried Agents," "Aggressive Marketing," and "Professional Support." To the naked eye, the postcard differs little from the kind mailed from a company like Century 21 or Realty Executives, with the exception of the large "2% Commission" statement. Because the difference is transparent to the uninitiated consumer, the odds that they'll go for the low-price firm are very good.

Because of this, the no-frills approach to real estate is taking at least some market share from traditional agents, whether they admit it or not. Most full-service agents will tell you, however, that it's the FSBO market—the one they probably wouldn't be reaching anyway—that's being chipped away by discounters, not the folks whose normal course of action when they are buying or selling a home would be to go to a full-service franchise or independent real estate brokerage (see Figure 5-1).

Most traditional agents would also argue that while discounters' Web sites and billboards may tout cheap real estate commissions, a closer look at the fine print in their ads reveals that the difference between full commission and their rates may not be as significant. That's because unless the homeowner opts not to list in the MLS, the sellers are still required to pay a co-brokerage fee of whatever the going rate in the market is, usually 3 or 3.5 percent; without this, very few selling agents will even show the home. That means that sellers who list with a discounter will pay the discounter's flat fee or low percentage plus the 3 or 3.5 percent, bringing the total commission to 5 percent or more.

Coldwell Banker, well known for its full-service approach to real estate, is using such a strategy by offering a 2 percent listing fee through its Blue Edge Realty offices in Pennsylvania and Illinois. For the fee, sell-

Figure 5-1.

WHERE THE FSBOS ARE

Many full-service brokers feel that discounters are chipping away only at the FSBO market. Here are the areas of the country where those brokers are probably finding the most opportunity right now, according to statistics from ForSaleByOwner.com, which offers a multitiered rate package for home sellers who want to play a larger role in the sale of their own homes:

City	No. of Listings, 2002	Share of Total (percent)
Houston	2,400	8
Charlotte, N.C.	1,923	6.41
Indianapolis	1,788	5.96
Raleigh, N.C.	1,371	4.57
Virginia Beach	954	3.18
Wilmington, N.C.	954	3.18
Omaha	918	3.06
Atlanta	783	2.61
Jacksonville, Fla.	747	2.49
Orlando, Fla.	711	2.37

ers get a home seller kit, home marketing services, marketing support services, and closing and contract services. The seller who agrees to pay "a market-competitive commission" also gets "the same services and materials as the flat 2 percent, plus an MLS and REALTOR.com listing," according to the firm's Web site.

Blue Edge initially raised hackles in the full-service real estate industry, but it has since become thought of as largely a lead generator for the company's full-service side. In other words, let consumers try it on their own, and when it doesn't work out the way they planned, they'll probably list with a Coldwell Banker agent.

MINIMAL BLIP

Cut-rate brokers who charge $200 and let the homeowner take ownership of the sales process are particularly bothersome for full-service agents at companies like RE/MAX, ERA, and Century 21. Some agents call them the demise of the real estate industry; others opt to completely ignore them. But if you ask most full-service brokers what they think about discounters, the answer is usually the same: "They've been around forever, and they don't make much of a dent in our business."

Is that good news for the individual agent who is out pounding the pavement every day in search of customers, or are brokers simply ignoring the truth? The verdict is still out, but one south Florida broker says that he really hasn't seen any upswing in activity among discount brokers in recent years.

"Those companies are still just a minimal blip that's not really making the radar screen," says the broker, who says that he has seen several traditional brokers test out discounts and flat fees rather than the traditional commission structure, but adds that it's mainly small offices that are trying to up the volume and need a "hook to get the customer in the door."

Where many discount brokers tend to fall short, it seems, is in the level of service that they can and will provide to their buyers and sellers. Unlike the traditional agent, who focuses closely on each sale, establishes strong bonds with customers and business partners, and has a real interest in seeing the sale through to the end (mainly because the agent doesn't see a cent until the checks are cut at the closing table), the broker who collects $200 up front has little incentive to do the same. That leaves a pretty big doorway open for the full-service agent who can handle the buying or selling process from concept to completion.

Whether discounters are making a serious dent in full-service agents' business is perhaps not as important as the fact that they're definitely changing the industry and giving consumers choices that they didn't have in the past. In the next two sections, we'll look at two different companies that are affecting the changes in the industry. One has been around since 1987—long before the word *Internet* was widely used—and the other was born as a result of technology.

Unlike some online and discount brokers, both have stood the test of time and have carved their own niches in the industry, with many full-service brokers cringing at the mention of their names. Here, the leaders of two of the industry's best known nontraditional real estate brokerage firms, eRealty Inc. and Assist-2-Sell, reveal the philosophies behind their very different business models and the effects they're having on the industry.

TOO MUCH FOR TOO LITTLE

The Internet was purely an educational tool when Assist-2-Sell came into being, but that didn't stop the company from planting its roots the old-fashioned way, then speeding up its reach with the advent of technology and the World Wide Web. The Reno, Nevada–based firm was formed out of sheer frustration on the parts of its cofounders, Lyle Martin and Mary LaMeres-Pomin, back in 1987.

"As real estate agents for ten years, we were tired of spending 80 percent of our time looking for customers to do business with," says Martin, the firm's co-CEO. "We figured that if we gave home sellers a price break, they would call on us."

The company has since grown from a single location to 281 locations in 45 states and Canada. Early on, customers paid a flat fee of $1,495—after their homes were sold—for the same services that traditional agents were providing. For an additional, competitive co-broker fee, customers could also have their homes listed in the local MLS.

Today, the firm's flat fee ranges from $1,995 to $5,995, depending on geographic location. The company began franchising in 1995, handles over a hundred transactions monthly from its Reno office alone, and operates in large and small markets alike. The concept works well in "hot" markets, where Martin says homeowners are more reluctant to pay a high commission, as they know homes sell easily. In slower markets, home sellers also welcome the concept, as the commission savings allows them to price their home more competitively.

Even after seventeen years of growth and expansion in the real estate industry, Martin says he still comes across traditional brokers and agents who bluntly ask him to "stop upsetting the apple cart." Martin blames their desperation on the fact that traditional brokers operate on razor-thin profit margins. "They can't afford to reduce their commissions," Martin explains. "Still, I don't see discount brokers affecting traditional rates, but I do see traditional brokers being forced to offer a better level of service as a result of companies like ours."

According to Martin, real estate commissions have been artificially high for years, with no correlation with supply and demand or any other economic basis. As technology and sound business principles prevail, he says, fees will come down. He describes menu options (discussed in depth in Chapter 6) as a "joke" and calls this alternative a "traditional broker's guise" of offering the seller choices. In other words, when it's all over, consumers are still paying the same amount of money for less service. "Ever notice that traditional brokers have a tough time valuing the individual things they do for a customer?" Martin asks. "That's because they've yet to come up with a way to legitimately get to their favored 6 or 7 percent."

Martin is equally skeptical about discount brokers' ability to fill the gap left behind by traditional brokers. "The so-called cut-rate brokers don't get it either; they think that charging less means that they get to do less," says Martin. "The reality is that sellers are demanding full service at competitive fees, which is where our company comes in: by charging less and doing more."

Typically more open-minded about change, flat-fee and discount brokers tend to be among the first to try new technologies and tools that will help them work smarter, better, and faster. Assist-2-Sell, for example, was one of the first to sign up to participate in a broker reciprocity system. Today, the firm's Web sites include information on or links to FSBOs, its own non-MLS (flat-fee) listings and MLS listings, and other brokers' MLS listings.

"We think broker reciprocity is a great opportunity for all brokers to gain greater exposure for their listings," Martin says. "Many brokers think they are protecting their livelihood by trying to keep the information on homes available proprietary, but we've always taken the position that an open exchange of information benefits our clients and customers (sellers and buyers), which ultimately benefits the broker."

To agents looking to make their way in the industry, Martin says, "Become a student of the industry and offer real value to your buyers and sellers." And remember, he adds, that just because you passed a test and got a license doesn't mean you're an expert in the industry. To overcome that hurdle, he suggests that all agents apprentice with a successful agent prior to going out into the market on their own. "We don't allow plumbers or electricians to run loose before they've apprenticed," says Martin, "but we expect homeowners to turn over their largest asset to a 'newbie' just out of real estate school."

When it comes to general industry trends, Martin says he's picked up on a few that are playing a key role in agents' success or failure. Most disconcerting, he says, is the fact that agents are accepting overpriced listings (those priced at above fair market value) in order to get the listings without realizing what a disservice they're doing to their clients. The answer to the problem, he says, is to do your homework to pinpoint the home's value and be prepared to pass on the listing if the seller is unrealistic.

The fact that agents work in an environment that thrives on an inefficient business model is also a problem, says Martin, who adds that brokers provide less and less support while their agents remain powerless. "An agent's most important role is to expose property to buyers and negotiate an agreement of purchase, yet agents fail miserably at this," says Martin. "They rely nearly 100 percent on the MLS for exposure and lack training in negotiation."

The influx of new licensees into the industry over the last few years has Martin wondering just what those new agents are really expecting from their new career, which is far from the "get rich quick" venture that some believe it to be. He says that most are looking for easy money and will leave the entrepreneurial endeavor at the first chance of getting a "real" job with a paycheck. "The new crop of licensees are mainly dislocated employees," says Martin, "who don't realize that real estate is a sales career. Those who last are salespeople, not employees."

Those agents who do survive and thrive will be the ones who discard the old "gatekeeper" mentality that their predecessors coveted with their MLS books, and instead focus closely on the marketing, service, and value that they can provide to buyers and sellers. Along the way, Martin says, they'll also have to rethink the traditional pricing model, which he blames mostly on brokers who are sticking to their "inefficient and unprofitable" business models. "Sellers are forced to pay high prices to sell their homes to subsidize this model," says Martin. "Interestingly, though, while sellers are paying too much, most brokers are making too little."

TAPPING TECHNOLOGY

If there was one event that triggered the influx of discounters into the market, it was undoubtedly advances in technology. Where in the past the home selling and buying process was highly reliant on newspaper ads, open houses, and individual agents taking time away from their families on Sundays to sell homes, the Internet is now the most popular starting point for the home search process. Because the Internet is such a level playing field (without some digging, it's hard for the average consumer to know if he's dealing with a large franchise or with an entrepreneurial agent sitting at home with the full, local MLS listed on her Web site), the opportunities for nontraditional real estate agency models abound.

Two of the highest-profile online brokerages to survive the dot-com bomb and thrive in the industry are eRealty and zipRealty, both of which offer a discounted commission price and use licensed agents in various areas of the country.

Emeryville, California–based zipRealty claims to save home sellers up to 25 percent in commission, based on the fact that it's "more efficient than other real estate companies and shares its operating efficiencies" with its customers. The company has been around since 1999 and calls itself "one of the nation's fastest-growing full-service real estate brokerages," using a 1 percent cash back at closing offer for buyers and a 1 percent discount for qualified sellers who list with zipRealty.

eRealty also uses a Web-based model based on the efficiencies it's gained through technology, and runs most of its business through the Web, with transactions being handled by licensed agents. Through eRealty, buyers receive full attention from local eRealty agents, a buyer's rebate up to 1 percent of the home's purchase price, online access to information on homes listed on the local MLS, and e-mail alerts on new listings and property status changes. Sellers pay a negotiable "full-service" commission for personal assistance from a real estate agent, who helps them market their home to potential buyers using both traditional and high-tech methods: a local MLS listing, yard signs, and flyers, and multiple photographs, virtual tours, and floor plans online.

Russell Capper, eRealty's president, says that the company has over 650,000 registered users and that it has saved consumers more than $8.3 million in commissions since it was founded in 1997. Capper says that the company's foundation was determined after its founders' analysis revealed that the real estate transaction could be improved by technology, that consumers were gravitating to the Internet for home-buying information, and that large real estate franchisers were turning up their noses at the trend and sticking with a "business as usual" approach.

To the eRealty mix, Capper brought a technology background, having worked for IBM in the 1970s, and a keen awareness of the role that technology could play in the future of real estate. "I've always participated where technology starts working, and where it starts making a difference," says Capper. What really motivated him to join eRealty's three founders was the reluctance to change on the part of the large franchisers who, at the time, basically ran the industry.

"It was hard to believe, but they were reluctant to provide their agents, brokers, and franchisees with improved systems and processes to address the new consumer," says Capper. That, he adds, opened the door for companies like eRealty to make their entrance into the industry.

Opening the door even wider was the speed at which technology was evolving, pulling consumers right along with it through personal computers and connections to the Internet.

The technology wave affected everything in the real estate industry, according to Capper—from the number of competitors to the number of agents to the prices they were able to charge. In fact, he says, in the last few years he's moved away from referring to eRealty as a "virtual office Web site" and more toward calling it a traditional brokerage that has integrated Internet technology into its operations quite extensively. "Besides that one fact, everything else about us is basically the same as any other brokerage," says Capper, adding that the firm still does some things "the old-fashioned way," but that the net result is still a much less expensive process, thus justifying the rebate-based discounts that the company offers its customers.

Where eRealty stands out, says Capper, is in its basic business model, which is based not on the traditional "I'll show you my office's home listings first" philosophy, but on one that allows consumers to pick from an entire MLS full of homes to find the one that's perfect for them. "There's a theory in the industry that an agent should show twenty homes, and that the consumer should be able to pick one from that pool," Capper says. "But that's not the way the consumer looks at the home-buying transaction anymore. To think that a modern consumer would like to do that transaction based on the opinion and judgment of somebody who, after showing them twenty homes, says pick one is simply ludicrous."

And that's where technology and nontraditional real estate business models come in. Over the last two decades, Capper says, real estate agents have gained access to tools that can help them break the mold and truly focus on customer service—helping their customers hone their choices down to the ideal abode. Looking ahead, Capper sees the overall role of the real estate agent as closely paralleling what VOWs are offering online right now—for lack of a better analogy.

"When I look to the future, I see agents who work much more efficiently, who have their own private, full-functioning Web sites, and yet who still meet consumers the old-fashioned way (in person), continuing to serve them well from their book of business and from the firms and family of their successful clients," Capper says. "When they meet with a buyer, however, they'll hand over a business card and ask them to visit that private Web site, access the listings via a password (hence the VOW scenario, which requires that a 'relationship' be established between the agent and the customer before any such information can be shared), and view the listings."

From there, Capper says, agents will be able to monitor closely whether or not their buyer is actively looking for a home, via a robust back-end Web system. "If the buyer isn't migrating to the process, then the agent can call her the old-fashioned way and light a fire under her," says Capper. "It's a matter of realizing just how smart the consumer really is, and letting her take ownership of the process in a way that hasn't been done in the past."

CAUGHT IN THE WEB

In Chicago, RE/MAX Suburban agent Mary Zentz closed a few transactions in 2003 that involved discount brokers. Not all of them went smoothly, she adds. "There are a few things that really bother me, and most of it lies in the quality of service that these companies provide to their customers—or lack of it," says Zentz, whose most recent discount transaction found her fielding inquiries by phone from a confused buyer, even though he had his own "discount" representation and she was the listing agent. "That's not my job," Zentz says, adamantly. (Legally and ethically, in Illinois, agents don't communicate directly with the other party; they answer questions agent to agent or through attorneys and do not contact each other's clients.)

On the other side of the transaction, Zentz recently sold a listing from a discount broker who wasn't even willing to send the closing statement to the client's attorney. "They wanted me to do it," says Zentz. Knowing that a full-service agent is not only knowledgeable, but also willing to go the extra mile to get the deal completed in a professional fashion, the discounter was obviously taking advantage of Zentz's good nature.

"I didn't even know what the listing commission rate was—how in the world could I make up a closing statement?" asks Zentz, who contacted her local Realtor association for advice and learned that her position was correct, and that it was not her position to draw up and circulate such a document. To make matters worse, she later learned from another agent that the broker in question was a full-time barber running a real estate brokerage out of his barbershop. "I couldn't believe it," says Zentz. "I was thinking, this guy has to stop cutting hair long enough to do some of the work on this transaction."

Nationwide, full-service agents are grappling with similar scenarios. In Washington state, for example, one broker says that his agents just don't see discounters as "viable competition" in the marketplace. To put it simply, no company has been able to prove that simply listing property on the MLS for a flat fee actually leads to the sale of the property.

In the end, he says, consumers are just wasting their $295, because many have to go ahead and list with a full-service agent anyway, particularly in areas where the housing inventory is plentiful (five to six months is considered the norm in most areas). "The success of listing a home with one of those low-service companies is so modest," he says. "The word is not getting spread that this is the way to go—in fact, it might be getting spread the other way."

Most full-service brokers and their agents feel that there has always been—always will be—a market for the no-frills brokerages that skimp on services in exchange for lower commissions or flat fees. That there are some legitimate companies out there cannot be denied, although it remains to be seen what long-term effect those companies have on the business that full-service brokers chase anyway.

According to NAR's 2003 Profile of Homebuyers and Sellers, customers' top considerations when selecting a real estate agent are the agent's reputation, the agent's knowledge of the neighborhood, the agent's association with a particular firm, and the professional designation held by the agent. Nowhere in the top four are commissions mentioned, which means that consumers are not as price-conscious—and therefore not as interested in looking for the best possible financial deal—as some might think (see Figure 5-2).

GRAPPLING WITH CHANGE

Carolann Flesch, president of King's Real Estate Services in Orlando, Florida, says that while many agents in her area claim to be full-service, some do little more than put a sign in the ground, a listing in the MLS, and one or two ads in the newspaper during the listing period. As a legitimate full-service agent, Flesch says that her approach has always been to, first, remember whom she's working for and what her ethical obligations are to the seller, and second, always strive to get those sellers the highest price possible.

"Listing with a full-service agent means that the seller will net more money at closing than he would with a discount broker," says Flesch, who always asks the following question during her initial listing appointment: Does it matter to you that I charge 7 percent commission if you know that you will still end up with more money at closing than you would

Figure 5-2.

WHAT MATTERS MOST?

When homeowners or buyers are looking for an agent, here are the top factors that they consider:

Reputation of the real estate agent	47%
Agent's knowledge of the neighborhood	23%
Agent's association with a particular firm	7%
Professional designation(s) held by agent	4%
Other	19%

Source: The 2003 National Association of REALTORS Profile of Home Buyers and Sellers. Used with permission.

with a discount agent? "A full-service agent gets a higher price for the seller by actively working the listing, which means not only placing ads but also following up."

Flesch calls that "follow-up" the most time-consuming part of her job, but says that it's undoubtedly the key ingredient in a quick sale at a high price. "Many times you can launch buyers and other agents into action by following up with them," says Flesch, who advises agents to bone up on their negotiation skills. "I tell agents to bring me any offer, but once I get it, it's my job to bring it up to acceptable terms for my seller."

As full-service agents, Flesch says, her team makes appointments to go into a home after a listing agreement is signed and help sellers clean, organize, and prep their dwellings for sale. Recently, she says, they even supplied the paint and pizza for a "paint and pizza party" with a local volunteer organization to help a financially troubled seller get the home ready for a foreclosure sale. "We really do earn our full commission," says Flesch.

Unlike flat-fee brokers, FSBOs, and many online brokerages, full-service agents are typically motivated to see deals through to closing. In fact, even a one-hour delay in closing time can send agents scrambling to fix last-minute problems and handle eleventh-hour negotiations in order to keep the financing, interest terms, and occupation date intact. Flesch says that most FSBOs, on the other hand (those sellers who would be most apt to use a cut-rate option), think selling real estate simply means finding a buyer.

"I once listed an FSBO who had found three different buyers, but all three contracts fell apart because there was no one to check out the pitfalls and hold the deal together until closing," says Flesch, who recalls that the homeowner admitted that she had been trying to save money by selling her home herself, but that it wound up costing her time and a delay in the start date on a new job. "In the end, she actually got more money at closing after paying my commission than she would have gotten if the other three deals had closed."

Despite the obvious benefits that a full-service agent brings to the table, Flesch says, she's noticed a surge in discount brokers in the last few years. One in particular advertises on television, she says, and advertises that it gives full service for a flat fee, with no hidden charges. "What the discount brokers don't advertise is that if their seller wants other agents to show and sell their property, they will still be expected to pay the selling agent a commission," says Flesch. "I don't have a problem with discount brokers as long as the seller is not deceived as to what to expect from the broker. Unfortunately, you do get what you pay for, and most sellers are upset after they are stuck in a listing and are left to solve their own problems."

On a recent transaction, for example, Flesch says that the listing agent was so busy trying to get more listings to make up for his lack of full commissions that it took him three days to present an offer from Flesch's buyers. He also took more than a week to return calls and had his own seller "very upset," she recalls. "I ended up having to meet with his seller to explain the offer, get the signatures, and answer their questions, because their agent wasn't available," says Flesch, whose experience closely parallels those of RE/MAX agent Mary Zentz.

And it's not getting any better for Flesch, who says she's not the only full-service agent in her area who has had to take up babysitting duties to make up for some nontraditional brokers' lack of experience and service. "Many full-service agents are running into this and try to avoid bringing in offers on listings with discount agents, because they know they will have to do twice the work for less money, while the listing agents are out doing their sales pitch to get more flat fees," says Flesch. "With a discount broker, customers are paying for little more than a sign in the ground and a listing in the MLS. There's no follow-up or representation, but the consumers often don't realize that until they need help and find out that their agent just isn't there for them."

CAN'T BEAT 'EM? JOIN 'EM

Whether a real estate agent should hang his license with a discount or other type of nontraditional broker is a very personal choice, and one that deserves treatment in a book about industry survival. In fact, a handbook for surviving and thriving in the changing world of real estate would be remiss if it didn't mention the opportunities that some of the nation's nontraditional brokerages are providing to their agents. As with most things in life, there are some quality companies in the bunch, supported by a network of real estate agents that enjoy their discount, flat-fee, rebate, or online status.

Andrew Boyd is one of them. As marketing director for eRealty's Houston, Texas, office, where he lists and sells property while also overseeing thirteen other agents, Boyd is a perfect example of how a full-service agent can make the switch to a nontraditional brokerage and succeed as a result. He estimates that he closed about sixty-five transactions in 2002, or roughly 5.4 per month (he says the average eRealty agent in Houston averages thirty-nine transactions annually).

Boyd got his start in the real estate business after watching his mother's successful career in the field. He calls his decision to get licensed a "natural progression," and he initially hung that license on the wall of a small, independent company. Within a few months he moved to a RE/MAX office, in search of 100 percent commissions, better branding, and a higher profile. He stayed with RE/MAX until May 2001—the month he joined eRealty as a field sales agent.

When asked why he made the switch to what at the time was still a fairly untested business concept, Boyd says the decision came after he heard about alternative brokerage arrangements at a mandatory continuing education class. "The instructor began talking about eRealty, which I wasn't familiar with at the time," recalls Boyd. "I went home that day and looked them up online and, quite frankly, figured that where the company was then—and is today—was where all real estate brokerages were going to have to be in the future."

By that, Boyd means that the days of charging high percentages for home listings are long gone, and that the Internet has become a key focal point for the entire industry.

"The information gathering on the consumer's part is just so much easier now, and consumers' housing knowledge has increased exponentially over the last five years," Boyd explains. "Consumers come to us already knowing what they want, and quite honestly, they want to be compensated for it."

And with that, Boyd again moved his shingle, this time to eRealty, a company that returns a certain percentage of a home's sales price to either the buyer or the seller in the form of a rebate. He says that he immediately saw a dramatic spike in the number of transactions that he was handling, as well as the number of clients he was working with at any given time. "It just went through the roof," says Boyd. "A darned good year for me at RE/MAX would be twenty or thirty transactions, and I found myself more than doubling that number very quickly."

Of course, one would assume that moving from a full-service, 100 percent commission firm to one where agents work on salaries would find Boyd taking a pay cut. (Capper called eRealty agents' salaries "substantial" and said that they're complemented by all of the tools they need to sell real estate, such as cell phones, laptops, and high-speed Internet access—the expenses that most traditional agents cover out of their own pockets. eRealty also offers its agents reimbursement for expenses and health benefits.)

"In essence, I took a gross pay decrease but not a net pay decrease because I was able to remove all of my expenses," Boyd explains, adding that during 2001 he did experience a slight decrease in income. He made it up the following year. "The company covers all of the agent's expenses, and my client base grew so dramatically for future referrals that it was well worth it."

Within eighteen months of joining eRealty, Boyd was promoted to his current market director position. The company has one such individual in each of its major markets, for a total of ten nationwide. For Boyd, shedding the old habits of farming and marketing was no easy task, particularly since he'd watched his own mother achieve success through those tried-and-true strategies. Instead, he says, eRealty agents wait for the customers to come to them. "I quickly found out not only that the farming was unnecessary, but that I also didn't have time to do it," says Boyd.

While eRealty's agents may be compensated differently, given the opportunity to obtain benefits, and not required to hit the pavement in search of customers, Boyd says that the interaction they have with customers is no different from that of a Coldwell Banker or RE/MAX agent. "What it all boils down to is, you can still take the computers out of our office; you still have traditional real estate agents and real estate brokers servicing each client in a traditional manner, just like they would at any traditional company," says Boyd.

At eRealty, agents list homes for a fee as low as 4.5 percent in the state of Texas, where 3 percent will go to a buyer's agent who brings a buyer to the table. Having been a traditional agent himself, Boyd says that giving the selling agent the commission that they're used to getting is absolutely critical. "If we didn't pay a 3 percent commission, they wouldn't show our listings," he says. eRealty then retains a 1.5 percent commission on listings, or a 3 percent commission if it's representing a buyer. Of the latter number, eRealty used to offer a rebate but now negotiates the commission on an "individual" basis.

Boyd admits that his decision to leave RE/MAX for eRealty evoked skepticism from his peers, but he says that's because at the time many thought that the online brokerage was going to be just another fly-by-night discount house. Their attitudes changed when they realized that eRealty was in it for the long haul, and that it was proving just how critical a role technology could play in the changing world of real estate.

"In my marketplace I was already pretty well known, but when listing agents saw that we were real-life agents with real-life buyers, they changed their minds about the company," says Boyd, who has received letters from traditional brokers praising eRealty's ability to bring qualified buyers to the table. Nor are those buyers as hard to come by as they were when Boyd was with RE/MAX. Back then, he remembers showing the typical buyer from twenty to forty homes to get the right one.

These days, he says his brokerage's comprehensive Web site and VOW capabilities allow the same buyers to whittle their choices down to a handful—ten at the most—of potential homes. The company also advises buyers to start the mortgage preapproval process prior to looking at homes, to keep the overall transaction time to a minimum. "That's how we can keep the volume up, since driving around in a car for weeks on end is what eats away at an agent's ability to close transactions," says Boyd. "Our counterparts in other companies have come to recognize that, and we've been able to develop wonderful relationships with them as a result."

Looking to the future, Boyd sees nontraditional brokerages—be they discount, online, or otherwise—growing in number and excelling. He says such companies provide a service that today's consumer is demanding, particularly the comprehensive online listing database that potential home buyers can access long before they ever have to get out and physically look at the homes. "All the information we're showing from the local MLS is the same as what consumers would see if they walked into a bricks-and-mortar company and asked to see a printout," Boyd says. "The world is moving to more efficient ways of doing business, and the consumers are demanding and we are providing it. I believe many other companies will be following right behind us."

STANDING OUT

So you know they're out there, but what can you do about them? Well, like any high-quality business, you must differentiate yourself from the discounters of the world and show home buyers and sellers why working with a full-service agent is simply the best choice. There are myriad steps that a full-service, full-commission agent can take to stand out from the pack of nontraditional brokerages that are vying for a slice of the market. Here are a few basic steps that all full-service agents should be taking when working with home buyers:

❑ For starters, you'll need a vast working knowledge of your real estate market, including price trends, neighborhood conditions and amenities, real estate law, zoning issues, financing, taxes, insurance, and negotiating. The most successful agents are also street smart in the psychology of home buying and the factors that accompany it (such as apprehension, buyer's remorse, and so on).

❑ Early on, you'll have to help your buyers determine the importance of their needs and wants when it comes to choosing a neighborhood and a specific home. That means helping customers learn how much they can afford, locating financing, and educating them on the current market conditions. (Is it a buyer's market? A seller's market?)

❑ During the "shopping" phase, you'll keep in close contact with your buyers as you tour (either online or in person) properties, discuss details, review floor plans, and educate your buyers about outside factors, such as proximity to schools, cultural entities, and work centers.

❑ Once a buyer decides on a home, your negotiating skills will have to kick into gear as you play advocate for the buyer (if you've signed a buyer agency agreement), trying to get the best possible price for the property.

❑ In keeping with your hands-on, full service approach, the next phase will involve obtaining disclosures, making sure home inspections and repairs are completed on time, and coordinating the activities of the lender, attorney, title company, and other key players in the process.

❑ Before you get to the closing table to watch those keys get handed over to your buyer, you'll help the customer make sure that all the i's have been dotted and the t's crossed.

THE FUTURE DISCOUNTER

David Jenks, vice president of research and development at Keller Williams Realty International in Austin, Texas, says that discount brokerages' track records don't bode well for their future prospects, mainly because of the thin margins that all brokerages are working on. He says that discounters have been in the marketplace since he got into the industry in the early 1980s, and that they haven't gained much ground since then. "They never last because the costs of doing business have cranked way up, and they just can't do business at that level," says Jenks, adding that the cost of doing business in real estate has escalated nearly as fast as home sales prices. As a result, the average broker barely has enough of a budget to keep operations going, let alone growing. So while agents thrive, the companies themselves tend to go in and out of business on a regular basis.

"There's not a lot of room to budge there, if you know what I'm saying," says Jenks. "That's why almost no discounters have lasted, even though they continue to do damage while they're actually in business. They will grab business because they are discounting, but they don't tend to last with the discount strategy, because the cost of doing business is higher than most people realize."

In real estate since the 1970s, Dave Liniger, founder of RE/MAX International, has also seen his share of nontraditional brokerages come and go, and says the trend is bound to continue well into the future—whether full-service agents like it or not. He sees menu options also growing in popularity (see Chapter 6), mainly because there is always a certain percentage of consumers who would rather handle parts of the transaction on their own.

"In reality, discount brokers have never had an impact on our industry, even though they've been around for well over thirty years," says Liniger. "They might appeal to a small segment of the market, but they've never really made much of a dent in our business."

That's because buying and selling a home is still a very personal experience for consumers, and one that can't be replaced by technology, flashy advertisements, or promises of cut-rate commissions, according to J. Lennox Scott, president of John L. Scott Real Estate in Bellevue, Washington. Scott says that real estate buyers and sellers are clearly divided between those who want to work with full-service agents and those who would rather do it themselves. Those agents and brokers who undercut their services, he says, are typically chasing the second market, or the FSBOs. "There has always been a certain percentage of FSBOs—that hasn't changed much in recent years," says Scott. "Many of the discount brokerages are dealing with the folks who want to be FSBOs anyway, and who don't want a true real estate consultant in their corner."

Most buyers, said Scott, want a trusted consultant to represent them, serve as advocate, and handle the transaction. "That alone is more valuable than discount or limited services because the consumers flat out get their money's worth," says Scott. "In going with those alternative services, they're giving up that trusted relationship." That desire for relationships might even be thwarting the "get them in the door" efforts of discount brokerages, Scott added. "It's been proven that the vast majority of customers want a trusted advocate and consultant," he explained. "As a result, these companies just aren't getting the huge numbers they thought they would by offering a discount."

The good news is that as an agent, the world is your oyster right now, thanks to the many new options that exist on the market. Whether a company is offering 100 percent commission splits, cut-rate commission rates and salaries, or a 50/50 split with most of the overhead and technology tools paid for, every one of them still relies on good real estate agents to make its engine run. Unlike in the olden days, when a 50/50 split was the norm and consumers turned up their noses at the cut-rate deals, today's business environment allows you to take your pick, so choose carefully.

SIX THINGS TO REMEMBER FROM CHAPTER 5

❑ Discount, cut-rate, and flat-fee brokers have been around for decades, but they have traditionally had little effect on the full-service broker's business.

❑ The advent of the Internet, technology, and a more price-conscious consumer have paved the way for a variety of different real estate business models, ranging from the $200-a-listing Internet sites to the more sophisticated flat-fee and percentage firms.

❑ Industry experts estimate that today's nontraditional brokers claim about 10 percent of the total residential real estate market.

❑ Many such companies go out of business or struggle to survive, mainly as a result of the slim margins that real estate brokerages operate on.

❑ Most full-service brokers deny that the discounters are having any effect on their marketplace, and feel that those nontraditional companies are simply chipping away at the FSBO market.

❑ Full-service agents looking to stay a step ahead of the low-price leaders should focus closely on the services and value that they provide to buyers and sellers, as well as the knowledge and expertise that they bring to the table.

CHAPTER 6

Selling Real Estate
Piecemeal

REAL ESTATE AGENT OR CAFETERIA?

Michael Lee knows all about menus, and not the kind that he opens up when he sits down at his favorite Castro Valley, California, restaurant. Lee, a licensed real estate agent and broker since 1977, is intimately familiar with the kind of menus that real estate agents are creating and using to sell their "unbundled" services to clients who don't want or need full service at a full price.

But that doesn't mean that Lee has sold out, nor does it mean that he doesn't first try to get his sellers to take the complete package for the standard commission fee. It just means that he is wise enough to know that some customers just aren't going to go full-service, no matter how hard he tries to convince them. He also knows that if he didn't offer the menu or unbundled option, someone else would.

To set the scene, you'll first need to know that Lee is no run-of-the-mill real estate agent looking for a way to increase his coffers. He's earned his Certified Residential Specialist (CRS), Graduate Realtor Institute (GRI), and Seniors Real Estate Specialist (SRES) designations and is broker/owner of Realty Unlimited in Castro Valley, California. As an agent, he's earned as much as $75,000 in commissions in a single month, and as a broker, he's owned both small independent companies and large franchised firms. A master instructor for the California Association of Realtors®, Lee is also one of only 300 Certified Speaking Professionals (CSPs) nationwide.

To say that Lee was an early adopter of the menu strategy would be an understatement. He's been offering customers unbundled services since the 1980s, and he says that the concept's biggest detractors tend to be the brokers themselves, who seem unwilling to educate themselves about the process. "It's a foreign concept to brokers, who are not overly creative to begin with," says Lee. "What they don't realize is that if their agents were making more money, they too would be benefiting and making more money."

Lee says brokers' uneasiness with the new concept has somewhat stigmatized it, even though it's one of the more obvious ways for a real estate agent to attract customers who would otherwise be out there struggling to sell their homes on their own. Instead of letting them flounder in the FSBO market, why not take the step that many other professionals in different industries have done and offer your services piecemeal on a perproject or hourly basis? From $250 for a comparative market analysis to $400 for a weekend of open houses, it's money that you get up front and that wouldn't have been yours if the seller had chosen the FSBO route. (Of course, there are arguments on both sides of this issue, and we'll get to the negative aspects of unbundling later in this chapter.)

A good example of an industry that went from being commission-only to including fee-for-service professionals is financial planning. Back in the early 1980s, a group of planners decided that they no longer wanted their compensation to be tied to the quantity of mutual funds, stocks, or bonds that they were selling to individual clients, so they broke the mold and started an industry known as "fee-only financial planning." They charge hourly or set fees for the services they provide, which the investors pay as they use the services. The movement was driven largely by the formation of the National Association of Personal Financial Planners (NAPFA), which advocates the fee-for-service approach to financial planning.

Agents and/or brokers started taking a similar approach to the real estate industry as early as the 1980s, but the strategy didn't gain in popularity until the late 1990s, when alternative brokerage models like discount, flat-fee, and online brokerages surfaced with the advent of the Internet. Still, Lee says that the savvy client who understands the complexity of the real estate sales process will probably opt for a full-service agent. Where he feels he's gained a competitive advantage is in the high number of listings appointments that he goes on as a result of the choices that he offers.

"People want choices," says Lee, "but when customers realize that they might actually have to pay me for the work I do even if the house doesn't sell, most of them don't want to take the risks, so they'll hire me on a commission basis anyway."

Lee says that he's relied on the same menu of options for the last twenty years, but adds that customers are "more interested than they ever have been in the past" in hearing about them. He says it all comes down to the fact that most consumers are wary of real estate professionals and the seemingly high commission rates that they tend to fetch for what looks like a minimal amount of work (little do they know!). "They think we do nothing, and that we make an incredible amount of money doing it," Lee quips. "Much of that stems from the perception that in the past, we've given them no choices: It was 6 percent or go do it yourself."

The happy medium between the wary consumers who think they want to handle much of the work and the ones who think real estate agents make too much money, it seems, is the agent who offers unbundled services based on client needs. "Real estate agents used to be like a computer store that only sold one type of computer," says Lee. "Then we realized that what people really want is a choice. The tide is turning, and people are really pushing for alternatives and finding them in some agents and brokers who are willing to break out of the traditional model."

How It Unraveled

Given the opportunity, most real estate agents would rather provide full service for a full commission that ranges from 6 to 7 percent of a home's selling price. Being in that position gives the agent control over the entire transaction, thus helping him limit—or at least stay completely aware of—his liability in the deal if he sees it through to the end. In fact, the traditional agent simply isn't wired to serve up menu-style everything the agent does for customers during the typical transaction.

Unfortunately for agents, consumers don't really care how they are wired. Consumers want more control over the transaction process, they want to try out new options that tout full service for as low as $200 or less, and they want to know that they're getting the best deal. Some full-service brokers and many more of their nontraditional competitors have found the answer to be unbundled services. Let's say a home seller needs you only to draw up a contract and disclosure statements, then be present at the closing table. Charge that seller $2,500 for the package, regardless of the home's price. Get the job done, take your check to the bank, and move on.

The idea is both tempting and gaining in popularity, particularly because the FSBO market is growing. In 2001, roughly 13 percent of the homes sold in the United States were FSBOs, which netted zero commissions for agents. That market is expected to grow to approximately 40 percent of the available property market in the next several years, which means that for every hundred properties on the market, forty will be FSBOs, and will be out of the reach of the full-service agents that those home sellers are trying to avoid.

But by unbundling your real estate services and dividing them into separate parts—a CMA, signage, advertising, open houses, showings, negotiations, and so on—you can fulfill the role of real estate consultant and get paid for it, regardless of whether the home sells or not. The key to keeping those customers from walking out the door could be the piece-meal services that agents like Lee are offering (right along with their commission-based services, mind you). Thus, the risk appears to be limited, especially because the FSBO wouldn't be your customer anyway.

WATCH OUT, IT'S GAINING

The menu option alternative is catching on with consumers, who are getting more savvy about the various types of real estate agents that are available to them in nearly every marketplace nationwide. On the REALTOR.com Web site, for example, the company's "Choose a Realtor®" advice page clearly tells consumers that if they require only limited services, some agents "will agree to help with the transaction for a predetermined fee." The site advises consumers to "call real estate companies and ask for the managing broker and see if they're interested in furnishing 'unbundled services.'"

A 2003 report from NAR, "The Future of Real Estate Brokerage," also confirmed what many agents already knew but didn't want to acknowledge: that fee-for-service providers are gaining in popularity. In the report, NAR predicted continued pressure on traditional brokerages from a number of directions, including a gain in popularity for fee-for-service providers and online transaction platforms. NAR refers to the piecemeal agents and brokers as "unbundled-service providers," or USPs, and says that their customers are most likely to be drawn from the FSBO clientele, which represented about $110 billion in home sales in the United States in 2001.

NAR says that the USP model was spawned several years ago when the increase in litigation associated with dual agency (the representation of both the buyer and the seller in the same transaction by the same agent) and the ensuing expansion of buyer agency contributed to a growth in the number of firms catering to the specific needs of buyers and sellers. Further exacerbating the growth of USPs, according to NAR, were the franchisers and start-up companies that recognized the consumer demand for lower-cost brokerage services, with the consumer taking over at least some of the control of the process.

By offering services individually rather than in a package format, NAR says, brokerages can evaluate single services to determine which of those services provide the most consistent satisfaction to the individual client. The USP model also allows agents to customize product offerings to again maximize their clients' satisfaction with the process.

As mentioned, NAR says that USP consumers—much like the kind of customers who flock to discounters—are most likely to be drawn from the FSBO market. In fact, NAR says that the USP model may be able to capture the FSBO client who would not otherwise choose to use a real estate brokerage. In 2001, FSBOs accounted for 13 percent of the residential market, but represented over $110 billion in transactions. According to NAR's Profile of Homebuyers and Sellers, more than 20 percent of sales in Alabama, Delaware, Indiana, Louisiana, Missouri, Oregon, and Oklahoma were FSBOs.

And while NAR reports that many USPs are operating and exhibiting some staying power, it predicts that it will take a "significant amount of time" for these companies to grow their businesses. In other words, the same lower prices that benefit consumers can put pressure on the brokerage firms, making them rethink the piecemeal or discount approach to a business in which margins are thin even for the largest, most successful, and age-old franchisers.

PUSHING THE OPTIONS

The first real estate educator, a practitioner of thirty years, to work with and develop fee-for-services consulting was Julie Garton-Good, the Orlando, Florida–based author of *Real Estate a la Carte, Selecting the Services You Need, Paying What They're Worth* (Dearborn, 2001) and founder and president of the National Association of Real Estate Consultants (NAREC). Founded in 1999 to assist real estate professionals in "reframing their focus as real estate consultants to better meet the needs of today's savvy consumer," NAREC offers the Consumer-Certified Real Estate Consultant (C-CREC) designation, which is awarded to agents who can analyze the consumer's needs and deliver timely and cost-effective results-based solutions.

According to Garton-Good, a good chunk of those solutions should center around the real estate agent as consultant, which means offering services in exchange for fees. Garton-Good defines unbundling as dividing real estate services into separate parts, resulting in greater flexibility, more potential control, and a lower cost to the consumer than the commission strategy. "Once unbundled," she says, each service or task that the consumer accesses is assigned its own value, with the intent being that using components separately will result in less overall net cost and greater flexibility.

"Real estate for almost a hundred years considered the end user to be the agent and the brokerage, not the consumer. With the advent of the Internet, the entire paradigm is shifting, and our end user is definitely the consumer, not the agent," said Garton-Good. "Consumers want more control over the transaction. They value the real estate agent's knowledge, but they resist paying for it as a percentage of the home sales prices. The fee-for-service model gives sellers what they want and compensates agents with what they're worth."

To put it simply, fee-for-service agents either attach a dollar value to each service or calculate an hourly rate, and the fee is paid regardless of whether the deal closes—an attractive thought for some agents, who sit on pins and needles until closing day comes. Garton-Good says that the model as a whole recognizes services that have typically been "given away" and identifies which services are more profitable than others. (The concept differs from discounting, which claims to offer full service while charging less than market-rate commission.)

Brokers nationwide have found different ways to integrate menu options into their real estate offerings. Some charge $100 an hour for their services, with the average real estate transaction requiring forty to sixty hours per side, according to Garton-Good. That means that the agent charging $100 an hour would earn $4,000 to $6,000 per transaction, which would be slightly more than 3 percent on a $160,000 house but significantly less than 3 percent on a $300,000 house. As Lee says, it's the owners of higher-priced homes for whom the menu services option seems to work best, particularly if the client has bought and sold homes in the past and has some knowledge of how to get to the closing table.

The nation's skyrocketing home prices in states like California, where housing appreciation has averaged 20 percent annually and affordable homes are becoming increasingly harder to find, has led sellers to question the rates that agents have charged for years. For example, the home that cost $300,000 a year ago is by now worth $340,000 and would generate an additional $2,400 in commissions, but the effort on the agent's part that is required to sell it is probably the same. Smart sellers can do the math, and they typically start the negotiation process by asking for a lower commission rate.

Garton-Good's support of à la carte real estate is rooted in one of the most basic business tenets: Customers want options when it comes to the process of buying and selling homes. She says that full-service, full-commission agents will continue to appeal to those consumers for whom time is at a premium. "For most consumers, selling a home is like taking on a part-time job for three hours a day, three to four days a week for two months," says Garton-Good. "Until they get into it, most of them don't realize how long it takes, and just how much of their time it takes."

Then there's the safety aspect of having people traipsing through the customer's home at all hours of the day, vying for a peek at the neighborhood's newest listing. That alone can drive what could have been an FSBO to list with an agent, whose job it is to screen potential buyers prior to showing them a home. "People are a little leery because it's kind of like loading your kids up in a car with a stranger and waving goodbye," Garton-Good says. "It's very tough for a seller to be in all parts of a home while they're showing it, and people who lack the knowledge or inclination to do this on their own are definitely better suited for a full-service agent."

Lastly, Garton-Good says, the consumers' level of knowledge concerning the transaction is often what keeps them working with full-service agents, who usually stand out in terms of their vast expertise not only in the transaction process, but also in the property disclosures and legal requirements that go along with it. "A lot of consumers I talk to are clueless about their state laws," says Garton-Good, adding that thirty-two states currently require sellers to fill out property disclosure statements prior to the sale. The property disclosure statement is designed to protect all persons involved in a real estate transaction and to encourage full communication so that, having as much information as possible, buyers will pay and sellers will receive a fair price for the property.

Where FSBO buyers tend to go wrong is in assuming that their attorney will handle such issues, without realizing that attorneys rarely visit the actual property to do their own due diligence and do not have the knowledge to point out what would be potential problems with the property. "With the preponderance of FSBOs out there, I think we're going to see a lot more consumer-to-consumer lawsuits in the future," says Garton-Good. "If someone purchases a home that wasn't properly represented on the disclosure statement, for example, and a problem turns up a few months down the road, then it's off to court."

First-time sellers, in particular, need the most hand-holding, according to Garton-Good. "Many times they're just concerned about finding someone to buy the house, and they're not taking the proper routes to represent the property and fill out the right forms—only to find out just how significant the financial damages can be in the long run."

While she makes a valid case for full-service agents in these statements, Garton-Good also says that for experienced buyers and sellers, the FSBO route can be the best choice. An even better choice, however, is the unbundled services that agents like Lee are offering to their customers. She says that the negotiation phase—in which consumers tend to leave "too much money on the table"—tends to be a particularly sticky area where an agent can step in and use her expertise, for a fee, to help the consumer. To make the unbundled approach work, she advises brokers and agents to draw up clear policies and procedures, and also to alert the consumer—and other cooperating agents or brokers—as to what is and is not being offered.

"Most consumers are 70 percent more visual than they are audial, so agents really need to work through these new business models in writing for their clients—including the listing information and contractual obligations," says Garton-Good. "That's going to be the real key to success, and the best way to ward off problems down the line." What customers want from this new option, she adds, are schematics, visuals, and even short, three- to five-question quizzes that help them determine whether unbundled services are in their best interest. For example: Do you feel comfortable conducting your own open houses? Do you consider yourself to be a proficient, successful negotiator on your own behalf?

Where customers tend to need the most help, according to Garton-Good, is at the point where the transaction is starting to wind down and the closing table is coming into clear view. The consumer who can place his own newspaper ads, field phone calls from prospective buyers, and show his own home, for example, could very well need your expertise when it comes to negotiating a fair price and filling out contracts and disclosures.

When someone says that she can handle three of the six main pieces of the puzzle, for example, the door is wide open for the enterprising agent to fill in—menu in hand—with his services. Garton-Good warns that the business is out there for the getting, provided the agent is proactive about recruiting such clients. Like Lee, who uses unbundled services to either (1) make money he wouldn't otherwise have made or (2) help homeowners realize that they really do need the full-service option, you too must put yourself out there, if this is the route that you choose to take.

That's because consumers often don't know any better, or are too fixated on that 6 or 7 percent commission price to even think about negotiating on a piecemeal basis. "I think most homeowners realize that they can't do it all, but they also feel that they don't want to pay X percent to have someone else do it," says Garton-Good. "Smart agents can offer to hold their hand and navigate them through the sticky areas."

RESTAURANT OR AGENT? IT'S YOUR CHOICE

Not everyone is enthusiastic about the trend of unbundling real estate services. In fact, most traditional full-service brokers feel that offering menu options puts yet another arrow in the heart of an industry that relies on long-time relationships and not on individual services like creating a comparative market analysis for $200 or producing an advertising and media plan for $1,000. Still, one can't ignore the fact that the idea of paying for only what they need is very alluring to the consumer.

Steven Pugh, a broker at Home Pride Realty Services, Inc., in Orlando, has so far steered clear of offering unbundled services, focusing instead on delivering full service at the market price. He's been in business for seven years and closed seventy transactions during his first year running his own brokerage in 2002. For 2003, the twenty-five-year-old agent was on track to close a hundred with four agents.

Pugh says that 95 percent of his business comes from working with first-time home buyers, most of whom need a lot of hand-holding and help with their first home purchase. However, Pugh says that he's noticed a number of "alternative" brokerage models sprouting up around him in the last year or so, including firms that list homes on the MLS for a flat fee of $499 and brokers who purportedly offer full-service for a flat fee of $2,500, regardless of the home's sale price.

It's not what Pugh had in mind when he opened his small boutique firm in 2002, but he does acknowledge the need to change with the times when it's warranted and consumer-driven. "I don't ever see myself changing my pricing structure, but I might not have a choice," says Pugh, adding that unbundled services haven't yet caught on in his region, though he does see a time in the future when more brokers and agents will do business in that fashion. "How long it will take to get there, I have no idea," he says.

Lyle Martin, co-owner of the flat-rate brokerage Assist-2-Sell in Reno, Nevada, sees menu options as nothing more than a way for full-service brokerages to retain their stronghold on the market, and says that the concept doesn't take a big enough step away from the traditional full-fee model. "Menu options are a joke," says Martin. "It is the traditional broker's guise of offering seller's choices." An avid believer that typical commission rates are entirely too high to justify the services that most agents offer, Martin says that the real key is to charge less and do more, not the opposite.

John Foltz, president of Realty Executives Phoenix, says that unbundling is typically the domain of real estate agents who lack the courage, the skills, or both to position themselves as a trusted adviser who can walk the consumer through the process of buying or selling a home from concept to completion. "It's those types of agents who feel that they have to compete with each other based on price and discounts," says Foltz, adding that prices and discounts only come into play when the clients themselves don't perceive value from their service providers.

"It's a known fact that agents who do well over the years consistently do not talk about price (meaning: commission rates) and consistently offer value, and the value they offer their clients is the value of being a trusted adviser," says Foltz. "Unlike agents who have to unbundle their services and offer them on a piecemeal basis, these trusted advisers gain additional advantages in the marketplace because of their counseling and negotiation skills."

BREAKING THROUGH

Curry Jameson, president of Realty Executives of North Nevada in Reno, with one office and forty-five agents, says that the proliferation of alternative brokerage models (unbundling included) is high in his marketplace right now. He says that while real estate commissions have always been negotiable (and continue to be), pressure is being placed on full-service firms by flat-fee and unbundled-services providers. "We've seen a significant increase in the advertising by such companies, which encourages the consumer to search for a better fee structure," says Jameson. "In my eyes, it hurts our industry. Not because of the commission issue, but because it's pushing consumers in a direction that they probably don't understand."

What Jameson means is that when a consumer opts to work with an agent who handles the transaction in a piecemeal fashion, the buyer or seller can risk missing key details and/or end up having to do too much work on her own. "If they understood in the beginning just how much work they'd have to do on their own, I don't think many of them would go for the alternative," says Jameson, who advises all of his agents to explain to customers exactly what they can expect from them and explain the difference between their options: full-service, discount, and unbundled, plus all of the hybrids that have surfaced in the last few years.

"It's a true education process on the part of the agent," says Jameson. "As brokers, we're determined to stay on track with a fee basis that provides the best full service that I think a consumer wants today, no matter what type of marketplace they're operating in." Where Jameson's agents have also found success is by offering even more than the typical real estate office, in terms of mortgage and insurance services. This trend toward vertical integration is spreading through the industry and is helping traditional brokers maintain more comprehensive control over both the consumer and the transaction itself.

Jameson is right on target. As profits in the real estate brokerage business get thinner and thinner, a number of firms nationwide have added ancillary services to their offerings. Recent research from NAR shows that 66 percent of recent home buyers reported that the next time they buy a home, they'll select a brokerage company based on the availability of one-stop shopping for a variety of products and services. Since it's in a full-service, full-commission broker's best interest to ensure that home sales go through to the closing table, offering everything from mortgage origination and title company services to home warranties and insurance is a natural for these offices (see Figure 6-1).

In the past, an agent would refer a home buyer to a good mortgage banker, an insurance firm for homeowner's insurance, and a title company for title insurance and closing. Today, it doesn't work that way for all companies; many of them have brought such services in-house, either by starting their own firms or pairing up with an existing company. In effect, the trend has gone in the completely opposite direction from unbundling services. By adding even more services to the list of "full-service" offerings, for example, the broker can more closely knit the entire process into one streamlined event.

The theory is that since harried, time-strapped consumers are leaning to the one-stop-shopping approach anyway, why not bring the concept right into the real estate transaction? Add to these services the ability to refer consumers to reputable moving services, landscaping companies,

Figure 6-1.

MENU OPTIONS, BROKEN DOWN

In the National Association of Realtors' 2003 report "The Future of Real Estate Brokerage," the organization breaks down the major functions that menu-options-oriented agents, or USPs, can offer their sellers as:

1. Developing a comparative market analysis that will help the seller determine market value, set a listing price, or make price revisions over time.

2. Suggesting repairs or cosmetic work that will significantly enhance the marketability of the property.

3. Exposing the property to the public and other real estate agents using the MLS and personal contacts.

4. Producing an advertising and media plan.

5. Screening potential buyers for qualifications and security risks.

6. Showing the home to agents or direct nonrepresented buyers.

7. Assisting in the review of offers and negotiation of the contract.

8. Assisting in the resolution of problems and closing details.

Source: National Association of Realtors' "The Future of Real Estate Brokerage," 2003. Used with permission.

and home improvement companies, and the brokerage firm and its agents can also exert some "after sale" control, thus ensuring future referrals and business from repeat customers.

NOT SO FAST

Not all industry studies concur about the growth and popularity of unbundled services in real estate. According to a 2000 report from the Real Estate Center at Texas A&M University, the fact that real estate has opted to incorporate unbundled services into its business models is directly correlated to the securities brokerage model. The hybrid scenario gives consumers a choice between a traditional full-service brokerage and discount broker-age packages.

The Real Estate Center's research economists say that consumers who wish to rely on their brokers to handle entire transactions will continue to choose full-service firms, while those who wish a more limited set of services—listing, showing, or contract negotiation, for example—will grab the chance to work with an agent who allows them to select from a menu of unbundled services. The economists predict that agents working for these firms will become specialists in various aspects of the business.

Where menu options tend to work best is with consumers who wish to control the process of selling and/or buying a home themselves. Armed with the Internet as an information source and a host of professionals to work with, the Real Estate Center says that the unbundling portion of the nontraditional real estate industry will "dominate" in the future, based on the fact that today's consumers wants to pay less for more choices and more control.

The Real Estate Center predicts that brokerage firms will offer servic-es for a fee as demanded by consumers, which may also shift some of the cost explicitly to the buyer. The predictions fall in line with Garton-Good's assumptions in that the economist says that agents will become more like consultants and will be involved in the home search process and the closing transaction details in a more limited way.

Three years later, however, the same College Station, Texas–based real estate center reports that real estate professionals are an independent lot and are largely resistant to change and new trends. In a 2003 survey of real estate licensees conducted by the Real Estate Center, the findings revealed that while some have adopted new ways of doing business and go with the latest trends, others prefer to stick with tried-and-true practices.

The Real Estate Center reports that the real estate field has been "largely resistant" to the trend of discounters who offer no-frills services and products at discounted prices. It says that allowing clients to pur-chase brokerage services piecemeal is one way of discounting commis-sions, and that while the limited-service option may appeal to some home sellers, only 12 percent of respondents offer limited-service options, and only 15 percent of franchised firms do so.

OOZING CUSTOMER SERVICE

Laurie Moore-Moore, an industry speaker and consultant as well as the cofounder and former coeditor of *REAL Trends*, points to Coldwell Banker's introduction of a Concierge Service, which offers consumers an entire spectrum of homeownership services and products, as the innovation that caused other firms to consider the value of diversifying and to feel some pressure to act quickly in order to compete. But does this mean that agents will be asked to sell these added products and services? Probably not, says Moore-Moore.

"Instead, agents will introduce their buyers and sellers to a customer service expert who will offer a list of homeownership-related products and services from affiliates of the firm or from suppliers who have been screened by the brokerage firm and may pay the brokerage a fee," says Moore-Moore, who adds that the Real Estate Settlement Practices Act (RESPA) will ultimately govern how the trend toward cross-selling develops. (RESPA is a HUD-enforced consumer protection statute designed to help home buyers be better shoppers in the home-buying process. It requires that consumers receive disclosures at various times during the transaction and outlaws kickbacks that increase the cost of settlement services. RESPA is covered in more detail in Chapter 8.)

In fact, Moore-Moore says, the trend is already well underway, and companies no longer call these "ancillary" services, but rather see them as core services because the profits they represent are critical to the companies' survival. These companies are repositioning themselves from brokerage firms to "homeownership" companies.

At Realty Executives of Nevada, consumers have access to in-house mortgage services via an outside service provider who set up shop within the company's offices. "It's a huge benefit for our agents as well as for the customer," says Jameson. "We can accommodate financing within a short time frame—something that's not so easy to come by in the industry these days." Agents gain no monetary benefit from referring customers to the in-house mortgage provider, says Jameson, but they do benefit in terms of gains in customer satisfaction and a speedier closing.

Jameson says that his next charge is to get agents to make better use of the company's homeowner's insurance partner, who recently began offering policies to home buyers through Realty Executives. It's all in the name of providing total service, says Jameson, who is determined to keep his company's full-service offering intact, bundled, and successful well into the future.

CREATING A MENU

If the only time you use the word *menu* is when you're having dinner at a restaurant, and if you have a true interest in unbundling your services and offering them piecemeal to at least some of your customers, then you're reading the right book. Here, I'll give you a short primer on how a full-service agent can start unbundling his services to reach a broader customer base that's reluctant to shell out the 6 or 7 percent commission in exchange for the full Monty.

Across the country, real estate companies have quietly began altering the way they offer services, mainly by creating menus. These menus allow customers—who at one time could only opt for either full-service or do-it-yourself—the option to pick and pay only for the real estate services that they need. Through this system, sellers might pay a fee to the agent for listing the home in the local MLS, another fee for negotiating and writing the contract, and yet another for handling the activities that lead up to closing (home inspections, scheduling appraisals and surveys, and so on).

While these parts of the transaction are being taken care of, the sellers might be handling other pertinent functions on their own, such as fielding phone calls from potential buyers, preparing their homes for sale, or holding open houses. The biggest challenge for agents and their brokers is deciding which services to keep intact and which to unbundle and offer piecemeal.

When Lee instituted his menu option approach in the 1980s, he says that he first divided his fee structure into three parts: full-service (for the typical market-rate commission), an hourly rate (which for most agents runs from $100 to $200 an hour), and a menu of services. Once he determines where the consumer is coming from, Lee says, he offers all three options and allows the consumer to mull over the choices.

"I let them know that they'll obviously get a more complete and comprehensive package with the full-service option," says Lee, who began offering the other two alternatives during an era when an increasing number of people began buying and selling real estate without a real estate license. He points to the Internet as the main driver behind the need for options.

Even though the real estate transaction—unlike the purchase of an automobile or boat—is undeniably the most difficult financial process on earth, hands down, Lee says that the perception that real estate transactions are somehow easy to pull off has decreased the value of the agent in the eyes of the client. It's a perception that he says most agents do little to change.

"Real estate agents have never done a good job of explaining their value to clients, and no matter where I travel and speak across the country, people still believe that agents do virtually nothing," Lee says. "They also believe that agents get an incredibly large quantity of money for doing it."

Seeing these incorrect perceptions coming down the pike as early as the 1980s, Lee took a proactive step and developed a list of a hundred things that he does to help buyers purchase the homes of their dreams. He developed another list, this one giving sellers a rundown of everything he does when helping to sell a home. A third list, designed specifically for FSBOs, lists everything that he could do that they couldn't possibly do themselves (like producing a reliable comparative market analysis, or CMA). Lee created yet another list for expired listings, and on it listed a hundred ways that he could help a home sell faster, and at a higher price.

The lists haven't changed much over the last two decades, says Lee, and have certainly come in handy whenever a cynical customer approaches him and asks for a discount on commissions. "Since putting those lists together, I've never had to lower my commissions because people can see in plain English exactly what I do," says Lee, adding that most consumers will still question the agent's value proposition, based on the seemingly high commissions that they fetch. "At that point, I explain to them just how little we really do make. When I figured it out myself, it comes right down to the fact that we take home about one-half of 1 percent of the sales price."

Lee's original lists spawned a need to create a menu of services—complete with accompanying prices—targeted mostly at owners of higher-priced homes who balk at the thought of spending $60,000 to sell a $1 million home (based on a 6 percent commission). "It's no secret that commissions are inherently unfair as the homes go up in price," says Lee. "It doesn't take ten times as much money to market and sell a $1 million home versus a $100,000 home, and the American public has figured this out. As a result, on upper-end properties people are much more interested in alternative compensation structures."

Even with the myriad options that Lee offers, he says, the bulk of his clients go with the traditional, flat commission rate in exchange for full service, mainly because customers are afraid that if a property doesn't sell, they'll be out the amount of money that they paid for the services that he performed.

HITTING THE FSBOS

Agents looking for a place to start selling their unbundled services should look no further than the most overlooked and underserviced market, according to Garton-Good: FSBOs. The buoyant real estate market of the past several years has drawn agents to more lucrative targets for listings and sales, she adds, yet the prediction is that the number of FSBOS will more than double in the next ten years and could represent as much as 40 percent of all properties for sale in the marketplace.

"That's a statistic to pay attention to," says Garton-Good. "And even if online services help FSBOs to lease signage, write ads, and so on, there's still money to be made offering the personalized services of negotiating, advocating, and troubleshooting the transaction." Garton-Good advises agents and/or brokers to take the following steps in developing an unbundled-services option for those customers:

❑ *Do the math as a real estate consultant.* Crank out your calculator: How many hours would it take to negotiate between the FSBO and a qualified buyer and monitor the sale to a successful closing? Garton-Good's research shows a median time frame of ten hours for these tasks. What if the parties to the transaction were willing to pay you, say (for the purpose of example only), $150 per hour, capped at a maximum fee of $1,500? And what if they gave you a $500 retainer against that fee? (Passed through your broker's escrow account, of course.) So on a 50/50 split with your broker, you'd gross $750 per FSBO transaction as a consultant. And if you closed just two of these assignments per month, that would be an extra $18,000 a year. That's certainly nothing to sneeze at, and it's a professional activity that mixes well with commissioned-sales business. "And don't forget that satisfied FSBOs are an especially good source of recommending you to others," says Garton-Good. "After all, they've won, so they're willing to help you win."

❑ *Ease in with consultancy (or unbundled services) as an alternative choice.* Garton-Good says that since most real estate markets are booming, the average agent would probably rather have a root canal than spend time hammering (usually, cold calling from a newspaper ad or yard sign) an FSBO to list. But what if in lieu of listing, a consumer chose to actually pay you for services rendered? Would that be worth the effort?

"Give it a try the next time you have the opportunity," she says. "Offer it to an FSBO as an alternative to a formal exclusive listing (after receiving the blessing of your broker, of course). In my experience, you'll receive one of two responses from the consumer: (1)

'Read my lips, I want to sell my house myself' or (2) 'That's interesting. It could be exactly what I need. How much will it cost?'"

❑ *What to charge and how to decide.* Because different markets fetch
   different prices, Garton-Good says that figuring out what to charge
   for the menu options is a very personal decision. "One of the beau-
   tiful things about being a real estate consultant is determining the
   true value of your expertise," she says, adding that real estate agents
   have long been slotted as "just another real estate agent, charging
   the same X percent." Such perceptions can get thrown out the window when an agent uses the unbundling approach. "You can niche
   your market by being the best at a certain task while being rewarded in proportion to your ability," says Garton-Good, "much like
   the CPAs and attorneys you refer business to."

   Before coming up with a price for their services, Garton-Good says,
   agents and their brokers must first determine the following factors
   behind each unbundled service: (1) The skill level required to perform the service (broker, agent, licensed or unlicensed assistant),
   (2) the cost of any new training required to do the job satisfactori-
   ly, (3) the per-hour dollar value of the person performing the task
   (allowing for a factor of "lost opportunity" time that could better
   be spent doing or developing other higher-paid opportunities), and
   (4) the block of time it would customarily take to perform the
   unbundled activity (including a factor for additional administrative
   or clerical assistance, cost of supplies, technology required, and so
   on).

After performing this cost-analysis gyration, Garton-Good says, the
broker and/or agent might find that (1) it is unrealistic to believe that a
consumer would pay enough for the unbundled service to be profitable to
the brokerage, (2) it could work financially, but not with top producers,
or (3) it could make financial sense to begin the unbundling process with
"troubleshooting-the-sale services" for FSBOs, using existing administra-
tion personnel.

And remember, says Garton-Good, that it's ultimately the broker who decides whether this alternative form of real estate service is the right avenue for the company. "The alpha and omega in this situation is the principal broker, who not only makes decisions for the brokerage about whether unbundled services is a logical fit for the brokerage," says Garton-Good, "but also dictates the services offered and the range of fees for those services."

MORE À LA CARTE TO COME

Real estate professionals certainly aren't the only businesspeople who have been asked by customers to break down their fees, and they probably won't be the last. Whether you decide to create a menu of services to either replace or complement your full-service offerings is a purely personal choice, to be decided between you, your broker, and your customers, who will be most affected by the new choices. If you do decide to augment your current offerings, keep in mind that the challenge will be disclosing your service offerings to all consumers (you wouldn't want a savvy 7 percent commission customer finding out later that you sold your services to someone else piecemeal) without jeopardizing the amount of full service that you're accustomed to providing.

And remember that if you refuse to offer your services piecemeal, the agent down the street probably will. It's not a threat, but simply the reality of doing business in a competitive field. As many other business segments (such as those fee-only financial planners, for example) have come to realize, offering consumers exactly what they want, when they need it, and charging them what it's worth usually winds up as a win-win situation for both the consumer and the professional. Knowing this, it's easy to see why unbundled fee-for-service in the home-buying and home-selling field will become a much larger part of the marketplace and more readily available to consumers in the future.

"There's definitely going to be more fee-for-service in real estate's future," says Lee, who is quick to point out that the full-service concept will also continue to work well, as long as agents can explain and justify their value to the client in a meaningful manner that sticks.

"Unfortunately, I'd venture to say that no more than 2 or 3 percent of all agents in the nation know how to go about convincingly justifying the value of their services to the client," he adds.

Lee points to the 12,000 or so agents that he speaks to each year at various speaking engagements nationwide as the proof of these low numbers. He often asks the audience, "How do you justify your value?" Very few people raise their hands, and even fewer can actually explain in a meaningful way exactly what they do in exchange for their 6 or 7 percent commission. As a result, most buckle under the pressure and end up reducing their commissions.

"The only thing agents really know how to do is lower their commissions," says Lee. "The bad news is that when you look at the cost of doing business in this industry, if you lower them too much, you're out of business." And while menu options serve as a viable alternative for the agent who can't convince a customer to go the full-service route, Lee says, the concept doesn't replace the need for better justification of value in an industry where most consumers think that real estate agents make entirely too much money.

"In reality, we earn every dollar that we get," says Lee. "The clients would never be willing to be agents themselves if they understood all that was involved in doing our business. But again, we have failed to educate our clients, so the fault lies on our shoulders for not representing ourselves better in the marketplace."

The good news, says Garton-Good, is that demanding consumers are willing to compensate experts who can provide the services and products that they want. That's also the bad news, she adds, because only those real estate professionals who can provide the services at the right price and in a timely fashion will prevail in an industry where barriers to entry are as low as success rates. The good news–bad news scenario opens the door to agents and brokers who are willing to do what it takes to satisfy the customer without cutting their own throats.

"Since the real estate industry is the last of the financial industries to unbundle services, it's merely a matter of time before empowered consumers vote with their feet, and their wallets, in the move to unbundled, results-oriented, cost-effective real estate answers," says Garton-Good (see Figure 6-2).

REAL Trends editor Steve Murray chalks the menu-option trend up to the influx of new competitors in an industry where a single business model was accepted and flourished for decades. It was only a matter of time before someone developed alternative methods of delivery in a booming industry where billions of dollars of properties are sold nation-wide each year. "We have full-service discount brokers, we have online discount brokers, we have unbundled-service providers," says Murray. "I think there is a chance that each of them can earn a piece of the market.

SIX THINGS TO REMEMBER FROM CHAPTER 6

❑ Accustomed to offering their services in an unbundled format, most full-service agents just aren't wired to be able to break their services down piecemeal.

❑ Menu or unbundled services have both supporters and detractors within the real estate industry, with most traditional real estate brokers speaking out against such business models.

❑ Menu options tend to work best when the consumers have experience in buying and/or selling homes and want to control some or all of the process themselves.

❑ Some full-service brokers are using unbundled-service options to help consumers realize just how valuable their commission-based services are—particularly when it comes to paying for services up front, regardless of whether the home sells or not.

❑ Most experts agree that menu-option services do not chip away at the full-service market, but that they are making a dent in the nation's FSBO market, which would be most apt to test out a concept that allows them to pay for services piecemeal.

❑ NAR reports that many unbundled-service providers (USPs) are operating and exhibiting some staying power, but predicts that it will take a "significant amount of time" for these companies to grow their businesses.

Figure 6-2.

ARE UNBUNDLED SERVICES IN EVERY AGENT'S FUTURE?

Within the real estate business right now, there are a number of innovative business models competing for the customer's business, with some agents specializing in delivering just one piece of the puzzle at a time and others offering the full menu at once. According to Julie Garton-Good, the Orlando, Florida–based author of *Real Estate a la Carte, Selecting the Services You Need, Paying What They're Worth* (Dearborn, 2001), offering true value to your customers means being able to provide flexibility and greater control to your customers—all at a lower cost.

Garton-Good, who is also founder and president of the National Association of Real Estate Consultants (NAREC), says that when all is said and done, three primary "power groups" will stake their claims in the real estate industry: for sale by owners, aggregators, and fee-for-services consultants. Here are her thoughts on where each will stand in the real estate industry of the future.

Power group 1: For-sale-by-owners. These will dominate the market. Depending on the source and date of the statistics, Garton-Good says, FSBOs are expected to grow to approximately 40 percent of the available property market over the next several years. She also says that the power will lie in the hands of for-sale-by-owners.

Power group 2: Aggregators who strive to meet the needs of the consumer. (An aggregator is an entity that brings together various products and/or services in order to meet a need or solve a problem). The most prevalent aggregators today are the online aggregators like REALTOR.com, and Garton-Good expects their power to grow by 2010, at which point they could be providing as much as 20 percent of the nation's real estate services.

Power group 3: Real estate agents who reinvent themselves into fee-for-service consultants. Garton-Good, who has based her prognosis on research regarding the FSBO market, predicts that the high-pressure salesperson will gradually give way to the one who concentrates on results. She says that consultants will focus solely on the customers' needs, leaving troubleshooting and related tasks to the brokerage itself.

PART 3

JOB HAZARDS

CHAPTER 7

Risk Management for Agents

KEEPING YOUR NOSE CLEAN

Like the bartender who finds herself liable for pouring a drink for someone who gets behind the wheel of a car and hurts someone, real estate agents have been finding themselves on the wrong side of issues like property defects, poor disclosure of agency relationships, fair housing issues, and bad real estate deals lately. Our increasingly litigious society has created somewhat of a minefield for a number of professions, and real estate is no exception.

To put it simply, a real estate deal that goes awry can unleash a series of events that drag the agent and/or the broker down with the ship, regardless of how much or little they were involved. Even the most trivial of issues can turn into a major debacle once the lawyers and the courts get involved, and because most agents work as independent contractors (and not employees), their brokers aren't always implicated. As a result, much of the weight ends up on the individual agent's shoulders. It's a harsh reality, but one that can be navigated with knowledge of the most prevalent risks for agents combined with a basic ability to discern right from wrong.

Legal hurdles that agents have to contend with right now range from toxic mold claims and poorly executed property disclosures to fair housing law violations and relationship disclosures within the transaction. Most of the time these issues are pretty low on the average agent's priority list as he goes about his daily routines, blissfully unaware of the legal implications that could be waiting for him around the corner. That is, until one wrong move comes back to bite him in the rear. Not all issues escalate into serious cases, but when something unfortunate does occur, the agent can quickly find herself consumed by the legalities, drained of resources, and trying to repair her reputation in an industry that thrives on close, trusting, long-term relationships.

Take the recent case in which a Florida real estate agent supposedly steered a potential buyer away from a mobile home park that catered only to the over-fifty-five crowd. Such developments are popular in that state, which has a large retired population. The problem was, the mobile home that this mother and her nine-year-old son wanted to purchase was in a community that wasn't registered with the state of Florida (the state allows parks to discriminate based on age if at least 80 percent of the occupied units are occupied by at least one person fifty-five years of age or older), making it illegal for the park to turn someone away because of their age.

The buyer sued the mobile home park in federal court, and the area's fair housing center investigated the case. In the end, the fair housing center alleged that both the mobile home park and the agent who listed the home for sale violated federal housing laws. Because the agent was operating as an independent contractor, her broker wasn't implicated in the case. The case was expected to go to court in late 2003, with the buyer seeking $250,000 in damages. The case against the agent was pretty clear: By telling the buyer that the mobile home park was an over-fifty-five community without researching whether the claim was indeed true, the agent violated federal fair housing laws.

This case is just one example of why risk management is yet another critical tool in any successful agent's arsenal. Remember, however, that while this chapter will give you a sampling of legal issues that real estate agents are dealing with, the list is by no means comprehensive, nor is it meant to serve as a substitute for legal advice from a qualified attorney.

For more specific information about laws and recent legal issues affecting agents in your area, check with your Board of Realtors® or state association, or utilize one of the associations' legal hotlines for more in-depth assistance on sticky topics.

WATCHING YOUR BACK

Right now, it's words like *toxic mold* and *fair housing* that send shudders down a real estate agent's spine, mainly because of the national attention that such issues have been getting in the press recently. In the past, words like *radon* and *asbestos* had similar effects. To cover their hides, agents must educate themselves and keep up to date on recent trends in a number of areas. For example, agents must be aware of the public's most pressing concerns and should be taking steps to protect themselves from liability, primarily through good disclosure to both buyers and sellers throughout the entire transaction. As any good businessperson would advise, they should also get everything in writing—a step that most Boards of Realtors and state real estate commissions can help with through printed and/or online disclosures that cover a variety of topics.

Matthew Zifrony, an attorney at Tripp Scott and head of the firm's real estate department in Fort Lauderdale, Florida, has spent the last thirteen years of his career handling real estate transactions. He says that risk management has always been a priority for real estate agents, but he adds that concern over legal risks has increased over the last eight years. He identifies our litigious society and the sheer number of real estate agents and brokers operating in the field as the two primary culprits. "There's a larger number of agents out there, fighting harder for deals and competing against one another," says Zifrony. "Because of that, risk management has taken on an even greater importance."

When it comes to customer satisfaction, real estate agents are at particular risk, says Zifrony. Again, because the best real estate agents pride themselves on forging long-term relationships with buyers and sellers, they are open to blame when a deal doesn't go through properly, or when that $350,000 house doesn't live up the buyer's expectations. "On top of just getting the deal done, agents need to be aware that buyers who aren't as happy as they thought they would be will come after them after the fact," says Zifrony, who points to the recent toxic mold cases nationwide as examples of after-the-fact risks.

"If somebody buys a piece of property and it turns out that the property has mold in it, then given the society we're living in, that buyer is going to start thinking about who she can sue to recoup her losses," says Zifrony. "The seller is one target, and the real estate agent who facilitated the deal is a second target." Zifrony says that he's dealt with less publicized cases over the years, like the home buyer who assumed that he was purchasing a home with marble floors, only to find out that the floor was actually made of sheetrock.

In this case, Zifrony says the buyer said to the agent, "I told you that the only thing that mattered to me was that the floor be marble, and you told me I'd love this house. But it's not marble." Because the purchase agreement included no such specifications (i.e., that the floor had to be marble), the buyer had no recourse other than to allege some type of fraud—against both the seller and the agents involved, says Zifrony.

Zifrony pinpoints home defects and a lack of communication as the two basic areas that agents should be aware of right now in terms of risk management. In some states, for example, he says that issues like drainage problems—something that would hardly be noticed unless it happened to be raining hard on the day the buyer walked through or inspected the home and neighborhood—can go undetected until after closing. It's best to ask about such issues when listing or showing a home, he adds, to avert problems down the line when the monsoon comes and the land surrounding the home floods.

Open lines of communication are equally as important, according to Zifrony, who warns against trying to deceive a buyer into signing on the dotted line without first covering important issues like the possibility of home defects. A buyer who makes the purchase "as is," for example, may not realize that a major home leak that surfaces a week after they walk away from the closing table is his problem, not the seller's. Typically, however, contracts include clauses that force a seller to repair any defects detected by a home inspector or other professional prior to closing, or risk losing the deal.

FAIR HOUSING

I couldn't believe my ears. Did a real estate agent that I know really just tell me that one of her colleagues was upset because she had "accidentally" rented a condominium to an African American couple, and that her "Jewish condo owners" were going to be even more upset about it? It was a casual recounting between friends, but one that could be devastating for the agent who did the renting, should word of the prejudice and possibility of fair housing law violations ever get out. The point is, this agent should have never made the decision to rent (or not to rent) to anyone based on race, color, or creed.

As a professional operating in an industry where "steering" buyers to certain neighborhoods is an ethical violation, that real estate agent should have known better. In this day and age, there's simply no excuse for such blatant prejudice in a nation where the melting pot is becoming more and more varied by the day. But while treating everyone equally in the business world sounds simple enough in concept, it's apparently not as easy as it looks in practice. According to the National Fair Housing Alliance, the nation's leading housing advocacy group, housing discrimination figures have remained high over the past year, despite what seem to be movements toward fair and equal treatment of all home buyers and sellers.

The alliance found that 23,500 claims of housing discrimination were filed in 2002, and that approximately 16,500 of those were filed with local fair housing groups, 5,000 with state and local civil rights agencies, 2,000 with the U.S. Department of Housing and Urban Development (HUD), and 64 with the U.S. Department of Justice.

The leading claim remained race discrimination (32 percent of all claims), followed by disability discrimination (24 percent), family status discrimination (15 percent), and national origin discrimination (10 percent). The group also reported that HUD estimates that two million instances of housing discrimination occur each year, which means that only about 1 percent of all instances of housing discrimination are actually reported.

According to the National Association of Realtors®, fair housing violations account for only 1 percent to 2 percent of litigation but can result in costly judgments for the agent. NAR calls the area "tricky," however, because state and local laws can add protected classes (such as gays and lesbians) to the federal discrimination laws.

Much the way retail stores and restaurants use "mystery shoppers" to detect bad business practices on their front lines, fair housing groups often use "testing" to detect steering and other fair housing violations. That means that a seller who doesn't want to sell to a buyer of a certain ethnic background, age, or race should immediately raise a red flag for any good agent who knows the local fair housing laws and the implications of violating them.

But it happens. Take the agent mentioned a few paragraphs back who allegedly steered a potential buyer away from a mobile home park because she had a nine-year-old son and because the park was—at least in theory, and according to the owner—designed for residents who are fifty-five and older. Brenda Montague, a Realtor® with Coldwell Banker Residential Real Estate, serves on the Fair Housing/Equal Employment Opportunity Board for the county of Palm Beach (which includes the city of Boca Raton, where the incident took place). She says that the lawsuit could have been avoided with some diligent research on the agent's part.

"There's no excuse for this," says Montague. "If an agent is in doubt about what looks to be discrimination, it's just a matter of reading the community's bylaws (to ensure that it is registered with the state, if required) and making a phone call to the fair housing board. There are just too many resources—including cities, counties, and municipalities—that we have available to us as agents and brokers to make those kinds of mistakes." Once a potential fair housing violation is detected, Montague says, it's up to the consumer or the buyer or seller to "open the case" with the fair housing board.

To limit fair housing liability, NAR suggests getting both education and training concerning local, state, and federal laws and guidelines. For example, the group offers its members a twenty-seven-minute fair housing video for $19.95 that focuses on timely fair housing topics and the complex issues presented by fair housing regulations. The group also suggests documenting every part of the process to ensure equal treatment for all involved, and using its "model equal services report form" (one for sales and one for rental) as another tool for dealing with a claim of discrimination.

DUAL AGENCY AND BUYER AGENCY

The word *agent* in the legal sense means a fiduciary, one whose primary duty is to put the interests of the client first. (Doctors, lawyers, and accountants are examples of fiduciaries.) The courts have ruled that when real estate licensees act on behalf of others and represent them, they are accountable as fiduciaries. Obviously, buyers as well as sellers need protection and representation, which is why buyer agency and dual agency disclosures have become a major legal issue for the industry (see Figure 7-1).

That's because in the past, agents were pretty much always accountable to home sellers, while buyers would hire lawyers (in some states, a lawyer is required at the closing table) or fend for themselves. To put it simply, the agent owed loyalty, confidentiality, and fiduciary duties to the seller, and the seller alone. The concept is a hard one for consumers to grasp, since most of them are used to dealing with professionals like lawyers, doctors, and accountants, all of whom represent or work with their clients without dealing with such issues. The proof is in the pudding: A number of national surveys in the late 1980s and early 1990s indicated that most buyers of real estate thought that the sales agent represented them in the transaction, whereas agents who listed property and their brokers were in reality obligated only to the seller.

The problem erupted into a national concern in the 1990s, when brokers and agents nationwide sat up and realized that there was a need for expanded agency relationships. The realization came after a large private firm in the Midwest was sued in a class-action lawsuit involving the prac-

Figure 7-1.

AGENCY DEFINITIONS

Time was when real estate agents represented sellers, and sellers alone. In the last decade or so, the lines have blurred as terms like buyer's agent, exclusive buyer's agent, and dual agency have surfaced, making the agent's legal disclosure duties that much more complicated. Here's a rundown of the key terms you'll need to know in order to stay on the right side of the law when dealing with customers:

Agency. This is a relationship in which a real estate licensee represents a client in an immovable property transaction. An agency relationship is formed when a real estate agent works for a consumer in that consumer's best interest and represents the consumer in the transaction.

Designated Agency. This is a contractual relationship between a real estate agent and a client. As a designated agent, you are accountable to the client, regardless of which side of the transaction pays your commission. The law presumes that the licensee is the designated agent, unless there is a written and signed agreement stating otherwise.

Dual agency. This occurs when a real estate agent is representing both buyer and seller in the same transaction, and it's allowed only with the informed written consent of all clients. Since the agent has promised a duty of confidentiality, loyalty, and full disclosure to both parties simultaneously, it could be necessary to limit these duties in this situation, if both parties consent. Before receiving an offer, for example, both the buyer and the seller will be asked to consent in writing to the new, limited agency relationship. With dual agency, the agent deals with the buyer and seller impartially; the agent has the duty of disclosure to both the buyer and seller (with the exception that the agent doesn't disclose that the buyer is willing to pay a price or agree to terms other than those written in the offer, or the listing).

Buyer's agent. An agent, usually working in a "traditional" real estate office that takes listings, who spends most of her time representing buyers. However, the lines get blurry when a buyer wants to see a home listed by the same company; the buyer's agent then becomes a dual agent representing both the buyer and the seller. The rise of buyer's agency has raised a number of legal concerns in an industry where the seller once reigned as the sole person whom agents represented.

Exclusive buyer's agent. An agent who works for a real estate firm that takes no listings, but instead spends all of its time and resources working for buyers. Such offices do not wrangle with the issue of dual agency because the question of serving as both buyer's agent and listing agent never arises.

Listing agent. The person who signs a "listing agreement" with the home seller, and whose signs, newspaper ads, and Web site typically advertise the listing. As a listing agent, your job is to get the very best price possible for the seller.

---

tice of "undisclosed dual agency" in multiple transactions. Word got around about the very serious violation of customers' trust and loyalty, particularly after the firm lost the lawsuit and was forced to return all of the commissions it had collected from its customers.

As with most lawsuits of such magnitude, the event triggered regulatory scrutiny of agency laws and led to a growing interest in instituting a "buyer representation" category within the industry. The industry found its answer in buyer agency, a concept that helps buyers deal with the increasing complexity of the real estate transaction and educates them about the effects of customer or client representation. At the same time, it also helps agents deal with consumer protection laws and operate in an aboveboard manner in an litigious business environment. In most states today, real estate licensees are required to provide buyers with an "agency disclosure," in which they disclose to buyers whether they will be assisting them as seller agents, buyer agents, or some form of dual agent.

Steve Murray, editor of *REAL Trends*, a publication that tracks trends in the real estate industry, calls risk management in general an "increasing concern" for real estate agents, but points to the disclosure of relationships between those entities working on the deal and the disclosure of property conditions, the latter of which seems to be getting "substantial, and more complicated," as part of the solution.

To deal with the increased scrutiny, Murray says, successful agents should pay attention to compliance with the most critical areas. Other agents, it seems, are removing themselves from certain parts of the transaction in order to lessen the risk of being viewed as operating in a manner that is unfair to one or more of the involved parties. The industry as a whole, for example, is evolving towards associates as "transaction coordinators" or "facilitators" in the deals. Such individuals do not act as an agent of either the seller or the buyer, but provide services to complete a real estate transaction.

These transaction coordinators may or may not be acting in the role of agent as commonly understood and may not owe a fiduciary duty to either party, and they may not be an advocate of either party. Thus those operating as transaction coordinators or facilitators may have a lower level of duty to either the buyer or the seller, says Murray, "and that may remove them from having formal agency responsibilities."

HOME DEFECTS

Ah, if only every home was free of defects, structural problems, and wood-destroying insects. Wouldn't every agent's job be so much easier? Unfortunately, mistakes are a part of life and even the newest dwellings come with their share of problems, making it that much harder for an agent to enjoy a good living. Agents aren't always implicated when an air conditioner breaks down or a roof leaks, of course, mainly because it's up to the seller to completely fill out a property disclosure form before the sale. Often, however, agents do get tangled up in the mess as a result of their close relationship to the sale.

Take a recent case in Tennessee in which the state's appellate court ruled that property sellers were liable for a real estate agent's "negligent misrepresentation" to the home buyer. At issue was a property that was prone to flooding—a fact that was not disclosed on the purchase agreement. The purchase agreement stated that the property had not been damaged by flooding and did not require flood insurance. The property flooded more than a dozen times in the years after closing, with the water completely surrounding the home on several occasions, prompting the buyer to file a lawsuit against the sellers for negligent misrepresentation.

While the listing agent who provided her expertise on the likelihood of flood and the flood insurance issue wasn't implicated in the lawsuit, it's still easy to see how valuable accurate information, education, and research can be—as well as getting everything in writing—when representing sellers and buyers. Right now, toxic mold is the newest environmental scare on every agent's list, although in 2003 the issue waned some because many insurance firms decided to pull mold coverage from their homeowner's policies, so the lawsuits against insurers subsided.

Mold came to the forefront in 2001 when a family in Texas won a $32.1 million (later reduced to $4 million) lawsuit over extensive mold damage to their home. The effects of mold contamination haven't been medically or scientifically proven as yet, though mold is thought to be a health risk for children, adults, and even pets, but they are scary nonetheless, given the recent rash of media attention to the issue.

Realizing the implications for broker and agent members, NAR in 2003 began marketing an informational guide created by the American Industrial Hygiene Association to help consumers understand the basics about mold. "The Facts About Mold" is a twelve-page quick reference for real estate practitioners that helps answer questions from prospective homeowners and tenants about mold "that agents should not attempt to answer on their own." The brochure includes information about mold and health, suggestions on how to prevent mold from growing in the home, and tips on what to do if mold is discovered. In addition, the guide tells when it is necessary to contact a professional.

Some states have already taken measures to protect real estate agents from issues involving mold. In Louisiana, for example, a new bill under consideration would effectively shield Louisiana's real estate agents from liability in mold cases. HB 193, which is supported by the Louisiana Association of Realtors, provides for the adoption of the "mold informational pamphlet" by April 2004. The literature will be distributed to buyers by real estate licensees in connection with any real estate transaction entered into on and after July 1, 2004. As long as those licensees deliver the pamphlet to the buyer at the time the lease, rental agreement, or contract for sale is entered into by the parties, then the agent will not be required to provide any additional information concerning mold. (Problems involving mold are discussed in more detail later in the chapter.)

INFORMATION-AGE LIABILITIES

Risk management in the real estate world goes beyond making sure that homes are defect-free, sellers aren't discriminating, and mold isn't growing behind the living room walls. Thanks to technology, the real estate professional's liability also extends into areas created by the information age. Examples include the 2003 federal Do Not Call Law, which limits a company's ability to cold call (or even "warm call") past clients to rekindle business relationships, and a slew of consumer protection laws cropping up around the nation.

At Century 21 Award in San Diego, bold letters at the top of the disclosure form spell out its purpose clearly: Century 21 Award Privacy Policy Disclosure. The brokerage introduced the form to its 725 agents in April 2003, right around the time that consumers were receiving similar notices from their banks, financial institutions, and credit card companies. "We knew we needed a privacy policy," says Ann Throckmorton, the company's chief compliance officer, "so we went ahead and implemented our own."

After reading about the types of information that the brokerage collects; what its primary business is; how it uses documents like deeds, notes, or mortgages that are involved in the transaction; and how the brokerage does not share that information with service providers outside the marketing and transaction process, the buyers or sellers and a Century 21 Award agent are asked to sign the document and retain a copy for their records.

The disclosure also covers information protection—a key issue in California (that promises to radiate out to other states), which recently passed a computer data security breach law—and alerts customers to the fact that the brokerage restricts access to nonpublic personal information only to those associates and employees who "need the information" to provide products or services to the customer. "We maintain physical, electronic, and procedural safeguards that comply with law to guard your nonpublic personal information," it continues, "and we reinforce the company's privacy policy with our associates and employees."

Throckmorton says that keeping consumer information private has been a key issue for Realtors and brokers for years, as a result of the information-intensive nature of the real estate transaction. Everything from social security numbers to driver's license numbers and tax identification numbers to credit reports is swapped back and forth amongst the service providers in the process of closing the deal. The problem is, every time the information is shared or accessed, it increases the risk of a security breach or identity theft. In the electronic age, where information flows freely and is stored on a computer for an infinite amount of time, the risks are exacerbated even further.

"As Realtors, we come to know a lot of personal data about our customers," says Throckmorton. "We're responsible for protecting and respecting that information." She points out that California's new security breach law—which was signed into law on July 1, 2003, and is aimed at combating the growing threat of identity theft—didn't necessitate any new actions on the part of the brokerage, which already had security and firewall protections in its computer system and uses information technology professionals to "watch and monitor" any unusual activity within the system.

Protecting consumer privacy is not so much a growing concern for agents and brokers as it is a "fully grown" concern, says Dick Clark, senior partner with Denver-based law firm Rothgerber Johnson & Lyons LLP, which represents both the Colorado and Wyoming Association of Realtors. E-mail, in particular, can be an Achilles heel for Realtors, who don't always realize the implications of any information sharing they do via computer, or simply of the manner in which they store the critical data.

"Agents tend to treat e-mail much more informally than they would paper-based mail, using slang and writing things that they might regret

down the road, should that transaction become the subject of litigation,"
says Clark. "They also don't understand that data don't just disappear
once they're off the computer screens, and that they're usually stored on
their hard drives. We see too many agents put information in an e-mail to
their clients that they would never put in writing on a broker's letterhead."

With the advent of cross-state real estate transactions and systems like
broker reciprocity, Clark says, the issue is becoming even stickier for brokers and agents who share reams of data with service providers and business partners via computer. After all, who's to say whether the title company you do business with is as diligent about protecting data as you are?
And while the "paperless" transaction has yet to rear its head in any significant way, Clark says that when it does, the issue of consumer privacy
will play an even larger role in the typical real estate transaction.

"Right now it's a matter of treating and protecting your e-mail just as
you would treat your paper mail," says Clark. "The issue is sure to
become more complicated as real estate moves to a true paperless transaction, particularly when it comes to verifying that the recipient on the
'other end' of the transaction is really who he say he is."

To avoid legal problems with misuse of information, Clark suggests
that agents treat their e-mail—no matter how informal a note may seem
when they're pounding it out on the keyboard—just the way they would
treat paper mail. "It's just amazing how embarrassed and surprised an
agent can be when she sees an entire electronic mail exchange over six or
seven months retrieved and revealed during litigation," says Clark, who
also suggests retaining paper copies of all e-mail communications, just to
be on the safe side.

"It not only creates a paper trail," he says, "but it also forces agents to
stop and think about what they're writing and sending."

OTHER STICKY ISSUES

The list of potential legal risks for agents in the real estate field is long, and
it's getting longer. Those discussed here happen to be the ones that are
pushing agents' hot buttons right now, but there is a litany of other liabil-

ities that all real estate professionals should at least be aware of, if not somewhat educated about. One of the key areas is antitrust law, designed to prevent unreasonable restraints of trade.

You may read about price fixing and group boycotts on a global scale, but most agents don't relate to these issues on a day-to-day basis until they stop to think about how their commissions are determined. Because such fees are considered negotiable, the law prohibits competing brokers from talking about their commission rates or the level of commission that they offer cooperating brokers. It's not that the information isn't handy enough on the local MLS system, it's just that "discussion" of such issues between brokers could be construed as being antitrust. For agents, that means no preprinted commission rates on standard forms, and no discussing commission rates with competitors.

According to NAR, misrepresentation (the misstating of some material features of the property) is by far the legal issue that brokers need to be most aware of. In 1998, for example, 57 percent of the lawsuits brought against practitioners who were insured under the NAR-endorsed errors and omissions program were for misrepresentation, and 12 percent were for failure to disclose (not revealing an important feature of the property). The stickiest misrepresentation areas for agents included the home's foundation and structural features, property boundaries, roofs, and termite infestations, while disclosure lawsuits usually concerned easements, renovating without a permit, environmental problems, and title problems, according to NAR.

To limit the chance of getting involved in such lawsuits, NAR suggests using seller disclosure forms and always ensuring that the seller— not the agent—fills out the form. Get in writing or document all seller sources of information, and encourage the use of other professionals, like home inspectors and attorneys, as backup. And no matter how badly you want to get to the closing table, always avoid rash predictions like the one the agent in Texas made when she told the home buyer earlier in this chapter that the home was on a low flood plain, but that it "shouldn't flood."

Another critical—and growing—area of concern for brokers and

agents involves Real Estate Settlement Procedures Act (RESPA) violations. RESPA is covered in more depth in Chapter 8, but it deserves mention in a chapter on legal risks, since such violations occur when mortgage
brokers, lenders, title services, or real estate brokers give or receive anything of value in return for referrals. RESPA is designed to inform home
buyers about the costs of closing and eliminate kickbacks to settlement
service providers—real estate brokers included—for referrals.

RESPA is not actually a fully mature concept yet at this point, but
rather a work in progress that promises to gain more teeth as regulators
and groups like NAR push to get it modernized and amended. For now,
it's important that agents know that RESPA does permit referral fees
between two real estate brokers, but does not allow most other referral
fees. Also, if agents have ownership in another service provider—such as
a lender or an insurance company—to which they are referring a consumer, they must disclose it.

The good news in all this mess is that, despite the increasingly litigious society and a growing number of lawsuits, a 2002 report from
NAR's Legal Affairs staff revealed that real estate licensees are found "not
liable" in nearly 75 percent of those cases. That means that those agents
who steer clear of legal issues but who end up getting sucked into litigation have a three-in-four shot at being vindicated in the case, and being
free to go about doing what they do best.

YOUR BEST DEFENSE

If calls to the South Carolina Association of Realtors (SCAR) legal hotline
are any indication, agents and brokers in that particular state are concerned
about the care and handling of property disclosure forms. Hotline attorneys
received several calls in 2003 about the issue, and are charged with walking
members through the confusing disclosure maze.

To most agents, their advice is simple: "When dealing with the public, create a paper trail of agreements and disclosures." Several calls to the
hotline involved Realtors who did not pay attention to detail in getting
agency disclosures, buyer agency agreements, seller listing agreements,

seller disclosures, and dual agency forms signed. These oversights can cost members money or result in fines, remedial educational courses, reprimands, license suspension, probation, and commission checks.

For agents who are concerned about protecting themselves on the disclosure side, SCAR suggests using inspections as a liability shield. Create a checklist of all the different types of inspections available, the hotline attorneys advise, and let home buyers and sellers know that you highly recommend getting each of the various inspections listed. When presenting the form to the client, let them know that you understand that getting all the inspections may be cost-prohibitive, and have them initial the inspections that they want to have made and sign the bottom. Then keep this form in your file to order the inspections and to defend against any future lawsuits.

For real estate agents, the risks of getting sued or otherwise entangled in a lawsuit are much greater than for other sales-related professions. Because of the high dollar value of the home compared to, say, an automobile, the propensity of a buyer or seller to place blame on the service providers she relied on to get her through the transaction is high, and is something that can't be ignored.

One of your best defenses against such problems can be summed up in three simple words: disclose, disclose, disclose. Much as location, location, location is the key in commercial real estate, the "D" word should be rehearsed in triplicate in your industry. Because everyone from the individual agent to the real estate licensing board to NAR believes that buyers and sellers are entitled to fair dealings in their real estate transactions, the latter and its state and local constituents have created property disclosure statements, and recommend that agents use them for every single transaction—no exceptions. The general consensus is that as long as the seller has filled out the property disclosure form to the best of his knowledge and signed the form, then the service providers are effectively shielded from any potential liability, particularly when it comes to property defects.

To put it simply, the property disclosure statement is designed to protect everyone involved in a real estate transaction and to encourage full communication so that, having as much information as possible, buyers will pay and sellers will receive a fair price for the property. Unless certain important details are confirmed in writing on the property disclosure statements—such as an "as is" purchase, in which the seller is not responsible for any repairs or defects—sellers will be challenged to prove that a problem was disclosed to buyers, and buyers will probably be unable to recall whether a statement like "the pool pump doesn't work" was made, or whether that information was withheld.

The disclosure statement assists sellers in reviewing the condition of their property and provides a written record of the representations that were either made or not made. A complete disclosure statement reduces the risk of misunderstandings with the buyers, who often complain that a particular problem was not disclosed to them prior to the purchase. It's important that sellers don't just skim through the form but consider each question carefully to ensure that the most up-to-date, relevant information is reflected on this very important form.

Ultimately, it's up to the seller to decide whether she'll provide a disclosure statement to buyers, although most sellers realize the importance of it and know what it's like to be on the buy side of the transaction and be hungry for such information. Most sellers also realize that a complete disclosure statement will help increase the appeal of their property and reduce the risk of future complaints from the buyer.

As an agent, it's in your best interest to inform your sellers about the property disclosure form and why it's important. Since one of your primary roles involves communicating information between sellers and buyers, your position as an intermediary can quickly become undesirable when a buyer claims misrepresentation or claims that information was improperly withheld. In such a case, the sellers may claim that they relied on you to provide the necessary information to the buyers, leaving you stuck in the middle of a messy situation. To avoid such debacles, it's in your best interest to make sure that a properly completed disclosure statement that covers all relevant aspects of the property that's listed for sale is presented to the buyer. This ensures that all parties have access to the same, documented information.

Knowing that she's operating in a business environment where lawsuits run rampant and unhappy buyers are quick to blaze a trail to the door of the nearest law firm, Joyce Gomoljak, a Realtor with Champion Realty in Annapolis, Maryland, says that she advocates good property disclosures, gets everything in writing, and ends up with big, fat files of notes, records, and documents for every closed sale in the event that a problem arises, whether in the middle of the transaction or months down the road. Ultimately, she says, agents must be honest and aboveboard with every move they make during the sale, regardless of how badly they want to see it closed and moved off their "to do" list.

"Go with your gut instinct, even it if means going back and checking to see if a property floods in a hard rainstorm—even if the homeowner tells you that it doesn't," says Gomoljak, who also advises agents to inform sellers about home warranties, which cover the major appliances and systems in a home for a certain period of time (typically one year) after the sale (some can be extended at the buyer's cost and request once the initial period is over). "Get your sellers to take out home warranties," says Gomoljak, who asks buyers who decline a warranty to sign a document stating that they don't want one. When working with buyers to make an offer on a home that's not in too much demand (one that has been on the market for several months, for example), she also asks—in the contract—that a warranty be furnished, as further insurance for the buyer.

"A lot of sellers think that their homes are perfect, but if the furnace dies or the air compressor breaks a week after the sale, there could be implications," says Gomoljak, who gets no benefit financially from advocating home warranties, except peace of mind for all parties involved. "It's all in the name of disclosing, paying attention, following through on your promises, and just being completely honest from the start of the sale to the finish."

WHERE THERE'S MOLD

Everywhere David Pingree looks, he sees signs of potential litigation over toxic mold in homes. A broker-Realtor with Regency Real Estate in Mission Viejo, California, Pingree says that he's heard of brokers using mold disclosures and mold contract addendums to mitigate the risk, and says that home inspectors are getting more "mold savvy" and learning how to do moisture checks, take air samples, and carry out other tests to detect mold, even in homes where the visible walls might appear to be clean and mold-free. Pingree calls mold the top legal concern for agents right now, and adds that he and his team are working closely with buyers to ensure that the proper testing is done before the deals are signed and sealed.

"Mold is just the latest hot spot when it comes to potential litigation, and everyone in real estate is becoming more sensitive to it," says Pingree. "If we find any moisture or suspicious areas of a home, we get a mold inspector in to evaluate it immediately."

Of course, Pingree isn't surprised by the latest risk management issue for agents. He's been in real estate for seventeen years, and he says property disclosure statements were just beginning to surface when he closed his first deal. Since then, he's seen a proliferation of disclosure forms, addendums, and other paperwork involved in the deal—all in an effort to protect not only the home buyer and seller, but also the agent and other service providers, from potential litigation (see Figure 7-2).

To deal with it, Pingree says, agents need to stay on their toes and be more diligent about inspections and verifications of documents and files. In the past, home inspectors had gained a reputation as "deal killers" because revelation of the defects they found in properties sometimes killed the deal. Today, a good home inspector can be an agent's best friend, particularly if he ferrets out an undisclosed problem that the seller knowingly hid from the agent, broker, or buyer.

In 2002, for example, the Georgia Association of Realtors (GAR) added a mold-related question to its seller's property disclosure statement. Other states have taken a similar stance and added such a question to their own property disclosure statements, particularly in areas like Florida, California, and Texas, where mold problems have been especially prevalent. On the GAR form, the question is: "Are you aware of any recurring problems of mold in any dwelling on the property other than

Figure 7-2.

LEGAL Q&A

Across the country, state and local Realtor organizations provide legal advice to their members by phone on a daily basis, through attorneys that staff and monitor the groups' legal hotlines. Here's an example of a legal question that was recently fielded by the one Board of Realtors' legal and ethical hotline attorneys:

Question: I had a contract fall through because of a home inspection obtained by the buyer. The report indicated structural and mold problems with a particular listing. If I represent a second buyer under an exclusive buyer representation agreement, and the second buyer is now interested in the same listing, am I required or forbidden to give that buyer the information that I am privy to from that earlier inspection?

Answer: Normally, information obtained in your earlier representation (of the first buyer) would remain confidential. The law, however, says that the need to disclose any adverse facts about a property overrides your obligation to preserve the confidentiality of such information. Any licensee under Tennessee Code Annotated 66-5-206 "will be subject to a cause of action for damages or equitable relief for failing to disclose adverse facts to which the licensee has actual knowledge or notice." You are on notice that this particular piece of property has a mold and structural problem; therefore, you need to disclose these facts to the potential buyer to shield yourself from any liability.

We would caution you, nevertheless, not to convey any more information than the first inspection report conveyed—in other words, avoid interpretation of it—and advise the second buyer to consider his own inspection to confirm the property condition. [The original inspection report itself remains the property of the first buyer and therefore may not be passed along to any subsequent buyers.]

bathrooms?" Other states have posed the questions in different formats—all in an effort to shield their real estate professional members from potential liability risks should a mold issue surface at a later date.

According to Gomoljak, increased risk from legal liabilities has not only made the agent's job harder, but also forced agents to be much more cautious when working out in the field. Like Pingree, she too has seen her share of mold-related issues in the last year or so. Most recently, she says, she was attending a home inspection on a condominium that she'd just put under contract when the buyer noticed mold growing on an outer wall, near a furnace.

"She wanted to know what it was, and I said straight out, 'It looks like mold,'" says Gomoljak. "Then she wanted to know if it was 'bad' mold." Rather than taking a stab at the answer, Gomoljak informed the buyer that for an additional $250 she could have it tested to see how harmful or pervasive the problem was. The buyer opted for the mold test, and it turned out to indeed be "bad mold" of the *Staphylococcus* variety—something no condo buyer wants lurking around the outside of her dwelling.

The black stuff crawling up the wall didn't drive the buyer away, but it did prompt her to investigate several ways to eradicate the problem. It turned out she could either pay someone $1,000 to cut out a section of the outside wall and change out a piece of sheetrock or, at the abatement company's suggestion, simply spray Clorox on it. Gomoljak says that as an agent, she advised the buyer to do what made her most comfortable, and the buyer opted for choice number one.

"I didn't know a thing about mold, and I was very clear about that," Gomoljak says. "This was my first mold situation, and it worked out just fine, but it probably won't be the last. The key is to not make any assertions or suggestions and to instead point your customers in the direction of a professional who can help them solve the problem."

Whether the issue is mold, agency disclosure, property defects, or fair housing, Gomoljak says, an agent's best protection against potential litigation is to pay attention to what's going on in the home itself, be it a leaky basement, a flood plain, or an inoperable air conditioner. And while you're at it, keep a sharp eye out for sellers who could be a potential discrimination risk. (Remember the agent who was stressed over the rental agreement signed with an African American couple? Tsk, tsk.) And while it's certainly not the individual agent's responsibility to know everything that's going on, it's in your best interest to call customers on improper practices, potentially damaging defects, and other issues that could come back and bite you later (see Figure 7-3.)

"If you pay attention to the nuances of what is going on, you'll get a gut feeling as to whether it's right or wrong—that's a part of doing your complete job as an agent," says Gomoljak, who suggests that agents attend as many local educational courses as possible on timely legislative and legal topics, and that they look into getting certifications like the GRI, the broker's license, and other designations, all of which provide expanded educational options for agents.

"It's not so much about having the designation as about having this much education and background so that you know the right way to do things," says Gomoljak. "When you're up on the issues, people can't snow you, and you lessen your legal risks down the road. I'm always surprised at how many agents don't really know what they're talking about when it comes to the law, who they represent in the transaction, or when they should close their mouths and listen to the clients for a change."

GROWING CONCERNS

Dave Liniger, cofounder of RE/MAX International, says that the legal mistakes made in the real estate industry in the 1960s, 1970s, and 1980s led to a much keener attention to such issues in today's business environment. He adds that those early mistakes led to a "litigation explosion" that agents are now feeling the effects of and scrambling to shield themselves from, to avoid having both time and money tied up in costly legal suits.

One of their best defenses, says Liniger, is training. "The better trained agents are, even though they're busy doing more transactions and essentially increasing their risk, the better they're managing their business," says Liniger. "As an agent, you manage your legal risks by provid-

(text cont. on p.190)

Figure 7-3.

THE WHOLE NINE YARDS

For an idea of the overwhelming number of legal risks facing the real estate professional, check out the following list of article subjects. As of September 2003, NAR's library of Legal Connection articles included the following topics:

advertising

antisolicitation laws

arbitration

as-is clauses

boycotts

broker liability

buyer representation

caveat emptor

Code of Ethics

cold calling

commission disputes

committee reports

constitutional issues

consumer privacy disclosure regulations

copyright infringement

debt collection

designated agency

duties of agent

EIFS/synthetic stucco

employment policies

employment requirements for new parents/pregnant employees

federal facsimile regulations

group boycotts

harassment (sexual and hostile work environment claims)

homes magazines

independent contractors

ing superior service, dotting your i's and crossing your t's, and making sure that every commitment you make is covered."

Zifrony knows all about the litany of lawsuits spawning from hastily thrown together real estate deals of old. In fact, when he assembled his first home loan package for a bank in 1990, there were a paltry half-dozen documents for the home buyer to sign: a bank note, a mortgage, and a couple of disclosures. Today, he says, the typical home loan package includes about twenty-five documents for the homeowner to sign—each of which (with the exception of the original six documents) was created in response to some type of lawsuit that banks have been involved in over the years. "To make sure that never happened again, they created a document," says Zifrony, who singles out "communication" as the most important risk management tool in an agent's toolbox.

"When there's a lack of communication, problems arise," says Zifrony. He advises agents to always communicate information in writing, and—when they deem it necessary—have the buyer and/or the seller sign off on the communication. That will provide proof of the information sharing, should a legal problem develop in the future. For example, if a buyer tells you that certain home features are most important to her (remember the buyer of the sheetrock floor who says he wanted marble?), have her sign off on the document, which Zifrony says should be included in the purchase agreement.

When working with sellers, Zifrony says he's seen an increasing number of agents using property disclosures and ensuring that the seller signs such documents. To protect themselves, he advises agents to include in the disclosure language a statement like, "The only information that the real estate agent has is what the seller has revealed to him or her." That way, if an undocumented defect rears its ugly head, the agent can't be held liable because he knew nothing about it.

Looking ahead, Zifrony sees more legal issues coming down the pike for the real estate community, mainly because there are more practitioners in the field trying to grab a piece of the real estate pie. Everyone from retirees to ex-dot-comers to laid-off business executives is trying her hand at the business (see Chapter 1 for more specifics on the number of new entrants into the field), which means more potential legal hazards for those agents who would rather get a commission check than concern themselves with some mold growing on the outside of the wall of a condominium that they're ready to sell.

"There are more and more agents out there, and when you have that kind of influx into any profession, you're bound to get more and more bad ones," says Zifrony. "In the economy of the early 2000s, we've seen a lot of retirees take up real estate on the side, yet they have no experience in the field or knowledge of the various risks involved. Instead, they're focused on closing the deal. It won't take long for those who just jumped into the field to start falling into traps."

On a positive note, Zifrony points to the massive stacks of paperwork generated by the good agents, brokers, banks, and industry groups as something of a buffer for those who don't pay as much attention to risk management as they should. Good communication with buyers and sellers combined with excellent disclosure and documentation can probably shield even the uninitiated agent from the most basic risks.

Liniger also points to disclosure as the cornerstone of any agent's risk management approach. "As an agent, you can tame risk and legal issues by full disclosure—you do it through agency disclosure, advising the real estate customer that he ought to have a property inspection or that he needs to have representation," he continues. "As long as you are taking those steps, you're essentially removing yourself from risk. The better educated you are, the more professional designations you have, the better you understand the industry, the better service you are going to give and the better your risk management."

SIX THINGS TO REMEMBER FROM CHAPTER 7

❑ Managing risk and avoiding legal problems has always been a top-of-mind issue for real estate agents, but it's gained in importance in the last eight years.

❑ Operating in an increasingly litigious society as facilitator of one of the most important transactions a consumer will ever make puts real estate agents in a vulnerable spot when it comes to legal risks.

❑ Major issues that real estate agents are thinking about right now include property defects, agency disclosure, and fair housing law violations.

❑ In the information age, risk management for agents extends beyond just ensuring that homes are structurally sound and that agency relationships are properly disclosed; it also includes issues like consumer privacy and information sharing via electronic means.

❑ A real estate agent's best defenses against potential litigation include good disclosure, proper documentation, and an eye for recognizing potentially harmful practices like discrimination and fair housing violations.

❑ Despite the increasingly litigious society and a growing number of lawsuits, a 2002 report from NAR's Legal Affairs staff revealed that real estate licensees are found "not liable" in nearly 75 percent of those cases.

CHAPTER 8

Answering to a Higher Power

TRANSPARENT ISSUES

Most agents go about their daily business without too much interference from the outside forces that affect the real estate industry. And while knowledge of Real Estate Settlement Procedures Act (RESPA) violations, Brokerage Relationships in Real Estate Transactions Act (BRRETA) standards, and NAR's code of ethics may not help you net new customers, it can certainly put you into a small group of agents who not only know how to market and sell properties but also are intimately familiar with the rules and regulations of their industry. Unless you happen to violate one of the rules, you probably won't have to worry too much about them.

That is, you won't have to worry about them unless you want to go beyond customer-facing issues like technology and discount brokerages and become part of the small pool of agents and brokers who truly understand the industry they're operating in. That means knowing when to be concerned about your own safety while operating in the field; paying attention to what's going on with the nation's largest mortgage lender, Freddie Mac; and understanding how the Patriot Act could affect you and your company.

Those of you who don't have the time or the impetus to research and bone up on each of these topics one by one are in luck. In this chapter,

I've compiled a few of the "higher-power" issues that are affecting your industry right now—the kinds of things that could have long-term implications for successful agents. Like many changes going on in the industry, most of these are consumer-driven in that they're designed to protect the consumer from nasty stuff like predatory lending, high-fee loans, and collusion between the various parties who push the real estate transaction through to closing.

So this is where we look at the pertinent outside forces swirling around the real estate industry and break them down into digestible chunks that actually mean something to you as an agent. That includes acronyms like BRRETA and RESPA and issues like skyrocketing homeowner's insurance rates, taxes, and fees being placed on everything from new homes to your own income, and a federal do-not-call registry that threatens to do away with cold calling people with FSBO signs and expired listings (see Figure 8-1).

If this sounds a bit intimidating, you're right. That's because as a modern-day agent, you have issues to grapple with that your predecessors probably never even thought of. Your time is probably taken up with farming, marketing, showing and listing homes, and closing transactions. And while it's next to impossible to know each of these laws, regulations, and professional standards intimately, it is vital that agents know how to play by and follow the rules of the game.

NAR's Code of Ethics

Here's where we start, right at the root of the industry itself: the code of ethics that all Realtors® must follow. Adopted in 1913 and amended various times over the years, it's what sets Realtors apart from agents who are not NAR members, and it establishes obligations that may be higher than those mandated by law. But according to NAR, in any instance where the code of ethics and the law conflict, the obligations of the law must take precedence.

In its code of ethics, NAR acknowledges the real estate agent as a key player in the creation and sale of adequate housing. As such, Realtors have

Figure 8-1.

NO MORE LICENSES ON THE WALL IN TEXAS

It used to be a common sight: You would walk into any real estate office, and at least one full wall would be adorned with the framed licenses of every agent and broker working for the company. In 2003, real estate brokers in Texas learned that they could take down those licenses hanging on their office walls. The new law is H.B. 1508, and it updates the Texas Real Estate License Act. The law eases the burden on brokers, who for years have been forced to keep all of their agents' licenses hanging on the wall in clear view.

Bill Stinson, vice president of government affairs for the Texas Association of Realtors, says that the purpose of the original law was for agents to be able to prove that they were licensed. The law also provided consumers with information about the Texas Real Estate Commission as a place where they could file a complaint against an agent or broker.

"In this information age, most people know that on their own," says Stinson. "It was an old law that needed updating." He says that TAR lobbied successfully to have the antiquated law updated. The new law went into effect June 1, 2003.

"It's favorable for our members, particularly those brokers who have multiple offices and thousands of agents," says Stinston. "You can imagine what it's like trying to display and manage that many licenses on the wall."

---

a grave social responsibility and a patriotic duty to dedicate themselves to that cause. While working in the field, Realtors are expected to "maintain and improve the standards of their calling and share with their fellow Realtors a common responsibility for its integrity and honor."

NAR enforces the code of ethics and also assists appropriate regulatory bodies to eliminate practices that may damage the public or that might discredit or bring dishonor to the real estate profession. According to NAR, Realtors who have direct personal knowledge of conduct that may violate the code of ethics, such as misappropriation of client or customer funds or property, willful discrimination, or fraud resulting in substantial economic harm, should bring such matters to the attention of the appropriate association.

To put it simply, NAR's code of ethics should serve as something of a bible for every Realtor who wants to stay aboveboard in a changing industry. The document is updated regularly, and its most recent iteration is available online at www.realtor.org/mempolweb.nsf/pages/code.

LICENSING LAWS

Within each state there is one or more government departments or groups that are charged with overseeing real estate licensing, ensuring that licensees are practicing within the parameters of the law, and fielding consumer complaints about real estate professionals. Usually one department issues licenses (a bureau of professional licensing or division of real estate, for example), while another oversees the agents' and brokers' activities (usually a real estate commission). The setup varies by state, and here's a look at how the task is handled in a few different states.

In Utah, for example, a real estate commission determines the qualifications required for all applicants for a Utah real estate license. Each applicant is required to provide evidence of honesty, integrity, truthfulness, reputation, and competency, and must pass an examination covering the fundamentals of the English language, arithmetic, bookkeeping, real estate principles and practices, the rules established by the commission, and any other aspect of Utah Real Estate License Law that is considered appropriate.

Utah also has a Division of Real Estate (within the Department of Commerce for the State of Utah), which provides public protection in the real estate marketplace through the education and licensure of real estate brokers, sales agents, and appraisers and the registration of mortgage lenders. The Division of Real Estate issues real estate licenses and dictates that, in order to obtain a license, ninety hours of education from a certified school and completion of a national and state licensing test are required.

In California, the Department of Real Estate is charged with protecting the public in real estate transactions and providing related services to the real estate industry. It also issues and renews real estate licenses, while the state's Real Estate Advisory Commission (REAC), presided over by the commissioner, meets and consults on policies of the Department of Real Estate.

In Florida, the Department of Business and Professional Regulation, Division of Real Estate, handles the licensing of real estate agents and brokers, while the seven-member Florida Real Estate Commission (FREC) administers and enforces the real estate license law, Chapter 475, Part I, Florida Statutes. The commission is also empowered to pass rules that enable it to implement its statutorily authorized duties and responsibilities.

Groups like FREC play key roles in changing license laws, and this can be very important for real estate licensees, who often learn of the changes and updates through their continuing education courses. In Florida, the commission recently overhauled its Chapter 475 license law, which hadn't been amended in any significant manner since the land boom of the 1920s forced the state to enact it. Key changes in 2003 included a clarification that customers are not responsible for the acts of a transaction broker and that the licensee will not work for one party to the detriment of the other, and gave the department the ability to license a broker associate or sales associate as an individual, a professional corporation, or a limited liability company.

Continuing Education

For real estate agents, it's the same drill every two years: Sign up for a fourteen-hour continuing education (CE) course (the requirements vary by state, so check with your local licensing department or real estate commission for specifics) before your license expires in order to keep your license current. It's a lot like a visit to the dentist for most agents: They don't enjoy it, but they know they have to do it. Call it drudgery if you will, but there are strategies for choosing the right CE course, then maximizing the experience so that you take away valuable knowledge and information that you can use in your day-to-day business.

In Florida, for example, according to the Florida Real Estate Commission's (FREC) prescribed CE requirements, real estate brokers and salespersons are required to complete fourteen hours of CE every two years after their first license renewal, and prior to their license expiration date. Chapters 1, 2, and 3 of a course generally meet the commission's "core law" requirement, while the remaining chapters are "specialty education" sections that are of use to real estate professionals.

As a real estate agent with ERA Mount Vernon Realty in Sarasota, John Souders has been using correspondence courses to fulfill his CE requirement for the last eight years. Every time he goes through the fourteen-hour regimen and takes the exam, he learns something new. The last time around, it came in the form of several "case studies" that were worked into the course. Rather than telling Souders what was right and what was wrong, the course prompted him to make choices, then determine how good or bad they were.

According to Souders, each case study highlighted an agent's actions and the ramifications of the agent's individual choices. "It was very interesting because I was able to make my own judgment on how the particular situation should have been handled," says Souders. "I read some of them and thought, 'Well, that's not so bad,' when in reality it was bad, and the agent would have gotten slammed for it in a real-life setting."

Souders says that those anecdotes, taken from a correspondence course produced by The Real Estate School, Inc., opened his eyes because he could relate to them on a very personal level. He then took his new-found knowledge out into the business world.

"You can do all the reading you want, but when you get out into the field and see things going on, it's a different story," says Souders, adding that the fourteen-hour CE courses have been invaluable for keeping up with new real estate laws. "As real estate agents we tend to relax and take things for granted, but when we see these cases in black and white, we come away with a whole new perspective."

RESPA

In 1974 Congress enacted the Real Estate Settlement Procedures Act (RESPA) to address problems in the real estate settlement process that were seen at that time. Those problems included abusive practices that increased costs to home buyers and a lack of understanding on the part of home buyers of the real estate settlement process and the costs associated with it. Enter RESPA, an act with a double purpose: (1) to provide the consumer with information about the real estate mortgage transaction and the costs associated with it, and (2) to prohibit certain practices, such as referral fees between settlement service providers, that result in higher costs and reduced quality to the consumer (see Figure 8-2).

From RESPA came the good-faith estimate (GFE) and the HUD-1 closing document, which mortgage companies now use with all of their customers. To fight high transaction costs, Section 8 of RESPA makes it a criminal act for settlement service providers to pay each other fees for the referral of business. Section 8 prohibits anyone from giving or accepting a fee, kickback, or anything of value in exchange for referrals of settlement service business involving a federally related mortgage loan. In addition, RESPA prohibits fee splitting and receiving unearned fees for services not actually performed.

Violations of Section 8's antikickback, referral fees, and unearned fees provisions are subject to criminal and civil penalties. In a criminal case, a person who violates Section 8 may be fined up to $10,000 and imprisoned for up to one year. In a private lawsuit, a person who violates Section 8 may be liable to the person charged for the settlement service for an amount equal to three times the amount of the charge paid for the service.

To help consumers become better shoppers for settlement services and to eliminate kickbacks and referral fees that unnecessarily increase the costs of certain settlement services, RESPA requires that borrowers receive disclosures at various times. Some disclosures spell out the costs associated with the settlement, outline lender servicing and escrow

Figure 8-2.

RESPA REQUIRED DISCLOSURES

Here's a snapshot of the RESPA disclosures that home buyers are entitled to when purchasing a home, and that real estate agents should be aware of:

At the time of the loan application:

When borrowers apply for a mortgage loan, mortgage brokers and/or lenders must give the borrowers the following information. If the borrowers don't get the documents at the time of application, the lender must mail them within three days of receiving the loan application:

❏ A Special Information Booklet that contains consumer information regarding various real estate settlement services and a good-faith estimate (GFE) of settlement costs

❏ A Mortgage Servicing Disclosure Statement, which discloses to the borrower whether the lender intends to service the loan or transfer it to another lender

Before closing occurs:

❏ An Affiliated Business Arrangement (AfBA) Disclosure must be given to the consumer at or before the time of referral whenever a settlement service provider (such as a title company) involved in a RESPA-covered transaction refers the consumer to a provider with whom the referring party has an ownership or other beneficial interest. This disclosure outlines the business arrangement between the two parties, and gives the borrower an estimate of the second provider's charges.

❏ One day before the actual closing date, borrowers can request a HUD-1 Settlement Statement, a standard form that clearly shows all charges imposed on borrowers and sellers in connection with the settlement.

Disclosures at settlement:

❏ At the closing table, the HUD-1 Settlement Statement is provided, showing the actual settlement costs of the loan transaction. Separate forms are typically prepared for the borrower and the seller. If either party is not at the table, the HUD-1 is typically mailed or delivered right after the closing.

❏ The borrower is also given the Initial Escrow Statement, which itemizes the estimated taxes, insurance premiums, and other charges that will be paid from the escrow account during the first year of the loan. (The lender has forty-five days from closing to deliver this form).

Disclosures after settlement:

❏ Every year, loan servicers deliver to borrowers an annual escrow statement that summarizes all escrow account deposits and payments during the servicer's twelve-month computation year. It also notifies the borrower of any shortages or surpluses in the account and advises the borrower about the course of action being taken.

❏ If the loan servicer sells or assigns the servicing rights to the borrower's loan to another loan servicer (essentially "selling" the loan to another mortgage company), then borrowers will receive a Servicing Transfer Statement within fifteen days of the effective date of the loan transfer.

---

account practices, and describe business relationships between settlement service providers.

RESPA also prohibits certain practices that increase the cost of settlement services. In addition to the provisions in Section 8 of RESPA just described, Section 9 of RESPA prohibits home sellers from requiring home buyers to purchase title insurance from a particular company.

RESPA covers loans secured with a mortgage on a one- to four-family residential property. These include most purchase loans, assumptions, refinances, property improvement loans, and equity lines of credit.

HUD's Office of Consumer and Regulatory Affairs, Interstate Land Sales/RESPA Division, is responsible for enforcing RESPA.

RESPA has been revised and amended over the years to address new business practices, yet it continues to exist in somewhat of a state of flux, as not everyone really knows which fees are and which are not prohibited. For example, can a lender set up a contest for real estate agents under which the agent who provides the lender with the most business will win a trip to Hawaii? No, says HUD, because under RESPA, the trip itself, and even the opportunity to win the trip, would be a thing of value given in exchange for the referral of business.

But can a lender give a real estate agent note pads with the lender's name on it? Yes, says HUD, because such note pads with the lender's name on it would be allowable as normal promotional items. *However,* if the lender gives the real estate agent note pads with the real estate agent's name on it for the agent to use to market its real estate business, then the note pads could be a thing of value given for referral of loan business, because it defrays a marketing expense that the real estate agent would otherwise incur.[1]

The fact that the lines are somewhat blurred make it difficult for settlement service providers to conduct business together, knowing that a Section 8 violation could result in both criminal and civil penalties. RESPA, which is currently undergoing regulatory reform, can be a real spider web for individual agents who get involved with referral fees.

BRRETA

Another acronym that comes up in the real estate profession is BRRETA, or the Brokerage Relationships in Real Estate Transaction Act, which lays down the law on the representation relationships between brokers and consumers (which can include buyers, sellers, landlords, and tenants). BRRETA provides for disclosure to all parties in a real estate transaction and sets forth the obligations of licensees to their customers and clients.

---

[1] HUD Web site, www.hud.gov/offices/hsg/sfh/res/resindus.cfm.

BRRETA was adopted in 1994 to codify the common law of agency with respect to real estate brokerage transactions. The law has been beneficial in that it has clarified the duties and obligations of real estate brokers when they are working with buyers, sellers, landlords, and tenants. This law provides for agency relationships to be established when buyer or seller (or a landlord or tenant) authorizes a broker, by executing a brokerage engagement, to represent that buyer or seller (landlord or tenant) in a real estate transaction. BRRETA further provides for disclosure of representation to parties to the transaction and sets forth the obligations and responsibilities of the parties. The law allows each real estate company to incorporate specific BRRETA provisions into its agency policy.

BRRETA defines terms relating to a real estate transaction, including *agency*, which includes every relationship in which a real estate broker acts for or represents another person by the latter's express authority in a real estate transaction; and *broker*, which includes any individual or entity issued a broker's real estate license by his or her state real estate commission.

In a real estate transaction, brokerage engagements are established when a buyer or seller (landlord or tenant) engages a broker for representation. The roles of each party are described in the brokerage agreement (for example, either an Exclusive Seller [or Landlord] Brokerage Engagement or an Exclusive Buyer [or Tenant] Brokerage Engagement). When a buyer or seller, landlord or tenant enters into a brokerage engagement, that person becomes a client of the broker.

For the most part, following BRRETA rules will rest on the shoulders of your broker, whose job it is to develop and maintain a written office policy that sets forth the agency and brokerage relationships that agents can establish with clients. Under BRRETA, the broker must disclose in writing the types of agency and brokerage relationships the broker is offering to a particular person and allow that party the right to refuse or choose among the various real estate relationships. The following real estate relationships are valid under most state BRRETA laws, though it's best to check with your own state real estate commission or association for specific information:

Single agent—seller's/landlord's agent. This agent works on behalf of the seller or landlord and owes duties, which include good faith, loyalty, and fidelity, to the seller or landlord. The agent will negotiate on behalf of and act as an advocate for the seller/landlord. The agent may not disclose confidential information without the express authority of the seller or landlord.

Single agent—buyer's/tenant's agent. This agent works on behalf of the buyer or tenant and owes duties, which include good faith, loyalty, and fidelity, to the buyer or tenant. The agent will negotiate on behalf of and act as an advocate for the buyer or tenant. The agent may not disclose confidential information without the express authority of the buyer or tenant.

Disclosed limited agent. This agent works on behalf of more than one client to a transaction; before doing so, the informed written consent of the clients is required. A limited agent may not disclose confidential information about one client to another without written permission releasing that information.

Transaction broker. A transaction broker exercises reasonable skill and care in assisting one or more parties with a real estate transaction without being an advocate for any party. Although the transaction broker will help facilitate the transaction, the licensee will serve as a neutral party, offering no client-level services (such as negotiation) to the customer.

FEDERAL NO-CALL RULES

Cold-calling numbers captured from FSBO yard signs, telephoning customers who bought a home seven years ago, and faxing a page of current listings to prospective customers are common business strategies in residential real estate. Thanks to a new Federal Trade Commission law (which was supposed to go into effect in October 2003, but was still under consideration at press time as a result of attempts by state judges to block it), these and other business practices risk being made illegal, and worthy of hefty fines.

While many states already had their own "do not call" laws on the books before 2003, the issue went national when the FTC decided to give consumers a choice as to whether they want to receive telemarketing calls. On October 1, 2003, it began enforcing the National Do Not Call Registry provisions of the Amended Telemarketing Sales Rule. A violation by a company can result in a fine of up to $11,000. By July 2003, more than 23 million people had already signed up to have their phone numbers registered.

While telephone solicitation isn't the most popular form of marketing for real estate agents, most of them do keep in touch with former clients, contacts, prospects, and other sources of leads or information. On the bright side, the rule does allow companies—and that includes you—to continue contacting existing customers, whether they're in the registry or not, for up to 18 months after a consumer's last purchase, delivery, or payment. The rule also allows for contact with prospective customers who initiate contact, as long as the call takes place within three months of the initial inquiry.

The problem is that homeowners typically move every seven years, which means that the agent who picks up the phone to call a customer to whom she sold a home five or six years ago would have to check the "do not call" list to make sure that the customer's number isn't on it before dialing, or risk a hefty fine. Under the FTC-approved fee schedule, the annual cost to companies for accessing phone numbers in the registry will be $25 per area code, up to a maximum annual fee of $7,375 to access numbers for the entire country. There will be no charge to companies for accessing the first five area codes of data.

The new rule hasn't sat well with the real estate community, and both NAR and state groups have scrambled to gain exemptions for their members, particularly on the fax side of the issue. Joe Ventrone, managing director for regulatory and industry relations for NAR, says that the group is not opposed to the federal do not call registry, but adds that it has "operational concerns regarding the use of fax transmissions," as well as policy clarifications on the registry as it relates to expired listings and FSBOs.

"NAR does not want to send or receive unsolicited faxes, but simply wants the FTC to clarify how one can give express consent, and wants a realistic amount of time to come into compliance," says Ventrone. In response to petitions for stay filed by NAR, CAR, and other organizations, in August the FTC ordered an eighteen-month delay (until January 2005) in the implementation of its do-not-fax rule in order to give businesses more time to comply with the rule.

For now, agents who engage in cold calling would be wise to get their hands on the national registry. Developed and maintained by the FTC, the list will have to be purchased every three to four months, then checked against your database to make sure that new folks haven't been added since the last time you checked. It's burdensome, to be sure, but it has a good intent—after all, who really wants all of those annoying telemarketing calls during dinner?

Greg Herder of Hobbs/Herder Training says that many real estate agents think that the new rules mean that they can never call past clients, FSBOs, expireds, or people in farm areas without first checking to see if these people are on the do-not-call list. For those agents who think that these valuable business avenues will disappear as a result of the new rules, Herder suggests that they familiarize themselves with the actual FTC rules and regulations for the national do-not-call list. Pay particular attention to Section VI 109–119, which deals with established business relationships, and Section IX 136–145.

Herder says that agents clearly have the right to indefinitely call past clients to follow up, provide information, educate, and build or reinforce the relationship with those clients, even if they are on the do-not-call list. The regulations say that during the first eighteen months after a transaction, agents are also free to call them purely to solicit new business. After eighteen months, however, you can no longer call former clients to solicit new business. This probably includes calling them purely to ask for referrals, but it doesn't prohibit agents from making calls to provide them with information that they value or making purely relationship-building calls that show clients that you truly do care about them.

"The good news is that the regulations allow agents to send relationship-building and informational messages by voice broadcast as well," says

Herder. "I have found that this type of call creates a positive image for you in the client's mind and will enhance the effectiveness of your complete marketing campaign. In fact, these are the only types of past-client calls we have ever taught agents to use as part of a past-client marketing plan."

For example, Herder says, agents can make informational calls and voice broadcast calls to farm areas with messages like the following: "Hi, this is Mary Agent with XYZ Realty. I wanted to let you know that the home at 13345 Oakview Lane sold for $349,000. The home was highly upgraded with a newly remodeled kitchen. I just wanted to keep you up-to-date on home values in your area."

Herder admits that there are persistent unanswered questions regarding calling FSBOs and people with expired listings. For the latter, the previous listing agent has eighteen months during which it can call and try to relist the property. However, he says, the rules are unclear about whether another agent from the same company—as well as the first agent—can also call. "This issue will probably end up being decided by the courts," says Herder, adding that whether an agent can pick up the phone and cold-call an FSBO is also ambiguous. However, he says that because an FSBO is soliciting buyers for the house, an agent could call if he was representing a buyer that had an interest in the home.

"If you are calling purely to try to sell your services as a listing agent," Herder explains, "you probably should not call." Overall, Herder says, the federal do-not-call rules should help improve real estate professionals' image, mainly by getting rid of calls that irritate consumers and undermine the callers' professionalism.

SKYROCKETING INSURANCE RATES

As senior vice president of residential lending for Borel Private Bank and Trust in San Francisco, Martha Johnson hears a lot of home buyers griping about the cost and availability of homeowner's insurance. "I've seen everyone from the clients who have trouble lining up insurance at rates that they feel are affordable to those whose insurance companies refuse to insure properties at all," says Johnson. "The issue has not derailed any purchase or prevented anyone from buying a home, but it has caused people to have to search around quite a bit more and pay more than they thought they would have to for insurance."

The cost of homeowner's insurance jumped by a median of 13 percent in 2002, with mold being blamed as the leading cause, according to the Consumer Federation of America. The group surveyed state insurance departments in late 2001 and early 2003 to determine why homeowner's insurance was becoming so costly. Price hikes in 2002 ranged from 4 percent in Oregon to 57 percent in Texas. The states listed mold as the leading cause of increases, followed by catastrophes, decreases in investment income, and costly reinsurance.

That homeowner's insurance rates are rising so quickly as the providers are getting pickier about which properties they insure is a national issue. In May 2003, NAR approved a five-point policy on homeowner's insurance in response to the national crisis in premium costs and access to affordable insurance for consumers. The policy addresses NAR assistance for state association legislative/regulatory insurance dealings, federal policy recommendations, alternative insurance product recommendations, Realtor education efforts, and recommendations for state associations' consideration and activity.

TAXING MATTERS

Also raising concern in real estate circles is the increasing number of taxes and impact fees being placed on real estate concerns. (Impact fees are fees that cities or counties charge developers or builders for each new house that is built in a community. Builders pay the fees and typically pass on the cost to buyers.) When the economy dipped into recession, most states felt the pinch of less revenues and began seeking out areas where they could raise funds. Real estate was one of the first places they looked, and a number of builder and real estate associations have been fighting tooth and nail to keep those fees away from the consumers' pocketbook.

Their actions are justified: A 1998 study by the Real Estate Center at Texas A&M University determined the degree to which an increase in cost of $1,000 could affect someone's ability to buy a new home. Researchers concluded that if the median cost of new homes went up by $1,000, then 24,000 potential home buyers wouldn't be able to afford homes in that median price range. NAR research backs up the claim, and revealed that for every $100 home price increase, between 1,575 and 1,800 households in any particular state would be priced out of the market. Were the price of a home to be increased by $500 as a result of added taxes, for example, it would prevent as many as 9,400 households from being able to afford a home.

In Arkansas, two bills that would have added to homeowners' tax burdens were effectively defeated in the 2003 legislative session. HB 2367, which would have increased the current real estate transfer tax by 10 cents, and SB 697, which would have instituted a $1.75 per parcel of land property tax, were both shelved.

"These two pieces of legislation were very important to our industry, and we were even criticized by some of the legislators for not helping them pass the bills into law," says Bob Balhorn, Arkansas Realtors® Association (ARA) executive vice president and lobbyist, who admits that the amounts of both taxes were fairly minor. "But once you open that door for more taxation, it just keeps growing."

On the transfer tax issue, Balhorn says that ARA was adamant about keeping the state's rate of $3.30 per $1,000 in property value, which he adds is "right in line" with what states around the country are charging. As for the $1.75 per-parcel tax, which would have been levied against all property owners, Balhorn calls it inequitable because it was a flat rate for all property owners. The owner of a single-family home, for example, would have paid the same amount of tax as the owner of a shopping mall.

HOUSING AFFORDABILITY

It's the great oxymoron of the real estate world right now: Low interest rates are driving more first-time home buyers into the market, yet in many areas of the country, fewer households can afford to buy homes. The news doesn't bode well for agents working in states like California, where the percentage of households able to afford a median-priced home stood at a dismal 27 percent in mid-2003, a 1 percent decrease compared to the same period in 2002. The minimum household income needed to buy a median-priced home at $369,290 was $84,980, up from $81,510 in mid-2002. The state was well below the national average of 59 percent (up from 56 percent in 2002).

The state numbers concern Leslie Appleton-Young, California Association of Realtors'® chief economist, who says that if the current downward spiral continues, homeownership in the state will be out of grasp of the middle class within twenty years. "It would be a tragedy for the state, but we seem to be headed that way," says Appleton-Young. "It's hard to imagine how many college graduates could afford to buy the median-priced home in many California communities today without significant help from their parents. It's a huge issue here in that we're certainly much less affordable that the rest of the nation. Our homeownership rate is 10 percent lower than the national numbers, and our median home price is twice the national median home price."

The problem isn't limited to California, with its 20-plus percent housing appreciation rates, although the national numbers do paint a prettier picture, at least for now. Nationwide, NAR reported that housing affordability slipped by 0.7 percent during the second quarter of 2003, though appreciation rates were still at their highest level since 1973. NAR's second-quarter composite Housing Affordability Index was 143.4, down 0.7 percent from a thirty-year high of 144.1 reported in the first quarter. The West posts the lowest housing affordability rate, followed by the South, Northeast, and Midwest, respectively.

For real estate agents, housing affordability is a key measure, mainly because not every buyer will have cash in hand and excellent credit. The typical first-time buyer, in fact, is just like everyone else: He has a few credit blemishes, had to scrape together a down payment, and is probably scared silly about the thought of owning a home of his own. While most states have managed to keep housing affordability high enough for potential home buyers to gain access to homes that they can afford, agents would be wise to keep an eye on this measure in their own region for any major fluctuations. NAR releases both monthly and quarterly data online at http://www.realtor.org/Research.nsf/Pages/HousingInx.

FREDDIE MAC SHAKEUP

Somewhere in the middle of 2003's booming home sales, historically low interest rates, and rising home appreciation, something went terribly wrong at the nation's second largest U.S. mortgage finance company, leaving the real estate industry up in arms about oversight of government-sponsored enterprises (GSEs).

Established in 1970 to help address the nation's housing finance needs, Freddie Mac is a stockholder-owned corporation focused on creating a continuous flow of funds to mortgage lenders in support of homeownership and rental housing. Freddie Mac doesn't make individual mortgage loans to consumers, but it does ensure that there is a continuous flow of funds to mortgage lenders. As a secondary market for mortgage loans, Freddie Mac purchases mortgages from lenders across the country and packages them into securities that can be sold to investors.

Freddie Mac's accomplishments took a back seat to its problems in 2003, when the corporation announced a series of dramatic exits by key members of its executive staff. The mainstay of the mortgage industry came under unprecedented scrutiny, firing its president and COO over his apparent unwillingness to cooperate with an audit of the firm. The firm's CEO and CFO followed in Glenn's footsteps, leaving the industry wondering what in the world was going on at Freddie Mac.

The shake-up came after it was revealed that management was not fully cooperating with internal auditors who were examining earnings statements from 2000 through 2002. The Office of Federal Housing Enterprise Oversight (OFHEO), the federal agency that oversees Freddie Mac, stated in a letter to Freddie Mac's board that the management shake-up "only goes part of the way toward correcting serious problems." The OFHEO currently has a special team looking into Freddie Mac's re-audit.

As the investigation continues, the real estate industry is scratching its head over the level of congressional oversight being exerted over the mortgage powerhouse, and whether it's high enough. As this book went to press, many real estate professionals, mortgage brokers, and homeowners were watching closely as events unfolded at Freddie Mac because of speculation on the effect the situation will have on the housing market, given Freddie Mac's size and prowess.

BLOWING BUBBLES

There's been talk of a real estate bubble—similar to the technology bubble of the late 1990s that swelled to unbelievable proportions before bursting all over everyone—but so far it has yet to show its face. In fact, home sales remained one of the strongest sectors of the U.S. economy through 2001 and 2002 and well into 2003 and don't appear to be letting up anytime soon.

What worries some economists is housing appreciation. In some areas of the country, housing values have risen by over 20 percent from 2002 to 2003. California tops the list with a range of 17 to 23 percent appreciation during that time, followed by certain pockets in Florida (17 percent), Massachusetts (14 percent), and New Hampshire (13 percent).[3]

The Federal Reserve has good news for real estate agents who are challenged enough trying to operate in a changing business environment without worrying about their bubble bursting. In remarks at an economic conference in San Francisco sponsored by the Federal Reserve Bank of San Francisco and the Stanford Institute for Economic Policy Research on February 28, 2003, Federal Reserve governor Donald Kohn said that there was little reason to worry that the current low interest rates might cause a potential bubble in the rate-sensitive housing market.

"The rise in housing prices and the increase in household investment in houses and consumer durables do not appear out of line with what

---

[3] Office of Federal Housing Enterprise Oversight, a division of the Department of Housing and Urban Development.

might be expected in the current environment of low interest rates and continuing growth in real disposable incomes," Kohn said. (See Chapter 9 for NAR's take on the future of home sales).

THE PATRIOT ACT

Thanks to the increased emphasis on national security and oversight of financial transactions in the wake of 9/11, real estate agents, brokers, and other professionals who handle money and financial transactions have found themselves at the center of a complex issue: money laundering, or the process of converting funds that were illegally obtained into funds that appear to be legally earned (see Figure 8-3).

That's right. When this book went to press, Realtor groups were closely watching and lobbying over a provision that requires financial institutions (which, by definition, include persons involved in real estate closings and settlements) to implement programs designed to help the government prevent, detect, and prosecute international money laundering and financing of terrorism. The Patriot Act amends the Bank Secrecy Act, which already requires real estate brokers and other businesses to file notices with the Treasury when they handle cash transactions of $10,000 or more and conduct other transactions that meet "suspicious definitions."

Should Uncle Sam decide that brokers should have a key role under the Patriot Act, your neighborhood real estate office would have to designate or hire a compliance officer; develop internal policies, procedures, and controls; establish an employee-training program; and implement an independent audit function to test the anti-money laundering programs. NAR has taken a stand against this interpretation, claiming that the burden of compliance would far outweigh any benefit in terms of detecting money-laundering schemes. NAR also says that real estate licensees shouldn't be considered financial institutions because they don't receive or distribute money on behalf of the parties to a real estate transaction, other than holding earnest money.

Through NAR's efforts, the real estate industry is seeking an exclu-

Figure 8-3.

WHAT'S THE PATRIOT ACT?

For those of you who thought that stopping money launderers was mostly left up to organizations like the FBI and CIA, think again. Since April 2002, the government has enlisted financial institutions to help in thwarting these criminals. That includes banks, savings and loans, credit unions, securities brokers, credit card firms, and others, who now are required to institute antimoney-laundering programs (AMLs), per Section 352 of the Patriot Act.

The programs must include the following:

- ❏ Written policies, procedures, and controls for customer identification, reporting suspicious activity and large currency transactions, and customer due diligence
- ❏ An AML compliance office
- ❏ An ongoing employee training program
- ❏ An independent audit function to test how efficient the AML program is

---

sion from the anti-money laundering provisions of the Patriot Act. If it loses the fight, agents could be required to verify the identity of clients by obtaining drivers' licenses and other records, and to look for clients' names on the governments' antiterrorist lists. Keep a close eye on this issue, as it could increase the burden on everyone, from the large brokers to the individual agents, who are likely to find themselves helping in the hunt for terrorists and suspicious activity during the home-buying process.

BE CAREFUL OUT THERE

A book on how to survive and prosper in the challenging world of real estate would be remiss if it didn't include mention of agents' safety while they are working out in the field. As a very visible bunch who use everything from billboards to colorful photo business cards to magnetic vehicle signs to get the word out about their businesses, real estate agents aren't always aware of how vulnerable they are when they are working in the community.

The Real Estate Safety Council, a nonprofit organization dedicated to improving safety in the workplace, reports that twenty-one real estate agents were murdered in the United States while on the job in 2000. A total of 206 agents died as a result of violent assaults from 1982 through 2000. In 2003, NAR—which doesn't track such numbers itself—adopted a philosophy of "safety in numbers" and announced the first safety product selected for its ongoing initiative to improve agent safety. The product, Mobile Callback (produced by trade publication *Realty Times*), allows Realtors to receive prearranged calls on their mobile phones to monitor their location.

The system is programmed to call back within five minutes of an agent's establishing a showing location. If for some reason the subscriber does not answer her phone after three attempts, live operators are notified that the user needs emergency response and alerts the closest authority.

Agents can also protect themselves in a more basic manner: by doing due diligence up front and developing relationships before getting into a car to drive around showing homes. If your gut tells you that something could be fishy about a certain buyer (say, someone who knows that you're a single woman and calls at odd hours of the night to ask about "properties"), then think twice before putting yourself in a compromising position.

Due diligence means finding out how serious people are and whether they're prequalified, and doing it without alienating a potential client. If possible, make your first meeting with a client on your turf, at your office, even though it may be an inconvenience. And because visiting vacant properties in unfamiliar neighborhoods—very often at night—is a normal part of an agent's job, bring a buddy along with you when you do so, particularly if it's your first visit to the home. Follow precautionary safety rules, always carry your cell phone, and be aware of your surroundings.

Open houses, where potential buyers are free to roam through homes, touching and feeling along the way, open yet another door for potential harm. Such situations call for precautionary procedures, including a mandatory sign-in or registration sheet and the presentation of identification. Set up a time to check in with someone at the office every hour to verify that everything is going well, and again, bring someone along if possible. Remember that no matter how badly you want or need the deal, it's not worth your health or your life.

MORE TO COME

In the interest of consumers, you can expect more oversight and regulation of the real estate industry, since NAR reports that all aspects of the housing transaction are controlled through either law or regulation. Insurance and taxes are both necessary evils, so expect more of both to sneak into the transaction. Stay up to date on licensing laws and your continuing education requirements, and keep your fingers crossed that you won't have to hunt down money launderers. All of these issues and more make up the outside forces that you have to deal with in order to be a successful, conscientious professional in an changing industry.

And while it's your broker who ultimately has to comply with the Patriot Act, it's still up to the individual agent to follow the rules and stay on the right side of the regulators and rule makers in order to maintain a healthy, steady income flow. Remember that this book isn't meant to be a comprehensive aid in your conquest, but rather a primer that you can add to your toolbox when working. If these or other issues arise during your career, your best bet is to consult with the governing body or an attorney for more help on how to deal with them.

As the complexity of the process increases, NAR says, consumers will look to real estate professionals for answers. That will make real estate agents even more valuable for their ability to explain the requirements and process the paperwork. However, the increased disclosure requirements and other regulations have also raised the cost of doing business for all real estate professionals, says NAR, which adds that every time a new regulation is issued, real estate brokerage firms must consult with their lawyers and train their sales agents, adding to the challenge of operating a profitable real estate firm.

Going forward, you can probably expect more, not less, oversight of the real estate industry. In NAR's report "The Future of Real Estate Brokerage," the group states that the growing number of regulations may be designed to protect consumers, but can have the unintended consequence of increasing the complexity of the real estate transaction. To assist consumers as they navigate the myriad regulations involved in the real estate transaction, says NAR, agents need to understand the requirements of the process and educate consumers on them. That means being able to gather and disseminate information and knowledge on everything from RESPA to housing affordability, taxes, and good faith estimates, and everything in between.

Six Things to Remember from Chapter 8

- ❏ Over the years, a wide range of rules and regulations have been placed on the real estate industry, mainly in an attempt to protect consumers from unethical or unfair practices.

- ❏ Many agents go about their business blissfully unaware of these regulations until they happen to violate one or more of them and get into trouble.

- ❏ As responsible licensees, real estate agents and brokers are expected to comply with everything from NAR's code of ethics to state real estate licensing laws to continuing education requirements.

- ❏ Acronyms like RESPA and BRRETA may sound intimidating to the average agent, and their concepts may not be fully developed and honed, but that doesn't mean that agents can afford to ignore them.

- ❏ Going forward, you can expect more, not less, oversight of the real estate industry, according to NAR, which reports that the growing number of regulations may be designed to protect consumers, but can have the unintended consequence of increasing the complexity of the real estate transaction.

❑ To assist consumers as they navigate the myriad regulations involved in the real estate transaction, agents need to understand the requirements of the entire process and educate consumers on them.

CHAPTER 9

Spotting Real Estate Trends

TRACKING CHANGES

Every industry has its share of experts and analysts who like to talk about the hottest trends and what's coming around the next corner. Real estate has a lot of these people, although the individual agent who is toiling away in the field probably doesn't realize just how closely the industry is being tracked. Most of the key trends were covered in other chapters of this book, but there are a few others that don't warrant as much space but that still deserve coverage in a text designed to help agents navigate the industry.

In real estate, industry trend spotters include most of the major real estate industry groups (NAR, the Council of Residential Specialists, and so on), several independent firms (like REAL Trends), publications like *Realty Times*, and large universities like Texas A&M, which has its own real estate department. While no single source can reveal the future of the real estate industry, individual agents would be wise to watch the key trends that appear across several sources, then factor these trends into their own business models.

TREND SPOTTING

In the summer of 2001, G. Donald Jud and Stephen Roulac put their heads together and produced an article entitled "The Future of the Residential Real Estate Brokerage Industry." Jud, a professor in the Bryan School of Business and Economics at the University of North Carolina at Greensboro, and Roulac, CEO of The Roulac Group, Inc., a strategy and financial economics consultancy in San Francisco, came up with a few profound predictions that are already coming to fruition in the industry.

At the time, Jud and Roulac said that the real estate brokerage business was on the cusp of a radical transformation, brought on by the revolution of cyberspace technology and the globalization of business. The new technology is crushing established institutions (such as the MLS monopoly on information), they said, and opening new venues of change. They also examined how the new cyberspace technology was altering the residential brokerage business, how it will change institutional structures, and how it will shape the ways in which brokerage business will be conducted in the future.

So far it looks as if Jud and Roulac were on the money with their predictions, although the MLS still has control of all listing data, be it paper- or computer-based. They saw a number of changes coming down the pike, based mainly on the fact that historically, the real estate brokerage business existed because of the *lack* of market information. Buyers and sellers needed brokers to assemble market information because it was too costly and time-consuming for them to amass it on their own. Up through the mid-1800s, lawyers, bankers, and other such professionals were the most common intermediaries in the real estate transaction.

As the size and the complexity of the real estate market increased, so too did the need for someone specializing in the area to handle the transaction, and hence the independent contractor–agent model was born. With the advent of the Internet and a variety of new brokerage models that range from discount to menu and everything in between, the need for the full-service agent who holds all the cards fell by the wayside, opening the door for major changes in the industry. And while the size and complexity of the real estate transaction has continued to grow, so too have consumers' options for either buying the home of their dreams or selling their current dwellings. This means that to survive in the future, individual agents will have to stay a step ahead of their customers, stay on the cutting edge of the industry, and understand key industry trends, or risk obsolescence.

WHAT'S HOT

Right now, the most important real estate trends are the franchising movement, industry consolidation (small firms being consumed by larger ones, and independents merging to gain market power), historically low interest rates (which most agree has been a huge market driver since 2001), and a push by financial institutions to get into the real estate business (also referred to as the "big grab" by NAR). In this chapter we'll look at each of those trends and tell how they're affecting real estate agents. Most are not so much challenges as they are industry trends, which don't necessarily affect you right now unless your local board of Realtors® needs your support in lobbying against them.

As with any industry, key trends are usually just a plain fact of life that professionals have to deal with. Every profession has its own personal set of issues, and while we've already looked at the legal and regulatory hurdles that agents are dealing with, there's still room to examine the top few trends that agents should be aware of in today's market (see Figure 9-1).

As you are an independent contractor whose livelihood is largely determined by your own knowledge of and expertise in the market, it's safe to say that even a surface familiarity with these trends will put you ahead of the pack in the race to the finish line. Some of them, like banks' push into real estate, are clearly unfavorable for real estate agents, whereas trends like industry consolidation, if they hit too close to home, can be dealt with by going with the flow or finding a new company to work for. Then there's the historically low interest rates, which are helping sales close faster than ever. Read on.

Figure 9-1.

IMPORTANT BROKERAGE TRENDS

In "The Future of Real Estate Brokerage" (2003), NAR outlined both challenges and opportunities for Realtors. When it comes to brokerage size and prowess, the group's researchers uncovered the following findings:

❑ The 30,000 traditional brokerages represent the largest number of real estate brokerages.

❑ Technology use varies among traditional brokerages; as of 2001, half of traditional firms lacked Web sites, but 7 percent generated more than 20 percent of their leads from the Internet.

❑ Traditional firms require little capital, and their limited access to capital may inhibit growth opportunities associated with investment in technology and infrastructure.

❑ Vertically expanded firms are brokerage firms with more than 200 agents that have broadened their operations and product lines to include ancillary services.

❑ Referral networks allow vertically expanded firms to tap into the resources and leads of a much larger organization.

❑ Concentration is low in real estate brokerage, but the share of the top firms is increasing: In 2001, the Top 250 firms represented 24 percent of all agents and one in six home sales.

❑ Vertically expanded firms represent less than 1 percent of all real estate brokerage firms.

❑ Middle market firms—smaller firms that offer ancillary services—are more likely to be franchised firms and use this affiliation to offer the same services as larger firms.

❑ The agent service bureau model is an extreme form of the traditional model, offering a 100 percent commission to agents in return for a monthly service fee.

❑ Compensation of agents with 100 percent commission was more than 50 percent higher than that for agents earning commission splits, as of 2001.

Source: National Association of Realtors, "The Future of Real Estate Brokerage," 2003. Used with permission.

Franchising's Foothold

When Dave Liniger, cofounder of RE/MAX International, thinks back to the 1960s, he remembers how the first national real estate company ever, Red Carpet, came to be. Started in Walnut Creek, California, the company posted some initial success until the 1970s, when there was a push to franchise companies within the lucrative industry. Early entrants included Liniger's own firm, plus ERA, Realty World, and Century 21. The franchising movement worked its way across the country slowly, beginning with one or two dominant franchise players doing business in an environment where hundreds of independent mom-and-pop shops had a strong foothold.

Liniger says the allure of franchising was too great for many of those smaller entrepreneurs, who knew that if they agreed to hang out a national sign in front of their offices, they'd not only attract better agents and more market share, but also gain brand name recognition and better buying power. By the end of the 1970s, Liniger and his competitors were operating in a very different landscape from the one that had existed just ten years earlier.

"The idea was the franchisees could look like one big company and gain efficiencies by sharing training and privileges like better newspaper advertising prices," recalls Liniger. "At the same time, however, the offices would still be independently owned and operated, so the interest was very high and the concept started out well."

Soon, companies like Sears, Merrill Lynch, and Prudential, all successful in their own respective industries (retail, financial services, and insurance) came on the scene, ready to make new inroads into real estate. Initially, those three firms had no intention of using franchising to get there, according to Liniger, who says that each had a business plan in hand and aspirations to set up shop in the top seventy-five U.S. markets and become the dominant player in each.

"What they wanted to do was grow market share by acquisition and by purchasing major regional companies and creating major national brands," Liniger says. "Eventually, of course, they spent billions of dollars, only to realize that they could actually do better by franchising." At a 1978 Realtor trade show, Liniger remembers, there were well over a hundred national real estate companies in attendance, all sharing the gospel of franchising and telling show attendees that within five years there would be five major real estate companies claiming 80 percent of the U.S. real estate market.

"They were telling people that if they didn't buy one of their franchises or join the national company, they would be out of business," Liniger recalls. Five years later, their claims proved untrue. In fact, some of those hundred or so companies seemed to use tactics similar to those the dot-coms used with investors in the late 1990s, and only about eight of them are left. Today, the remaining national firms account for 50 percent of the U.S. real estate market, half of NAR's membership, and over one-quarter of the total offices nationwide, according to Liniger.

Look a little more closely at those numbers, he adds, and you'll see that it's not the mom-and-pop shops that are franchising (mainly because they can't afford the $25,000-plus franchise fees) but the larger offices—a sure sign of industry consolidation. Consolidated under a single brand but run as separate companies are the Cendant's/NRT Inc., Century 21, Coldwell Banker (which evolved from Sears), and ERA brands, competing against the likes of RE/MAX, Prudential, GMAC (formerly Better Homes and Gardens), Keller Williams, and Realty Executives.

"It's a classic case of consolidation," says Liniger, "headed up by two major players (RE/MAX and Coldwell Banker) and followed by a handful of other national players, and that's it." Looking ahead, Liniger expects the big to get bigger and continue taking market share, based on the fact that "the bigger you are, the more advertising you can afford and the more market share you can take." RE/MAX, for example, currently claims 36 percent of the Canadian market and 16 percent of the U.S. market, and represents 7 percent of NAR's total membership. He expects Coldwell Banker to continue on a similar trend, based mostly on acquisitions and mergers. "Much like what's happening in most industries, expect to see two major national companies claiming the bulk of the market share," says Liniger, "with the rest of the companies sharing what's left."

What does this mean for the individual agent who is looking for the right wall to hang a real estate license on? Liniger says that most of them continue to be attracted to the bigger companies, which can provide national referrals, a recognized brand name, and training support. He sees a place for smaller, independent firms, as they are where most agents get their start (RE/MAX, for example, has long stood on the principle that even its newest agents join the organization armed with years of industry experience and sales success), but he says that most agents wind up going to a larger firm because they get weary of fighting against firms with national brand awareness.

"Agents want the competitive market advantages of lead generation, they want the advantages of market share and brand name awareness when they talk to a customer, and they want the customer to know that they're indeed working for the biggest company in town," says Liniger. "Those are definite advantages for the individual agent who wants to survive and thrive in the changing industry. The push for consolidation has ultimately meant that more agents have gone to the major regional firms and major national companies. It's a trend that hasn't missed a step since 1966."

TRACKING THE ROLL-UP

So, you know what it took to get this whole industry started, and now we get into where it's at today and how this applies to you, the individual agent, who would probably rather see that sign outside your office window stay the same. Since it's human nature to resist change, it's common sense that any agent would be at least somewhat concerned to find out that his broker had been bought by a national conglomerate and that his yard signs, business cards, and entire identity would soon be replaced by the new ownership.

As Liniger mentioned, industry consolidation has been a key trend in an industry that for years was a highly fragmented industry of mom-and-pop shops. Today, Parsippany, New Jersey–based conglomerate NRT, Inc., holds most of the cards with its Coldwell Banker and ERA brands. Buying sprees throughout 2001, 2002, and into 2003, for example, saw the company consuming independent brokers like the Corcoran Group in New York and Florida-based Arvida Realty Services.

The good news is that the 300-pound gorilla may rule on the brokerage and ownership side, but the small office continues to reign in the industry. According to NAR, out of an estimated 80,000 real estate firms in the United States, just 4 percent have fifty or more agents. Those numbers include many small-town brokerages, but 60 percent of all U.S. real estate companies have five agents or fewer. Still, NAR predicts that consolidation of the industry will continue. Already, it says, out of some 50,000 firms, the top 250 companies represent 24 percent of the agents and one of every six transactions. That means that while your small office is still the norm, the chances that it could roll up into another firm in the coming years are very good.

With every new acquisition or merger come changes for the real estate agents who hung their shingle with the original companies. Consolidation can mean changes in leadership, more or less support from the broker and managers, increased or decreased access to national leads, integration of the two companies' infrastructure and systems, and either more or less brand recognition.

Some industry experts feel that consolidation is less of an agent issue and more of a broker concern, yet the simple fact that a change in ownership can set off a chain of events that may or may not work out in the agent's favor is proof of the importance of staying on top of consolidation-related news and events, and knowing how to react to them when they hit close to home. If there's one thing I learned from covering daily and weekly real estate news for a national publication, it's that rumors of a sale or acquisition within the industry are probably true, even if everyone denies them up until the minute before the news goes public. Keep an ear to the ground and keep on top of what's going on in your industry, and you won't get caught off guard.

CONSOLIDATION SNAPSHOTS

You're not convinced that the real estate business is taking the same track that the "Big 8" accounting firms did back in the late 1990s? You're wondering why these companies joined forces in a merger or decided to sell out to larger competitors? You'll find the proof, and the answers to those nagging consolidation questions, in this section, where we'll look at a few of the major consolidations that took place in 2003.

In June, two long-time, independent regional real estate firms decided to join forces and merged into one. The deal found one-hundred-year-old Cleveland-based Smythe, Cramer Co. merging with forty-year-old Pittsburgh-based Howard Hanna Company to form a combined organization with 150 offices and more than 3,000 sales associates and employees in six continuous metropolitan areas in Pennsylvania, Ohio, West Virginia, and New York. Prior to the merger, Howard Hanna and Smythe, Cramer ranked twenty-fourth and twenty-fifth, respectively, in the 2003 REAL Trends 500 report. The firms now estimate that they are the country's ninth largest full-service real estate organization.

During this particular merger, disruption of agents was kept to a minimum because top management at both real estate companies agreed that although the firms were merging into one operation, they would keep their existing policies, management teams, real estate agents, and employees in place. Each company also agreed to continue operating under its existing brand, making the transition easier for agents.

In a press release sent out when the merger was announced, Howard "Hoddy" Hanna III, the newly formed organization's president and CEO, said that by combining the two firms' strengths, talents, and resources, the new firm would have an automatic advantage in the marketplace that would translate into greater opportunities and enhanced services for people buying and selling properties with the firm. The merger's expanded geography and the 50 percent growth of sales associates were expected to provide a strengthened and expanded internal sales referral network, he added, and there was also expected to be expanded agent enrichment programs, providing valuable support to associates as they market properties.

About a month after the Howard Hanna–Smythe, Cramer marriage was announced, HomeServices of America Inc. (a Berkshire Hathaway affiliate) acquired South Florida–based Esslinger-Wooten-Maxwell Realtors (more commonly known as "EWM"), along with its related entities, Embassy Financial Services, Columbia Title, and First Reserve Insurance. Thirty-nine-year-old EWM was one of Florida's most respected brokerage firms, with more than $1.8 billion in closed transactions in 2002, 11 offices and 750 sales associates.

That's precisely why HomeServices was so interested in the company, which followed a path similar to that followed by another Florida company, Arvida Realty Services, the prior year when it agreed to be acquired by NRT, Inc., and change its name to Coldwell Banker. In a July 2002 press announcement, Ron Peltier, HomeServices president and CEO, said that EWM would give his firm a stronghold in the south Florida market and a platform from which to expand its presence throughout the state. With the closing of the transaction, HomeServices had a presence in sixteen states and a combined annualized sales volume of over $45 billion, based on the closing of more than 180,000 transaction sides across sixteen companies.

Chew on those numbers, all of them emanating from a company that bills itself as the second-largest full-service independent residential real estate brokerage firm and the largest settlement services provider in the United States. The firm offers integrated real estate services, including brokerage services, mortgage originations, title and closing services, home warranties, property and casualty insurance, and other related services (see Figure 9-2). Its latest acquisition was founded in 1964 with the goal of providing clients with expanded, personalized real estate services. With that goal, the three founders' reputation for quality flourished as rapidly as the community in which they were located, and by the time HomeServices snatched it up in 2003, EWM was ranked as one of south Florida's largest real estate brokerage firms and the largest independently owned firm in the region.

The next consolidations involved Manhattan-based Cendant Corp., which serves as the residential brokerage arm for NRT, Inc., and is

Figure 9-2.

ANCILLARY SERVICES OFFERED BY VERTICALLY EXPANDED FIRMS

In its 2003 report "The Future of Real Estate Brokerage," NAR outlines the key ancillary services that brokerages have adopted as ways to boost profitability and create additional revenue streams. (The information is based on 2001 data, according to NAR.) Of those firms, the most popular and profitable ancillary services are mortgage services, home warranties, and title insurance. Here's how they break down among those firms that have integrated them into their service lineup:

Mortgage lender	91.7 percent
Title company/insurance	58.2 percent
Home warranty	48.7 percent
Homeowner's insurance	31.3 percent
Settlement attorney	27.0 percent
Home inspector	9.1 percent
Radon inspector	3.7 percent
Termite/insect inspector	3.7 percent

Source: National Association of Realtors, "The Future of Real Estate Brokerage," 2003. Used with permission.

arguably the 300-pound gorilla of the real estate industry. Throughout 2001 and into 2002 the company went on a buying spree, which cooled off somewhat with the national economy, but then picked back up in late 2003. In August, for example, Cendant purchased two Long Island, New York, real estate firms, Coldwell Banker Sammis and National Homefinder Signature Properties. They are two of Long Island's largest real estate firms, bringing in $2 billion in sales in 2002. Combined, they have six offices that were to be merged into one, to be called Coldwell Banker Residential Brokerage.

For Coldwell Banker Sammis, the sale meant the end of a one-hundred-year-old, family-run real estate firm, although NRT announced that both companies would continue to be run by the leaders who had helped to create the successful firms. The company took a similar stance in 2001 when it purchased the Corcoran Group, a thirty-year-old New York City firm that was founded with an initial investment of $1,000 and that has since evolved into the city's top residential real estate firm, with an impressive eleven offices, 600-plus agents, and over $4 billion in annual sales volume.

Consolidations in the real estate industry aren't limited to mergers of firms that are already working the same side of the business. Sometimes, the acquisitions make sense because they involve companies in complementary industries, such as the August 2003 acquisition of South Carolina property firm United Country-Land Made Easy Inc., by Century 21 Bob Capes of Prosperity, South Carolina. The property firm, which specializes in rural and development properties, was the sixth real estate company that Century 21 Bob Capes purchased between 2001 and 2003, and it was all done in the name of expanding into areas where the company "wasn't as strong as it wanted to be."

Not all consolidations receive the press attention that these examples did. Daryl Jesperson, RE/MAX International's CEO, says that because a lot of mergers and consolidations take place "below the radar screen," the odds that a real estate agent would hear about such movements outside of their region or state is pretty slim. "A lot of these actions don't even get media attention, but it's going on in every major city across the United States," says Jesperson. "There are basically two or three large brokers that are picking off their smaller competitors one by one and bringing them under their umbrella. The benefits come in the form of economies of scale."

SLICE OF LIFE

In a region of Virginia known as Hampton Roads, in 2002 six independently owned real estate companies merged into one company that's now known as Coldwell Banker Professional, Realtors. Prior to the group marriage, the six firms operated independently as Coldwell Banker Helfant (now the administrative headquarters) in Virginia Beach; Coldwell Banker Gifford of Norfolk; Coldwell Banker Harbor in Portsmouth; Coldwell Banker Suburban in Poquoson; Coldwell Banker Brooks of Williamsburg; and Hampton-based Harrison and Lear Realtors.

Dorcas Helfant, one of six general managing partners and the principal broker for Coldwell Banker Professional, Realtors, says that the combination is working so well that the 120-agent, seven-office company immediately went on the prowl for two more offices. She says each former independent broker remains as the broker of the new branch.

The merger helped the six smaller firms meet the demands of an increasingly competitive real estate market and the notion that bigger is better when it comes to recruiting and retaining good sales agents. "These days," Helfant says, "you must have mass in order to offer an effective career track for your associates."

Helfant says that the merger took time and patience, but that all of the independent owners came to realize the value of the power of being one large firm, rather than six small ones. "In looking at our markets, we all began to realize the strength we'd have as a single company," Helfant says. "But first, as independent brokers, we had to wake up and smell the coffee, then move on to meet the challenges of this century. That meant parking our egos at the door and going to work for the team."

It didn't take long for each office's individual agents to take to the team approach to real estate. In fact, she says, there were no repercussions from the company's associates as a result of the merger, and most of them understand the value of joining forces. "We think it's gone over pretty well," adds Helfant. "We're seeing good team spirit and a real willingness to work together."

AGENTS AND CONSOLIDATION

Consolidation has hit the real estate industry particularly hard as large companies grab for more market share and smaller companies converge to gain greater prowess in their own marketplaces. And while the thought of a new owner or management might put fear into an agent's heart, the overall effect of consolidation on those agents whose firms are pairing up seems to be positive. When NRT, Inc., bought Arvida Realty Services of Clearwater in April, Virginia "Ginny" Lomagno, managing broker of fifty-two agents in two St. Petersburg offices, found herself giving agents regular updates on the sale and highlighting the fact that the office management was going to stay intact.

As a result, she says, overall reaction from agents was very positive. "The best way to maintain stability is by keeping agents informed about exactly what's going on," says Lomagno. "The overall feeling from agents was that as long as there was continuity in management, then it would be okay. Ultimately, the additional benefits offered by the new company would become evident and would be appreciated."

Sometimes, when big gobbles up small, the smaller competitors in the immediate area benefit from the acquisition. With one office and forty-five agents who average sixteen years of experience, Realty Executives of Northern Nevada has picked up business as a result of recent consolidations. "The acquisitions tend to involve companies that have less experienced agents," says Curry Jameson, president, who urges his team to aggressively promote their experience and track records to customers. As a result, he says, "Consolidation drives business to more experienced agents like ours."

A branch manager at one of Dallas's largest independent brokerages with one office and seventy agents, experienced a similar phenomenon in her market and gained about twenty-five new agents in 2002 thanks to consolidation. She says that she attracted them by promoting her firm's lengthy track record as a company that's still owned and run by its original founder. "We've definitely had to do some reassuring, but our leader has no intention of selling," she says. "We've had many, many offers over the years, but the leader has turned them all down and is still in control. Once agents hear that, they feel better."

For agents, Jesperson says that there's little doubt that a larger brokerage that boasts the most toys and tools will be the one that wins an agent's heart, hands down. That's because the large firms often have nationwide referral networks (in which agents from within the "family" refer business to other agents in different geographies in exchange for set fees), broader name recognition (mom and pop versus Coldwell Banker, who wins out?), cheaper advertising rates and significant buying power, extensive training programs, and even the best copiers, computers, and fax machines.

While no brokerage's budget is limitless, the one with the more robust backbone definitely has the edge when it comes to attracting talent. On the flip side, however, a larger office with 250 agents means more competition, the need for better individual marketing on the agent's part, and, of course, more bureaucracy. For that reason, industry consolidation remains a key trend that all agents should be aware of in the years to come.

THE BIG GRAB

In 2002, the nation's banks took a bold step and showed the world that they'd really like to get a piece of the real estate market. Through a series of political moves, the real estate industry fought back pretty vigorously and won, at least for the time being. It all started in early 2001, when the Federal Reserve Board and the Department of the Treasury published a joint proposal soliciting public comments on whether real estate brokerage was a permissible activity for financial holding companies and subsidiary national banks.

The proposal, made at the urging of some of the nation's largest and most aggressive banks, would have allowed financial services holding companies and national banks' financial subsidiaries to offer real estate brokerage, management, and relocation services. The banks' plan was to get the government to define real estate as a financial activity, rather than a commercial one, and make it part of their ever-growing array of services.

But there was a hang-up: For 200 years Congress has mandated the separation of banking and commerce. Very simply, Congress determined that real estate was not financial in nature and, very emphatically, decreed that real estate activities are not financial or closely related to banking. The Gramm-Leach-Bliley Act (GLBA) was established to modernize Depression-era laws governing financial transactions. Prior to Gramm-Leach-Bliley, federal law not only separated banking and commerce, but also effectively divided the U.S. financial services industry into separate and distinct types of institutions, such as banks, mutual funds, insurance companies, and securities firms.

For the most part, the separate types of financial services companies were strictly prohibited from merging and from offering the other types' products. Thus, banks were not allowed to own securities firms or sell stocks and bonds, and insurance companies were prohibited from owning banks or taking deposits. But that didn't stop the banks from making a concerted effort to push into the real estate market with the Banks in Real Estate Bill, which—had it passed—would have done away with regulations spelled out in the GLBA and allowed banks to conduct real estate transactions.

NAR and its constituents were quick to act, sponsoring bills in the Senate and the House of Representatives that would effectively block banks from entering the real estate business. On the other side of the issue, groups like the American Bankers Association worked hard to make sure that these bills didn't come to fruition, but they were thwarted. In February 2003, the U.S. House and Senate developed a provision that prohibited the U.S. Department of Treasury from finalizing a rule that would allow banks to enter the real estate business. The budget provision, which was inserted at the behest of U.S. Rep. Anne Northup (R-KY), specifically precludes the Treasury Department from using any funds to implement the rule in fiscal year 2003. Calling the step a "major victory for Realtors, consumers, and communities everywhere," NAR referred publicly to the move as a testament to the sustained, proactive grassroots activities of local Realtors.

In May 2003—for the second consecutive Congress—a majority of the U.S. House of Representatives cosponsored legislation that would amend the Bank Holding Company Act and permanently prohibit big banks from entering the real estate business. The bill was reintroduced with strong momentum and the same level of bipartisan support that it had gathered in the last Congress. Over 175 members of the House and 10 senators have signed onto the Community Choice in Real Estate Act since it was introduced. The underlying premise, it appears, is that a good majority of citizens and politicians simply do not want to see big banks controlling an industry that has served as a backbone of the U.S. economy over the last few years.

"For the second Congress in a row, a majority of the House of Representatives has affirmed that banking conglomerates should not be allowed to add real estate brokerage to their ever-expanding list of business ventures," said NAR president Cathy Whatley, in a statement following the decision.

NAR isn't alone in its fight to keep banks out of the business. Organizations that voiced support for the Community Choice in Real Estate Act included the Building Owners and Managers Association, CCIM Institute, Consumers Union, Institute of Real Estate Management, International Council of Shopping Centers, National Affordable Housing Management Association, National Association of Home Builders, National Association of Industrial and Office Properties, National Auctioneers Association, National Fair Housing Alliance, National Federation of Independent Business, National Leased Housing Association and the National Community Reinvestment Coalition.

But the issue is far from over, and it's one that everyone in the industry needs to keep an eye on. One executive from a state association says that his own association originally fought and won a similar effort at the state level in the late 1980s, and he calls the delay a positive, but he adds that both CAR and NAR are keeping their eye on any new movement on the issue. "Our associations are both very firm on the fact that commerce and finance are two separate entities," he says. "Banks are in the business of finance and we are in the business of commerce, and never the twain shall meet."

MORE TO GRAB

The words "banks in real estate" can conjure up some pretty scary images for the average broker, who pictures himself going up against the likes of Bank of America or Wachovia for business. Since most of the U.S. population already has an established relationship with a bank, it's logical that at least some of that broker's potential customers would feel more secure going to the bank for their real estate needs. Real estate agents are most concerned with the fact that a bigger role for banks would reduce the control that agents have throughout the home buying process. With banks thrown into the mix, it could be harder for agents to usher the transaction through to closing, thus inhibiting their ability to charge the traditional commission rates that they're accustomed to. As you already learned in Chapter 4, those fees are already coming under fire from a number of different directions. Why allow another one to take aim?

Martha Johnson, senior vice president of residential lending at Borel Private Bank and Trust in San Francisco, says that her bank doesn't necessarily want to get involved in selling real estate, but she adds that because real estate brokerages get involved with the lending side of the business (by aligning themselves with mortgage brokers or lenders and offering financing as an ancillary service), it seems inevitable that some banks may want to reciprocate.

"The real estate community is very much against banks in real estate, and I can see why," says Johnson, whose institution specializes mainly in high-end mortgage lending. "It's interesting, however, since the real estate community is in the lending business at this point, in that many real estate firms have mortgage lending operations. It appears that the lines are blurring a bit."

Expect more on this subject, since banks aren't likely to give up easily on a piece of business that they feel they're entitled to. In general, it's larger commercial entities that are looking for a piece of the real estate pie, hoping to tie together the transaction into a neat bundle that can be run from concept to completion right under their own roof. That's precisely what agents are worried about.

"I do think the banking industry may pursue the issue again, but when they do, they'll probably discover the same thing they discovered when they tried to push into other, broader lines of diversified financial services," says Johnson. "Ultimately they'll find out that as banks, they're more profitable when they stick to their core business of lending, deposits, asset management, and trust services."

HIGH SALES + LOW RATES

If there was one recurring theme echoing through the real estate industry in 2002 and 2003, it was certainly "historically low interest rates." Nationwide, renters opted to buy rather than rent, young buyers plunged into homeownership much sooner than usual, and move-up and second-home buyers also jumped into the market to take advantage of the low rates.

In June 2003, rates on a thirty-year fixed-rate loan bottomed out at 5.21 percent, according to Freddie Mac's national average statistics, but they had risen to 6.24 percent by August. Leslie Appleton-Young, chief economist with the California Association of Realtors, says mortgage rates are bound to continue their slow climb, although she doesn't predict any drastic, double-digit increases in the near future. Instead, she says, rates will probably plateau at a somewhat higher rate, which will in turn slow housing sales slightly next year.

"Mortgage rates will start to become more of an issue in terms of people not being able to qualify for loans, and that in turn will slow home appreciation rates," says Appleton-Young, adding that the negative impact of higher mortgage rates will be offset somewhat by improved economic conditions and increases in household income, which tend to fuel residential real estate activity. She says that the California Association of Realtors®' outlook for 2004 calls for a 2 percent decline in sales, to 539,400 units, and a new record median price of $399,600, 10 percent higher than the 2003 median.

Nationwide, in mid-2003 the National Association of Home Builders predicted record sales of homes for the year, estimating a 985,000 total, which was up 1 percent from 2002's record-breaking number of 973,000. NAR was equally optimistic, expecting 5.73 million existing-home sales in 2003, up 2.9 percent from 2002's 5.57 million. At the same time, national median home prices were expected to rise 6 percent to $167,800, while the median new-home price was expected to rise 3.8 percent to $194,700, according to NAR. Put the numbers together and it's clear to see how an ambitious, conscientious real estate agent who plays by the rules and pays attention to what's going on in the industry can achieve success, both financially and personally.

Lawrence C. Yun, a senior economist with NAR, says that while low interest rates certainly fueled home sales in 2002 and 2003, the predicted slow, steady upswing in rates will have a minimal effect on national home sales activity. "There have only been three years in the past three decades in which mortgage rates averaged lower than 7 percent," Yun says, "so it's still one of the better times to buy a home."

After all, says Yun, rates haven't been in the 5 to 6 percent range since Dwight Eisenhower was in office. The low rates have fueled not only home sales activity, but also new home construction. Looking ahead, he sees overall favorable housing market conditions well into the future, particularly over the next ten years. Prices and interest rates aside, Yun points to the age structure of the U.S. population as a trend that all real estate professionals should be aware of, particularly that big chunk of the population aged forty to fifty (the baby boomers, of which there are a whopping 78 million), who are moving into what Yun calls "the prime home-owning" age group.

"As a higher percentage of the population moves into that age group, we can expect very stable housing demand throughout the next decade," Yun says. He singles out states like California, Texas, and Florida—where immigration plays a leading role in the state's population growth—as another positive for the industry. "Over time the immigrant homeowner-ship rate steadily climbs with the number of years they reside in the United States," says Yun, who advises real estate agents to keep an eye open for all these immigrants who will be turning into homeowners in the current decade. "We saw a surge in immigration in the 1990s, which means that in the current decade all those people who moved in the last decade will steadily be being transformed into homeowners."

BABY BOOMERS ON THE PROWL

Yun isn't the only industry expert who sees the nation's baby boomers as an opportunity for real estate professionals. The fact is, this section of the population is looking for second homes in record numbers, and one of their top destinations is the state of Florida. Born between 1946 and 1965, this 78 million–strong demographic group intends to retire and move, according to a recent report from NAR.

A full 21 percent of them are considering moving to Florida, says Tony Macaluso, broker/owner of Portside Properties, Inc., in Palm Beach Gardens, Florida. In real estate for twenty-five years, Macaluso is also chief administrator for the Realtors Association of Palm Beaches' Advantage Real Estate School. According to Macaluso, someone in the United States turns fifty every nine seconds—a trend he expects to continue for at least another two to three years, thus creating a larger pool of baby boomers who are thinking about retirement and lengthier vacations. He says that south Florida's real estate market is proof of this immigration: Five years ago the area had a glut of condos on the market that has since "all but evaporated."

Macaluso sees many areas of the nation benefiting from the trend, but he adds that real estate professionals looking to work with such customers will have to look beyond the traditional "schools, neighborhood, and work centers" home search, and instead help their older buyers find what they're really looking for: the right mix of quality of life, water and recreational opportunities, and cultural activities.

When asked if the rising interest rates will slow the boomers down, Macaluso says that only about 39 percent of such buyers take out mortgages when purchasing. "You have about 60 percent of them that actually buy without the need for financing," says Macaluso. "Many of them had pricey real estate up in the Northeast and Midwest, so they simply cash out and come down here and buy less expensive homes."

MAKING SENSE OF IT ALL

So what does this grab bag of trends really mean for you, as an real estate agent? Some of them may not affect you at all, while others may prove valuable when you're out in the field lining up deals, forming relationships, and getting the word out about your services. If any of them strike a particular nerve—such as the banks in real estate issue—it would be wise to bone up on any recent movements on the issue and get involved with a letter-writing campaign to your local politicians.

Or if you're living in an area where second-home sales are brisk, then you'll probably want to take Macaluso's advice and redirect your marketing efforts to focus on those activities that older buyers are looking for. And if you're worried that rising interest rates will affect your business, be assured that some of the nation's top economists don't see a few percentage points as making much of a dent in the brisk market.

SIX THINGS TO REMEMBER FROM CHAPTER 9

❑ Along with the legal and regulatory issues previously covered, there are a handful of key real estate trends that can have a significant impact on the real estate agent working in the field.

❑ The way the real estate industry has morphed over the last forty years is a trend in itself, having moved from being dominated by mom-and-pop shops to being dominated by a few large national franchises.

❑ Consolidation is rampant in the real estate industry and ranges in scope from large franchises buying small offices, to small offices banding together, to small and midsize firms pairing up with companies that offer complementary services.

❑ Rising numbers of home sales combined with historically low interest rates have brought a lot of new agents into the business and kept the experienced agents very busy over the last few years.

❑ Banks' push into the real estate business in 2001–2002 may have been unsuccessful (their effort was thwarted in 2003), but that doesn't mean that the large commercial institutions won't try again in the future.

❑ Though interest rates are rising, a steady flow of baby boomer buyers, immigrants, and second-home buyers is expected to keep the industry healthy and strong for at least the next decade.

PART 4

BRACING FOR SUCCESS

CHAPTER 10

Ensuring Your Future Survival

STRATEGIZE FOR SUCCESS

By now you know that forces like technology, consumer needs and demands, commission compression, legal and regulatory issues, and broader real estate trends are all playing key roles in the way successful real estate agents do business today. You've heard from the horses' mouths (i.e., the productive agents themselves) that keeping your nose clean is of utmost importance, as is standing by the going commission rates and entrenching yourself firmly as *the* guy or gal in your area to go to for anything related to home sales and purchases.

This is a lot to chew on all at once, but the bottom line is that customers are more demanding, and if you're going to stick with this career, then you'd better get used to them. Not only do they want more for less, but their experiences are often the driving forces behind the increased regulatory scrutiny and legal issues that agents and their brokers are facing in today's business world. Consumers are also driving brokers to rethink the way they price and deliver their services, asking for "all in one" service packages that include everything from home inspections to mortgage services, and picking apart the full-service packages that have been standard in the industry.

As you've read, technology can be either a blessing or a curse for the real estate agent, depending on whom you ask. By now, the bulk of the agents—even the old-timers—realize that they need a cell phone and e-mail to deal with an increasingly tech-savvy consumer. Just a few years ago, however, a high percentage of agents were dragged kicking and screaming into the technology age, unaware of the impact that it would leave on their industry. From the electronic MLS to wireless laptops to online comparative market analyses that can be put together in minutes, technology has put the industry through some sweeping changes, with no end in sight. That's where we'll start in this chapter, which will see you off with a few good ideas about how to be a successful agent in an era of change.

CATCHING THE TECH BUG

James Marsden knows that success in the real estate industry is all about survival of the fittest. That's why Marsden, the broker/owner of James Marsden Real Estate LTD, a full-service brokerage in Warwick, New York, adopted a tech-heavy approach to the business early, and hasn't let up on it since he opened the doors to his company in 1998. These early insights have paid off well: Marsden and his twelve agents sold $55 million in properties in 2003, which averages out to about $4.6 million in production for each agent.

But Marsden wasn't always so tech-savvy. When he got into the industry in 1990, agents still relied heavily on those MLS books to retrieve information about area listings. Marsden remembers receiving the books every two weeks and immediately calling around to the offices to find out which listings had since been sold (since the books were published one to two weeks ahead of time, the odds were good that a hot listing would be gone long before the books hit your desk). He then went through his "new" book, crossing out all of the sold listings.

When the Internet began gaining mainstream attention in the early 1990s, Marsden says, he became the first agent in Orange County to create his own Web site, realizing that being able to pull information from various sources in a timely fashion would benefit not only his business, but also his individual customers. At the time, Marsden was working for a traditional brokerage and was fed up with the way the "older" folks in his office were looking down their noses at his technological aspirations.

"The other agents in my office were much older, and they just didn't grab the Internet," says Marsden. "I knew none of them would spend time and resources developing a Web site or taking any other technological strides, so I broke out on my own and started my own company."

From day one, Marsden says, he made technology his company's cornerstone. He spent time learning how to write HTML code so that he could create his own Web site and—perhaps more important—update it on a daily basis. And when companies like IPIX were still just a twinkle in their founders' eyes, Marsden was stitching together his own still photographs into virtual tours that consumers could view on his Web site.

For the first three years, Marsden ran his business as a solo practitioner, relying heavily on technology to help him get each transaction completed in a timely, smooth fashion. Working out of the front bedroom of his home, he sold about twenty homes a year. At night, he would tinker with his Web site, updating and maintaining it in a way that few other agents in his area were doing at the time. In April 2001, when he found himself hitting that front bedroom from six o'clock in the morning until one o'clock the next morning, he knew that it was time to expand, hire help, and move out of the house.

"I hired a few people and we all just sort of blew the doors off," says Marsden, whose company has progressively leased out more space as it has grown. Marsden attributes much of his success to—you guessed it—technology. "Either you embrace technology or you won't be here," he states. Referring to NAR's most recent numbers, which show that 80 percent of home buyers start their search on the Internet, and that 66 percent of those who buy a home purchase it through the first agent that they interact with, Marsden says that those agents who ignore technology will quickly find themselves in the dark ages.

Where brokers and agents tend to go wrong, according to Marsden, is by sticking with a pack mentality based largely on the movements that their competitors are making. If a real estate office decides to add title services to its service mix, for example, the chances are good that some of its competitors will sit up, take notice, and follow suit. Lack of innovation hurts the industry, says Marsden, and a broker's unwillingness to try new, untested ideas can trickle down to the individual agents' performance.

"In this industry you rarely see people creating their own patch; they follow the path as a group," says Marsden, who has stuck with his habit of splitting from the group (much as he did when he left his tech-hampered agents in the dust back in 1998). "I, on the other hand, will not go down a path that's already there."

RADICAL CHANGE

Over the last thirteen years, Marsden has seen radical changes in the real estate industry, particularly when it comes to for-sale listings and the need for them. Time was when the agent who held the most listings held all of the cards in the game. Being named listing agent in the MLS meant that you could advertise the listing, field inquiries from all other brokers and agents in your area, and pretty much be guaranteed at least half of the commission (depending on your broker's split).

"Listings were a very important source for attracting buyers," recalls Marsden, who says that technology and the advent of buyer's agents have changed that traditional way of doing business. These days, technologies like IDX and broker reciprocity allow all offices to display all of their competitors' listings as if they were their own (at least to the unknowing consumer—and with some limitations, based on NAR and the individual MLS's rules). Because buyers can be easier to net than sellers (relationships with buyers can be formed with a simple phone inquiry in response to a yard sign that you pick up during floor time), getting listings is no longer as important as it once was.

At Marsden's firm, for example, roughly 75 percent of that $55 million in sales came from working with home buyers. The company has few listings, concentrating instead on attracting buyers with the complete

MLS data that Marsden advertises on the brokerage's Web site. The efforts have pushed the company into the top spot for market share in the Warwick, New York, area, up from number thirteen in 2001.

"The reason we are number one is that we get to the buyer before the buyers know where we are," Marsden says. "When some guy in Brooklyn spends an hour and a half on the subway and says, 'Honey, we have got to get out of here,' to his wife, that guy goes to his computer, and we're the only real estate company he finds."

KEEPERS OF INFORMATION

Marsden isn't the only one who has noticed the major changes in the way real estate agents do business. Across the industry, agents and their brokers are finding innovative ways to grab a piece of the real estate pie, with technology being one of the driving forces behind the movement. Ultimately, of course, the push is on to serve customers in the most effective manner without breaking the bank. Because consumers who come to an agent are often already educated on both the home-buying process and what kind of homes are available in their desired area, the agent's role has become that of trusted adviser and consultant rather then just keeper of information.

But that doesn't mean that real estate agents are being disintermediated—not by a long shot. In fact, as you learned in Chapter 1, the role of the agent has only been strengthened as the transaction itself has become more complex and mired in regulatory requirements. Combine that with the fact that lenders offer myriad loan options, ranging from 100 percent mortgages to mortgages that come with their own built-in equity lines of credit, and increased concern over issues like toxic mold, and it's not hard to see why the real estate agent has become even more important to the transaction.

"The role of the agent has really changed in that consumers used to have to go to an agent to find out what properties were available on the market," says Bryan Foreman, president of MLS software provider Interealty Corp., in Vienna, Virginia. "That's not the case anymore, since the bulk of the home-buying public now does its research online, narrows the search criteria down to a few properties, then selects an agent to work with." While new agents seem to "get" this new positioning, those who have been in the industry since the pretechnology days are often reluctant to embrace it. Those who continue on that path soon find themselves unable to communicate and do business with today's consumers.

"The more that an agent can serve customers in a manner in which they want to be served, by making the information available online or communicating with them electronically," says Foreman, "the better the odds will be that those customers will come to that agent."

The good news is that the value of the real estate agent does not—and never did—lie in access to the information. While that MLS book was certainly great bait for getting both buyers and sellers walking through the front door of a brokerage, the ultimate value was delivered to the seller when the agent launched advertising campaigns, held open houses, handled negotiations, and coordinated the actual contract and transaction process. For buyers, the value came from the hours spent whittling down their likes and dislikes to a handful of "perfect" homes; helping them learn all there was to know about neighborhoods, schools, and work centers; and assisting them in their quest to find the right home at the right price.

"The value of the real estate agent lies in helping the consumer interpret the information, and then adding to that information the agent's own knowledge of negotiating and marketing," says Foreman, who acknowledges that some agents and brokers feel that putting listing data on the Web for all to access is a bad move. Think about it logically, however, and it makes perfect sense. "Doing so has actually made the agent more efficient," he continues. "I can't think of any agent who wouldn't like a customer saying, 'You know, I have looked at these three houses, I found them online, and I have done my homework. Can you help me buy this house or help me decide between these two or three homes, as opposed to spending three days in the car with me driving me around the neighborhood?'"

Foreman says that agents should brace themselves for more change on the technology front in the next couple of years, particularly when it comes to the automation of administrative functions and the looming "paperless transaction" that is often talked about, but has yet to come to full fruition. Foreman says that the idea that a contract can be written up, signed electronically by both buyer and seller, shipped off to the bank along with a loan application via e-mail, approved electronically, and then sent off to service providers like title insurance and homeowner's insurance without using a single piece of paper has been slow to take off. However, he says, when someone figures out how to make it work in a streamlined, seamless fashion, the impact will be significant.

"The world is becoming much more Web savvy and the audience buying property right now is younger," says Foreman. "These types of consumers expect that kind of automation, and they expect access to information. The better the job that agents can do at facilitating that, the better the chances are that they'll create opportunities for themselves."

Put It to Work for You

Before we leave the subject of technology, let's take a look at how one technology-centric brokerage stands out from the pack by being up with the times. At James Marsden Real Estate LTD, agents use a mix of proprietary (developed in-house by Marsden himself) and off-the-shelf software. Marsden says that the proprietary software beats programs like Top Producer (a popular program among agents) hands down, and says that he's tried a number of real estate–specific programs over the years and always gone back to the systems developed in-house.

"I just get tired of the daily complaints and go back to our own software," says Marsden. At the heart of an operation where 81 percent of customers come in the door through the firm's Web site is a program that mines data from that Web site. That means that when a customer comes to the Web site and begins searching for a home, agents can monitor what types of homes the customer has zeroed in on, when the customer looked at the data, and how many times the customer has come back for another peek. With that information, agents can build a buyer profile and begin making predictions and assumptions that the customer hasn't even thought of yet. When a new listing that matches a particular buyer's criteria comes on the market, for example, the company can "push" that information out to the potential buyer via the Web, long before the buyer is even aware that the home has been put up for sale.

"The Internet was built for real estate," says Marsden. "It's a fantastic tool to be able to get someone tons of information at a time when they're in a position to look at it and pay attention to it, from their own computers." Agents who don't believe that technology is a friend, says Marsden, will quickly find themselves obsolete in an industry that's expected to continue on its trend toward automation in the future. Whether it means taking a few courses at a local college, bartering a day with a colleague who's tech-savvy for some pointers, or reading a software manual from cover to cover, the time spent will be well worth it.

Doing so will put you in an elite group of agents who have embraced technology as friend rather than foe and learned how to use it to their advantage. "I find real estate agents as a rule to be behind the curve in what the marketplace is doing," says Marsden. "Most thirty-year-olds today are using instant messaging online, shopping online, and even researching medical information online. That's the market you want to reach as an agent, so if you're not embracing technology and making sure that you are out there where they can find you, you're simply not going to survive."

If that $250 contact management software program you bought last month doesn't work to your liking, don't even think about going back to using your old paper-based Rolodex and day planner system. Marsden says that he's purchased and discarded more programs and technology tools than he likes to remember, but that hasn't stopped him from putting technology at the center of his very successful business. It's something to think about the next time you sour on technology because your new Palm Pilot refuses to sync with your desktop computer.

"All I can say to agents is, don't be afraid of it," says Marsden. "We've purchased software, used some successfully, and thrown out more stuff than you can imagine. We've also tried things that didn't come to fruition, and learned from all of those experiences."

One way in which agents can embrace technology and the Internet in a simple way is by using it themselves to shop for everything from books to movies to clothing. The experience will give you a hands-on look at a process that your tech-savvy customer base is using on a daily basis, and it will help you relate to those customers and serve them better.

"Shopping online gives you an idea of how the public is interacting with the Internet," says Marsden. "It'll give you perspectives that you've never thought of."

And remember, says Marsden, that the only constant in technology is change, which means that you need to upgrade and update your Web sites, hardware, and software regularly. As independent contractors, many agents are reluctant to shell out the money that it takes to keep updated, and that can be detrimental to their success.

"Agents will go out and buy something and expect it to have a five-year shelf life, whereas the shelf life sometimes can be as short as a few months," says Marsden. "They're out there using software or Web site templates that they bought from some company two years ago instead of constantly changing their Web sites, upgrading their technology, and figuring out ways to work smarter, better, and faster."

Ultimately, Marsden says, agents must spend money to make money—just as any small company would in today's competitive business landscape. "Someone will come to them and offer to put together a great Web site for $1,500 a year, and they'll say, 'No way, not for that kind of money,'" says Marsden. "What they don't realize is that by opting not to spend $1,500 a year, they could end up giving away $30,000 worth of business."

THE RIGHT STUFF

Mike Watkins knows what it takes to succeed in the real estate business. In fact, as broker with Mike Watkins Real Estate Group in Greenwood, Indiana, this guy has managed to break into an elite group of agents who sell over $50 million in properties a year *without* selling multimillion-dollar homes. The average home price for Watkins and his seven salaried, licensed assistants in 2002 was $151,000. In the business for twenty-five years, Watkins says he knows why more agents aren't in his shoes.

"A lot of people who are in real estate are just in the wrong profession," Watkins asserts. "They get into it with big aspirations, but they really have no clue what it really entails." Some of the requirements? Realizing this is not a nine-to-five job, says Watkins, nor is it the type of job that you can walk into without first learning the ropes. "Agents who want to be good really have to learn the craft, talk to the best, and get as many mentors as they can, while at the same time dismissing any naysayers who tell them that they can't do it," Watkins says.

Like many full-service brokers, Watkins and his team have felt the pressure of commission compression, coming mainly from discount brokers and those who charge flat fees to list homes, but who don't provide the full gamut of services. Watkins says that while the pressure is certainly there, he doesn't worry too much about it because he knows that there will always be consumers who will pay for quality clothing at stores like Nordstrom's and those who prefer to get their clothes at discount stores.

"We've chosen not to be the Wal-Mart of real estate because we know that there are people out there who are willing to pay for our services," says Watkins. "If that weren't the case, and if people were only after the best deal, then why isn't everyone in America driving Kias?" Watkins blames the real estate industry itself for not positioning itself better to make that case. "Most people don't go in and negotiate their doctor down in price, because they truly want the best doctor," says Watkins, "yet they will ask brokers to cut their price. In our market, most consumers are finding out that the cut-rate brokers are most often not that beneficial to them."

CHOOSE YOUR BATTLES

Dave Liniger, cofounder and chairman of the board of RE/MAX International, has some clear-cut advice for anyone looking to survive and thrive in a changing industry: Find the best company to work for. In doing so, he says, you should look for companies that have brand-name awareness, an austere reputation, healthy market share, and other competitive advantages that can help the individual agent better navigate the profession. Overlook such important factors, he says, and they can quickly turn into competitive disadvantages—something that no agent can afford to have in her corner.

"The better the brokerage, the more likely it is to have good training, excellent referral systems, and better lead generation systems than its competitors," says Liniger, who warns agents not to depend solely on their broker for training. Through private institutions, local and state boards of Realtors®, and other industry groups, agents can rack up their educational credentials without having to earn them through the school of hard knocks, which entails getting your training on a day-to-day, trial-and-error basis.

"You can do it that way, or you can look at real estate as a real career by determining what skills you need to develop (negotiation tactics or public speaking, for example) and working hard on them," Liniger says. "Get out into the market, talk to the best agents in town, and find out who the best trainers and speakers are. Focus closely on what motivates you as an agent and use it to your advantage."

So that every real estate agent doesn't have to reinvent the wheel, Liniger also suggests pairing up with one or more mentors (typically a successful agent or broker), then picking their brains for the kind of hands-on advice and information that can't be taught in any type of classroom setting. Such hands-on work experience can be critical to an agent's success. "If you can find someone whom you can look up to, and who is a top producer, you'll definitely learn more by watching that person work than you ever will by listening to trainers," says Liniger, who used mentors when he was an agent. He booked several breakfast meetings a week with a number of top producers from his office, then sat down with them and asked them for advice and help on how to be as successful as possible in the industry.

"I took the twenty best people in the office, bought them breakfast, and took a pad of paper and pen along," says Liniger, whose primary query to those agents was: If you had a limited amount of time and were new to this city, how would you build your business in the fastest, most efficient manner to ensure that it would last forever? He says that the answers—which the agents gave him willingly—helped him shape a real estate career that's spanned over three decades. To this day, Liniger still has the yellow legal pad that he took those notes on.

MORE THAN AN AGENT

Most real estate agents don't think of themselves as business consultants, but they probably should. No longer the keepers of highly coveted information, today's real estate agents have a very clear purpose in the biggest financial transaction that the consumer will make during his lifetime, and it's time to let the cat out of the bag and let everyone know it. Doing so will further entrench the value of the real estate agent in consumers' minds, it will minimize the effect that discount brokerages are having on the industry, and it will also help on the regulatory and legal side in that a true business consultant has only her client's best interest in mind.

J. Lennox Scott, chairman and CEO of John L. Scott Real Estate in Seattle, is one real estate executive who sees the real estate agent as a consultant, with the brokerage or company backing up that individual agent throughout the entire transaction, not just the sale portion of the process. "Our philosophy is about encompassing our agents as the entire transaction—with mortgage, escrow, title, and other service offerings—and positioning them in such a way that the customer sees the value in the relationship," says Scott, who expects more companies to adopt a similar stance in the next few years. He says that the industry as a whole is moving in the direction of customer relationship management (CRM), which will be administered and used by the individual agents and supported by the company itself.

Russell Capper, president and CEO of eRealty, Inc., in Houston, says that the successful agent of the future will be focused more on representing the interests of the buyer and/or seller and less on providing information that those consumers can access themselves online. A friend of mine in Indiana recently listed one home and bought another within a two-month period, and says that he was very often a full step ahead of his real estate agent during the process. "She'd come to us every week or so with printouts of homes for sale, and we told her that we'd already driven by them last week," he says. "Ultimately, however, she was a sharp agent who got both of the deals closed effortlessly."

Capper says that for the average agent, he sees much less phone, fax, and e-mail tag and racing around trying to find the right home for a customer. He also sees less prospecting, since the modern-day consumer is using a different set of criteria to choose agents from the one he used in the past. "The good professionals with a number of transactions under their belts will have no need to prospect, and will be able to handle the many clients that come to them," says Capper, who doesn't characterize eRealty as a discount brokerage, but rather as one that offers lower commission rates to its customers as a result of its own efficiencies, attained mainly through technology.

Capper says that he expects commission compression to continue across the industry, but he adds that agents' fees probably won't come down as much as some are predicting. "I don't think the listing side (typically 2.5 to 3.5 percent, depending on the market) will go much lower than where it is right now, and I really don't think the consumer minds paying a fair price," he explains. "When the transaction is complete, however, I do believe that consumers compare the amount of work the agent did to what he or she earned in commissions, and feel that the agent wasn't worth that much. At the same time, they also don't think they should have handled it on their own because it's much too complicated."

FIDUCIARY DUTIES

David Jenks, vice president of research and development for Keller Williams Realty International in Austin and coauthor of the 2003 book *The Millionaire Real Estate Agent*, says that maintaining a fiduciary position (a fiduciary is an individual, corporation, or association that holds assets for another party, often with the legal authority and duty to make decisions regarding financial matters on behalf of the other party) is absolutely critical for all agents, particularly because of the size and magnitude of the typical real estate sale. Act just as you would want your own attorney, dentist, doctor, or accountant to act, he says, and always put the interest of the client ahead of anything else.

Put that message out in the limelight in a compelling manner (say, by using word-of-mouth testimonials from satisfied customers), says Jenks, and you'll never lack for business, even in today's competitive environment. Add in a systematic marketing process for your individual business, he adds, and the combination can be downright magical. By systematic, he means contacting your sphere of influence (your database of business and personal contacts) at least twice a month—a process that the Keller Williams team calls "touching." At the same time, reach out to targeted geographic areas at least once a month, in an effort to build your reputation and attract business from those pockets.

Lastly, says Jenks, look at real estate as a business, not as a job. As an independent contractor, you're much more of a business owner than you are an employee, so why not act like one? And while your broker ultimately dictates how you operate, your position as business owner means that hiring assistants, outsourcing tasks, and completing your annual tax forms are ultimately in your hands.

CHANGE IS IN THE AIR

Working in an industry that's undergoing major changes is no picnic, especially when commission checks are few and far between, health and life insurance are a pipe dream, and even a day off on the weekend has to be planned weeks ahead of time. Even the most entrenched, experienced agents, who swear their business hasn't been affected by industry trends, have to think about issues like toxic mold, increased regulation, commission compression, technology, and demanding consumers. To survive, to enter the ranks of the top producers, the key is to be flexible and adaptive in an environment that isn't always friendly to agents who walk away from the closing table with 6 or 7 percent of a home's sale price.

"Any experienced agent has over the years proven that she can adapt to any circumstance and deal with any type of adversity that might come her way," says Daryl Jesperson, CEO of RE/MAX International in Greenwood Village, Colorado. "Once in a while she might get caught sleeping on the job, but overall she's very adaptive and entrepreneurial, which is why concepts like salaried agents have never really stuck in the real estate industry."

That the real estate industry comprises individuals working on their own entrepreneurial bents can be both a blessing and a curse for the industry as a whole, since not having an employer to answer to means that agents are largely on their own to either succeed or fail. Unfortunately, being too hungry (i.e., coming into the business with little or no savings) can hamper the path to success and lead some individuals to make unwise choices, given that no manager is breathing down their neck. Many times, as mentioned in Chapter 7, it's the individual agent who shoulders the responsibility for legal issues, for example, which leaves them on their own to make the right decisions while working in the field.

"Real estate agents wake up every morning and have to go out and find a job to do," says Jesperson. "That means that they're going to do what they have to do to succeed, or they are going to be faced with going to another industry and another job." For that reason, Jesperson says that the thought of banks in real estate, a trend covered in Chapter 9, could actually be a positive for the industry, but negative for consumers. Already used to working within stringent regulatory guidelines, Jesperson says, banks would probably institute great training programs, leaving the door open for larger, more established brokerages to recruit agents from them. For consumers, however, banks in real estate would be a raw deal.

"Consumers want banks watching their deposits and finances, not training real estate agents," says Jesperson. "For these types of trends, you really have to look at the bigger picture, and whether it really makes sense. It might work, but the reality is that real estate in late 2003 made up 12 percent of the gross domestic product (GDP), and I would say we're all doing a pretty good job without the bankers in the mix."

BRACING FOR THE FUTURE

Stay tuned, agents, there's more change ahead, which means being even more adaptive and flexible to ensure not only mere survival, but also success. NAR, in it's 2003 report "The Future of Real Estate Brokerage," assures us that the "only constant is change" and that new business models, increased regulations, and other interesting challenges are waiting right around the next corner. Given the sheer size and fragmentation of the real estate market, NAR says, changes that alter the balance of power take time. As Jesperson mentioned, NAR also says that agents' willingness to adapt and change will help them expand their businesses and achieve success.

Looking ahead the next few years, NAR says that the real estate brokerage of the future will be molded by the influences of technology, consumer preferences, and regulatory policy. In predicting what may come in 2008 and beyond, NAR says that current trends could result in technology-enabled markets (where buyers and sellers identify themselves and initiate the transaction), in which real estate professionals will specialize within the transaction and the dominant business models will follow vertically expanded or corporate models as their product range maintains the consumer relationship over time (see Figure 10-1).

So where in the world does that leave you, the individual real estate agent trying to make a living helping folks buy and sell their homes? In a pretty good position, really, since most of that jargon is hardly understandable to a real estate professional, let alone the average consumer. By fulfilling your professional role with the utmost ethics, getting educated and credentialed, boning up on what's going on (not only in your region but also industrywide), and striving to stay a step ahead of the consumer, you'll be well positioned to deal with whatever comes your way.

That's because even in the face of change, agents and brokerage firms are tied to consumer demands, and successful real estate professionals work continuously to serve those demands. The model that wins, says NAR, will be the one that provides services for which consumers are willing to compensate it, plain and simple. Successful real estate agents need to be agile; they must keep pace with the technology that adds to pro-

Figure 10-1. Future Trends.

What will the real estate brokerage of the future look like? According to G. Donald Jud and Stephen Roulac, it's not going to look much like your father's real estate industry, that's for sure. In fact, the pair predict that with the revolution in information technology and changing legal environment, we'll see the crumbling of the MLS informational monopoly, the abandonment of agency law (a consumer's legal rights when dealing with an agent or broker), the unbundling of services, and a rise in fee-for-service pricing.

Jud and Roulac outline five scenarios for the future of the brokerage industry. Here's a look at what these two real estate experts expect to see in the next few years:

❑ *The FSBO model.* In this model, the Internet becomes the medium through which buyers and sellers are able to interact directly, unaided by brokers or intermediaries.

❑ *The unbundled services model.* In this model, agents' service offerings are unbundled, and agents offer consumers a menu of services from which the consumers are able to choose, including pricing the property for sale, negotiating the contract, and managing the contract through to closing.

❑ *The alternative delivery model.* With this model, the full-service agent offers a mix of full-service and menu options to appeal to a broader range of customers.

❑ *The product extension model.* Brokers not only offer their traditional services, but also extend their service offerings to include complementary services such as help with financial planning and moving assistance.

❑ *The financial supermarket model.* In this model, large financial service firms recognize that they possess the human capital, financial capital, and complementary product offerings that real estate buyers and sellers want. As a result, real estate firms look for assistance from financial service firms for financial capital and technological expertise, while financial service firms look to the real estate brokers as a way to bring additional customers to their networks. In this situation, the traditional real estate broker evolves into a real estate marketing specialist, providing sellers with advice on pricing, showing, and negotiating.

Jud and Roulac won't speculate about which of these scenarios will come to dominate, and the final reality may very well comprise elements of all five. For now, it's important that agents are aware of the changing environment. The big winners will be the consumers: the home buyers and sellers who will be provided with better, more timely information at lower cost.

---

ductivity, while also keeping abreast of regulatory changes and ensuring that they are observing the laws. While many of the changes, trends, and challenges mentioned in this book may sound daunting to you, not a single one of them is insurmountable. In fact, the agent who works through these issues now—rather than pretending that they don't exist—is bound to emerge stronger, smarter, and more successful in the long run.

And remember, says Liniger, that the agent will always be more important than the brokerage company, the technology, the Internet, or anything else involved in the transaction. Know and learn this importance, and use it as a part of your unique selling position (USP). "People who deal with real estate agents are dealing with the biggest transaction of their lifetimes, and they want that transaction treated with a great deal of respect," says Liniger. "The service-oriented agent who treats the transaction with the respect that it deserves, and treats the customer with the respect that he or she deserves, will never be replaced by a computer."

SIX THINGS TO REMEMBER FROM CHAPTER 10

- ❏ A number of key issues and trends are taking place in the real estate industry right now, and it's up to the individual agents to educate themselves on how these trends will affect their businesses.

- ❏ Technology has been both a blessing and a curse for the real estate industry, depending on whom you ask.

- ❏ Ultimately, technology has helped real estate agents work smarter, better, and faster in an industry that's changing at a rapid pace.

❑ By embracing the role of consultant and viewing themselves as business entities rather than employees, savvy real estate agents can create value for their consumers that their competitors cannot.

❑ Looking ahead the next few years, NAR says that the real estate brokerage of the future will be molded by the influences of technology, consumer preferences, and regulatory policy.

❑ Because a real estate transaction is one of the most complex transactions anyone will undertake in his lifetime, good real estate agents will continue to play a starring role in the transaction process.

Resources for Real Estate Agents

INDUSTRY GROUPS AND TRADE ASSOCIATIONS

Association of Real Estate License Law Officials (ARELLO)

ARELLO comprises the official government agencies and other organizations around the world that issue real estate licenses/registrations in addition to regulating real estate practice and enforcing real estate law.

Post Office Box 230159
Montgomery, AL 36123-0159
www.arello.com

Council of Real Estate Broker Managers

The Council of Real Estate Brokerage Managers is a not-for-profit affiliate of NAR. The group provides benefits to enhance the productivity and profitability of its nearly 7,000 members nationwide and offers the CRB designation to Realtors® who have completed its advanced educational and professional requirements.

> 430 North Michigan Avenue
> Chicago, IL 60611
> Phone: 800-621-8738
> www.crb.com

Council of Residential Specialists

The Council of Residential Specialists is NAR's largest not-for-profit affiliate. It is composed of nearly 40,000 Certified Residential Specialists (CRS), Designees, and Candidates/General Members. The association was created to attract and retain those Realtors who were seeking the knowledge, tools, and relationship-building opportunities they needed in order to maximize their income and professionalism in residential real estate.

> 430 N. Michigan Ave, 3rd Floor
> Chicago, IL 60611
> Phone: 800-462-8841
> www.crs.com

Employee Relocation Council

Formed in 1964, the Employee Relocation Council (ERC) is a professional membership association focused on workforce mobility around the globe. Its current membership includes more than 1,250 representatives from corporations and government and military agencies and nearly 10,000 individuals and companies that provide relocation services targeted at both U.S. domestic moves and international moves.

1717 Pennsylvania Ave. NW, Suite 800
Washington, DC 20006
Phone: (202) 857-0857
www.erc.org

Graduate Realtors Institute

GRI is the symbol of the Graduate Realtors Institute professional designation series. Recognized nationwide, the GRI designation shows clients that the holder has a solid grasp of real estate fundamentals. The program is recognized by the National Association of Realtors (NAR) and individual state associations. Check with your state associations for more information, or visit NAR's Web site at www.realtors.org.

National Association of Realtors®

The National Association of Realtors ("The Voice for Real Estate") is America's largest trade association, representing approximately 880,000 members involved in all aspects of the residential and commercial real estate industries.

430 N. Michigan Ave.
Chicago, IL 60611
Phone: 1-800-874-6500
www.realtor.org

NAR has a list of state and local association information posted online at
www.realtor.org/leadrshp.nsf/webassoc?OpenView

NAR's Center for Realtor Technology

The primary goal of the Center for Realtor Technology is to serve as an industry advocate, implementation consultant, and technology information resource
for its Realtor members. The group also supports the NAR Leadership Team's
initiatives, its technology agenda, and its negotiations with potential providers
to members.

www.crt.realtors.org

Real Estate Buyers Agent Council (REBAC)

REBAC was founded in 1988 to promote superior buyer representation skills
and services. An affiliate of NAR since 1996, REBAC's membership now numbers well over 40,000, and it is the world's largest organization of real estate
professionals concentrating on buyer representation. Members who meet all
course and professional experience requirements are awarded the ABR
(Accredited Buyers Representative) and/or ABRM (Accredited Buyers
Representative Manager) designation(s). Both are the only designations of their
type recognized by NAR.

430 N. Michigan Ave.
Chicago, IL 60611
Phone: 800-648-6224
www.rebac.net

Women's Council of Realtors

This group was formed by NAR and is made up of women who are working Realtors.

430 North Michigan Avenue
Chicago IL 60611
www.wcr.org

REAL ESTATE NEWS AND INFORMATION SOURCES

Association Tech Helplines

Many of the state Realtor associations offer tech support to members via the phone. The Minnesota Association of Realtors®, for example (www.mnrealtor.com), offers a toll-free hotline at (866) 432-3024, with live tech support operators who offer help with operating systems, real estate–specific software, major Web design software, digital cameras, PDAs, and computer hardware. Check with your local or state association for similar services in your area.

The Economist

A magazine and online source for the analysis of world business and current affairs, providing authoritative insight into and opinions on international news, world politics, business, finance, science, and technology, as well as overviews of cultural trends and regular industry, business, and country surveys.

www.economist.com

Inman News

Inman News is a well-respected real estate news service that offers both online and offline formats. Billing itself as the nation's leading independent real estate news service and content provider for consumers and the real estate industry, Inman editorial content appears in over 250 newspapers throughout the country and is featured on over 10,000 Web sites.

> Email: editor@inman.com
> Phone: 510-658-9252
> www.inman.com

International Real Estate Directory

This site includes over 50,000 links to real estate–related Web sites nationwide. You can find links to real estate organizations, licensing commissions, news, and various other sources from this single Web site.

> www.ired.com

NAR's VOW Education Center

NAR's VOW education center contains an introduction to the VOW concept, the VOW policy, answers to frequently asked questions on the policy, and two implementation guides prepared by NAR's Center for Realtor Technology.

> www.realtor.org/realtororg.nsf/pages/VOWHome?OpenDocument

Realtor Magazine

Realtor Magazine Online is the online companion to *Realtor Magazine*, the business tool for real estate professionals. *Realtor Magazine Online* brings readers all the great articles from the print magazine, plus exclusive online columns and feature stories on topics and techniques not covered in print. The site also features weekly Web reviews and business book reviews.

www.realtor.org/rmodaily.nsf

Realty Times

Realty Times is a leading real estate news site on the Internet. Nearly half a million consumers and real estate professionals visit Realty Times each month to read the latest from its staff of award-winning columnists. From buying and selling advice for consumers to money-making tips for agents, the site's content, updated daily, has made Realty Times a must-read site for anyone involved in real estate.

5949 Sherry Lane, Suite #1250
Dallas, TX 75225
Phone: 214-353-6980
www.realtytimes.com

REAL Trends, Inc.

REAL Trends is a publishing and communications company that is considered to be a leading source of analysis and information on the residential brokerage industry. Founded in 1987 by Steve Murray and Laurie Moore-Moore, REAL Trends publishes a monthly newsletter highlighting events, issues, and challenges in real estate. Because of the tremendous response to the newsletter, REAL Trends has expanded to include four special publications that provide in-depth breakdowns and analyses of important industry information and weekly "Breaking News" e-mail updates reporting up-to-the-minute industry happenings. REAL Trends also produces other special industry reports, often in conjunction with other industry organizations such as the National Association of Realtors.

> 6898 South University Boulevard, Suite 200
> Littleton, CO 80122
> Phone: 303-741-1000
> www.realtrends.com

RISMEDIA

RISMEDIA was established in 1980 as The Relocation Information Service Inc. Since then, RISMEDIA has grown into the leading independent provider of news, information, reference publications, high-level events, and consulting services in the real estate and relocation industry. RISMEDIA's "Today's Real Estate News" e-mail reaches more than 200,000 real estate industry professionals every day, covering issues, trends, and leaders who are affecting change in the industry.

> 50 Water Street
> South Norwalk, CT 06854
> Phone: 203-855-1234
> www.rismedia.com

KEY REPORTS AND RESEARCH SOURCES

Alabama Real Estate Research and Education Center (AREREC)

AREREC is a state-of-the-art, comprehensive research and education facility designed to support Alabama's real estate community and economic development efforts throughout the state of Alabama.

www.arerec.cba.ua.edu

Bureau of Labor Statistics

The Bureau of Labor Statistics is the principal fact-finding agency for the federal government in the broad field of labor economics and statistics. From its Web site agents can access the latest unemployment rate and trend data for their respective states and regions.

www.bls.gov

The Federal Reserve

The Federal Reserve (the "Fed"), the central bank of the United States, has played a key role in the lowering of interest rates, which has led to a forty-year low in mortgage interest rates.

www.federalreserve.com

Harris Interactive

Harris Interactive is a worldwide market research and consulting firm, best known for the Harris Poll and for its pioneering use of the Internet to conduct scientifically accurate market research. The company combines the power of unique methodologies and technology with international expertise in predictive, custom, and strategic research.

135 Corporate Woods
Rochester, NY 14623-1457
Phone: 800-866-7655
www.harrisinteractive.com

NAR Surveys and Reports

"The Future of Real Estate Brokerage: Challenges and Opportunities for Realtors" is available for purchase from NAR Customer Service. To order, call 800-874-6500 and ask for item No. 186-72-LN. For more information, visit www.Realtor.org/research and click on "Business Research Products." The 2002 National Association of Realtors "Profile of Home Buyers and Sellers" is available at no charge from NAR's Web site at www.realtor.org/research.

The Real Estate Center at Texas A&M University (TAMU)

TAMU's Real Estate Center is the nation's largest publicly funded organization devoted to real estate research. The center's staff conducts research on financial, socioeconomic, public policy, trade, legal, land use, and local market analysis issues related to real estate.

2115 TAMU
College Station, TX 77843-2115
Phone: 800-244-2144
www.recenter.tamu.edu/

UCLA Center for Communication Policy

The organization produced the "Surveying the Digital Future" report.

Box 951586
Los Angeles, CA 90095-1586
Phone: (310) 825-3711
www.ccp.ucla.edu/

U.S. Census Bureau

The Census Bureau serves as the leading source of quality data about the nation's people and economy. This government agency shares its expertise globally and conducts its work openly. Real estate agents can find valuable data and demographic information about the country's population and related trends on the bureau's Web site.

www.census.gov

U.S. Department of Housing & Urban Development (HUD)

HUD is the nation's housing agency. It is committed to increasing homeownership, particularly among minorities; creating affordable housing opportunities for low-income Americans; and supporting the homeless, the elderly, people with disabilities, and people living with AIDS. The department also promotes economic and community development and enforces the nation's fair housing laws.

451 7th Street, SW, Room 5235
Washington, DC 20410
Phone: (202) 708-1992 x321
www.hud.gov

Links to Companies and Products Mentioned

ACT!: www.act.com

All Florida Referral Network: www.allfloridareferral.com

The Artasm Group, Inc.: www.artasm.com

Assist-2-Sell: www.assist2sell.com

Borel Private Bank & Trust Co.: www.borel.com

Buy Owner: www.buyowner.com

Century 21: www.century21.com

Champion Realty, Inc.: www.championrealty.com

Coldwell Banker: www.coldwellbanker.com

Coldwell Banker's Blue Edge: www.blueedge.com

The Competitive Edge (Stephen Canale): www.canale.com (From this site you can sign up for Canale's free Technology Tips & Tricks Newsletter.)

Desiree Savory: www.desireesavory.com

eRealty, Inc.: www.erealty.com

ERA: www.era.com

Exit Realty: www.exitrealty.com

For Sale By Owner: www.forsalebyowner.com

Foxtons: www.yhdfoxtons.com

Goldmine: www.goldmine.com

Help-U-Sell: www.helpusell.com

Homeadvisor: www.homeadvisor.com

HomeDiscovere.com: www.homediscovere.com

Interealty, Inc.: www.interealty.com

IPIX: www.ipix.com

James Marsden Real Estate LTD: www.JamesMarsden.net

Jim Casey Seminars & Consulting: www.jimcasey.com

John L. Scott Real Estate: www.johnlscott.com

John L. Scott Real Estate (Edward Krigsman's Web site): www.seattlecityhomes.com

Keller Williams: www.kw.com

King's Real Estate Services: www.kingsre.com

Microsoft Outlook: www.microsoft.com/outlook

MLSNow: www.mlsnow.com/html/cmareport.asp

Portside Properties (Tony Macaluso): www.tonymacalusoreschool.com

Realtor.com: www.realtor.com

Realty Executives: www.realtyexecutives.com

Regency Real Estate: www.regencyrealestate.com

RE/MAX International, Inc.: www.remax.com

Service Magic: www.servicemagic.com

Success Computer Consulting, Inc.: www.sccnet.com

Top Producer: www.topproducer.com

Trip Scott: www.tripscott.com

Yahoo! Real Estate: www.realestate.yahoo.com

zipRealty www.ziprealty.com

REAL ESTATE CONSULTANTS AND EXPERTS

Management Masters

Darla Scott, President
Philadelphia, PA

The Management Masters, a team of experienced consultants, provides commission plan analysis and new designs, as well as innovative recruiting and retention strategies and branch manager recruiting training. Contact Darla at 610-355-0111 or dscottMMI@aol.com.

Julie Garton-Good

As a syndicated columnist, author, and international speaker, Julie Garton-Good has been called "America's home affordability expert." She addresses more than 25,000 persons each year on the topics of real estate finance and home affordability. Visit her online at www.juliegarton-good.com.

Michael Lee

Seminars Unlimited
6550 Ridgewood Drive
Castro Valley, CA 94552
Phone: 800-417-REAL
www.seminarsunlimited.com

Laurie Moore & Associates

As cofounder of REAL Trends (a trend letter for real estate executives), real estate industry futurist Laurie Moore-Moore has kept her finger on the pulse of today's changing real estate business for over sixteen years. Each year, more than 10,000 people flock to her presentations on industry trends, business development, customer service, and marketing at conventions and other real estate meetings.

> 1409 South Lamar, Suite 355
> Dallas, TX 75215-1871
> Phone: 214-485-3000
> www.moore-moore.com

RELATED BOOKS

Negotiating

Roger Fisher, *Getting to Yes: Negotiating Agreement Without Giving In* (Penguin USA, December 1991).

William Ury, *Getting Past No: Negotiating Your Way from Confrontation to Cooperation* (Doubleday, January 1993). Paperback.

Peter B. Stark & Jane S. Flaherty, *The Only Negotiating Guide You'll Ever Need: 101 Ways to Win Every Time in Any Situation* (Broadway Books, September 2003).

Real Estate Sales

David McIntosh, *151 Tips for Realtors—By a Realtor* (David McIntosh, January 1998).

Gary Keller, Dave Jenks, and Jay Papasan, *Millionaire Real Estate Agent: It's Not About the Money* (Rellek Publishing Partners, LLC, February 2003).

Darryl Davis, *How to Become a Power Agent in Real Estate : A Top Industry Trainer Explains How to Double Your Income in 12 Months* (McGraw-Hill, October 2002).

Mike Ferry, *How to Develop a Six Figure Income in Real Estate: Superstar Selling the Mike Ferry Way* (Real Estate Educators Assn, November 1992).

Michael D. Lee, *Selling to Multicultural Home Buyers* (New Home Specialist Inc, January 2000).

Kenneth W. Edwards, *Your Successful Real Estate Career* (AMACOM, April 2003).

Frank Cook, *21 Things I Wish My Broker Had Told Me: Practical Advice for New Real Estate Professionals* (Dearborn Trade Publishing, June 2002).

Index

Look for These Exciting Real Estate Titles from AMACOM Books

Your Successful Real Estate Career, Fourth Edition by Ken Edwards
0-8144-7160-9 • $18.95 • Paperback

The Real Estate Agent's Field Guide by Bridget McCrea
0-8144-0809-5 • $19.95 • Paperback

Are You Dumb Enough to Be Rich?: The Amazingly Simple Way to Make Millions in Real Estate by G. William Barnett II
0-8144-7177-3 • $18.95 • Paperback

Real Estate Investing Made Simple: A Common-Sense Approach to Building Wealth by M. Anthony Carr
0-8144-7246-X • $17.95 • Paperback

A Survival Guide for Buying a Home by Sid Davis
0-8144-7196-X • $17.95 • Paperback

Mortgages 101: Quick Answers to Over 250 Critical Questions About Your Home Loan by David Reed
0-8144-7245-1 • $16.95 • Paperback

The Home Buyer's Question and Answer Book by Bridget McCrea
0-8144-7236-2 • $17.95 • Paperback

The Successful Landlord: How to Make Money Without Making Yourself Nuts by Ken Roth
0-8144-7228-1 • $19.95 • Paperback

The Landlord's Financial Tool Kit by Michael Thomsett
0-8144-7235-4 • $18.95 • Paperback

Available at your local bookstore and online or by calling 1-800-250-5308

Special discounts on bulk quantities of AMACOM books are available to corporations, professional associations, and other organizations. For details, contact Special Sales Department, AMACOM, a division of American Management Association, 1601 Broadway, New York, NY 10019. Tel.: 212-903-8316. Fax: 212-903-8083.

Web site: www.amacombooks.org

Prices Subject to Change